Sottsass **700** drawings

SOTTSASS
700
DRAWINGS

Edited by Milco Carboni
With an introduction by Hans Hollein

Provincia Autonoma di Trento
Comune di Trento
Comune di Rovereto

Museo di Arte
Moderna e Contemporanea
di Trento e Rovereto

First published in Italy
in 2005 by
Skira Editore S.p.A.
Palazzo Casati Stampa
via Torino 61
20123 Milano
Italy
www.skira.net

© 2005 Ettore Sottsass
© 2005 Mart – Museo
di Arte Moderna
e Contemporanea
di Trento e Rovereto
© 2005 Skira editore

Printed and bound in Italy.
First edition

ISBN 88-7624-093-4

Distributed in North America
by Rizzoli International
Publications, Inc., 300 Park
Avenue South, New York, NY
10010.
Distributed elsewhere in the
world by Thames and
Hudson Ltd., 181A High
Holborn, London WC1V 7QX,
United Kingdom.

Printed on
GardaPat 13 - 115 g/m²

GGARDA
CARTIERE

Provincia Autonoma di Trento
Comune di Trento
Comune di Rovereto

Museo di Arte
Moderna e Contemporanea
di Trento e Rovereto

in collaboration with
CSAS – Centro Studi e Archivio
della Comunicazione
dell'Università di Parma

This volume has been published in
occasion of the exhibition

**Sottsass progetti
1946–2005** →

Rovereto, Museo di Arte Moderna
e Contemporanea di Trento e Rovereto
February 26 – May 22, 2005

Curated by
Gabriella Belli and Milco Carboni

organizational Coordinatiom
Beatrice Avanzi

Registrar
Davide Sandrini

Installation Project
Sottsass Associati
Milco Carboni
with Iskra Grisogono

Superintendent of the Installation
Claudio Merz

Installation
Art Legno, Trento

Lighting
Raggi di Luce, Vicenza

Insurances
Epoca Insurance Brokers, Bologna
in collaboration with
Blackwall Green, London
National Versicherung, Zurich

Transportation
Arterìa, Cernusco sul Naviglio
in collaboration with
Möbel Transport AG, Zurich

Communication and Press Office
Luca Melchionna (Mart)
Villaggio Globale International,
Mogliano Veneto
Skira editore – Mara Vitali Comunicazioni,
Milan

Thanks to the museums, the art gallery
and all the private collectors that lending
their precious pieces made this exhibition
possible:
Maastricht, Gallery Mourmans
Milano, Photology
Massa, Ultima Edizione
Paris, Baccarat
Paris, Centre Georges Pompidou, Musée
national d'art moderne / Centre de création
industrielle
Pistoia, Poltronova Design
Parma, Centro Studi e Archivio
della Comunicazione dell'Università
di Parma, Sezione Progetto
Vicenza, Cleto Munari
Zurich, Galerie Bruno Bischofberger

For their help to the realization of the
exhibition, we are grateful to:
Gloria Bianchino
Egidio Di Rosa
Davide Faccioli
Chantal Granier
Marie-Laure Jousset
Simona Riva
Elvilino Zangrandi

The exhibition is made possible also
by the contribution of

With the exhibition "Sottsass. Progetti 1946-2005 →" the Museo di Arte Moderna e Contemporanea di Trento e Rovereto pays homage to one of the great protagonists of contemporary design and architecture. With this choice the Museum intends to reaffirm its interdisciplinary vocation and continue along the line of research it has been following since its foundation, exploring the different languages of artistic expression in our times. The interest in architecture, in particular, has characterized the events held in the historic Palazzo delle Albere, *where exhibitions of high scientific caliber have been dedicated to architects such as Luciano Baldessari (1985), Adalberto Libera (1989), Figini and Pollini (1997). Alongside this activity, the Museum has also been constantly involved in acquiring numerous architectural archives, including the archive of Ettore Sottsass Sr., whose son, Ettore Sottsass Jr., was a generous donor for the show dedicated to his father in 1991. More recently, the exhibitions dedicated to the ceramics of Fausto Melotti (2003) and to the sculptor and designer Isamu Noguchi (2003) have reemphasized the interest of the Museum for the different functional applications of art, in a field such as design, which touches our daily lives. In this field, Ettore Sottsass Jr. has affirmed himself as a master of international fame. The visitor will find ample testimony to this among the exhibits of furniture, ceramics, porcelain, crystal and jewels, accompanied by drawings and scale models of his architectural work, exhibited for the first time in all its completeness in Italy.*

Franco Bernabè
President
Museo di Arte Moderna e Contemporanea di Trento e Rovereto

For many years now — to be precise since 1991when I met Ettore Sottsass Jr. at the exhibition dedicated to Ettore Sr. — somewhere around Christmastime or shortly after New Year's I continue to receive word from him in various and unusual forms: photos, mini bios, heavier writings, short essays, chronicles of his travels.

It is his way of telling his friends that his life continues to be interwoven with our own, a message that is quite a bit more profound than the usual formal greetings and pat phrases.

I have learned a great deal about architecture and design from Ettore Jr., crowded next to him in a tiny car driving around Trentino on a hunt for the still living architecture designed and built by his father as a lucid lesson on measures and methods, and marked by a strongly Austrian character. But our conversations weren't about architecture. Those who know him well know that when you are with him you look at the colour of the sky, you smell the smells, you touch the stones and the stucco, but you talk very little of the theory of the discipline. Ettore Sottsass possesses mysterious sensorial, emotive and perceptive faculties that allow him to decipher — or better yet interpret — people's relationships, each person's relationship, to the space around them, to the places in their lives, to their being in the world. I don't know if when he was young it was more important to him to study the discipline or to fall in love with the paintings of Picasso, Matisse and Braque. What is certain is that the most precious elements in shaping the future of his architecture and his design came from these artists, and likewise it is from the encounters and experiences of his travels that issues the continuous flow of ideas and thoughts that are still at the base of the unstoppable outflow of creativity that nourishes his constant desire to experiment with, to draw, design, delight in and play with forms, colours and space.

I would like the exhibition dedicated to him to lead visitors to our museum in the right direction and not deceive them with explanations about his architecture and his design that are as useless as they are pedantic. If it's a rainy day we'll feel a little melancholy looking at the shadows of his masses — almost archetypical of his architectural design — perhaps a bit depressed near the all-black room where he decided to place his ceramics of gloom, *born of experimentation during a period of isolation and deep distress. If it is a beautiful sunny day we will see the shine of the surfaces of his ceramics, the glittering of his jewels, the colours will seem to smile at us from the façades of his inimitable architecture, and we will thus understand that the many projects of Ettore Jr. form 'a single, enormous, continuous project. A single, suave, tender, immense project that engages all of us, that unites us, that is the metaphor of our heroism and our errors, of our incredible daily desire to travel a few metres above the ground, and of our accursed weight that pulls us a little farther down with each passing day.'*

Gabriella Belli

Content

Ettore Sottsass. Thinking by drawing

The preface to this book should really be a drawing.

I sit in front of a vase by Sottsass.

For me the vase is a leitmotif in Sottsass's work and vision, embodying his attitude and philosophy.

Sottsass creates purposeless vases — flowers are rather an unwanted addition. The vase becomes an autonomous work of art.
Sottsass conceives vases in his mind, he does not throw them on the wheel.
They are a metaphor — a view of the world. The vase is a sculpture. Sottsass creates a sculpture which may be used — this is his social conscience — it also should be a useful object. A designer should make useful objects. Sottsass makes useful objects which are trailblazing. But he prefers imagining works of art. Sottsass draws vases in a variety of shapes. They are produced — and then they simply stand there — with a presence of their own. The vase as sculpture, as an image of man, as architecture.
Sottsass creates useless objects which will find their use. They are activated by imagination.
A sculptural framework can end up as a bookshelf.
Sottsass draws a variety of different shelves. They are simultaneously also models, models for possible realisation in completely different scales.

The shelf becomes a house, a skyscraper.

In his drawing on a small piece of paper, the decision has not yet been made if the shelf is to be a piece of furniture, or a building.

Sottsass is an architect.

And he dreams of architecture, of very simple architectural situations: a gate made of three posts and a lintel, or a piece of cloth fluttering in the wind that casts a shadow.

He not only draws these situations he builds them as well — himself.

Somewhere in the desert. And then he photographs them.

Sottsass's medium is not the drawing only but also photography. He is an explorer, who discovers innumerable things that others can't see. And he photographs them, making them part of his work of thoughts.

But here, in this book, we are talking about 700 drawings: drawings from the most diverse periods of his life and work, concerning a variety of topics.

Very early, Sottsass developed an original and unmistakable idiom in his drawings as well as in his objects and buildings.

Most of the drawings are reproduced here in their real size. The format is important. Sottsass thinks by means of drawings on an ordinary sheet, the size of writing-paper. A mental sketchbook accompanies him continuously.

Whether through fleeting, concise sketches or detailed representation an autarchic cosmos emerges.

This is particularly clear in his architectural drawings, which do not necessarily represent a building plan, but rather elements of life, cosmic concerns, fundamental human situations.

The volumetric is accentuated, color plays a key role. As do light and — most of all — shade. Shadow generates mood. Shadow is ambivalent too. In the hot South, people look for it, in the cold North they avoid it, preferring sunshine and light. There is an affinity here with de Chirico and Sironi. A concealed ambivalence is hidden in Sottsass's drawings. You can read them in two ways, like riddles, poised between cheerfulness and melancholy. Also, there are constant allusions to other cultures he experienced on his travels. Often with comments that jot down the drawer's mood at the time: personal, political and programmatic utterances passing through his head… while sitting on Filicudi island — thinking. Sottsass is a thinker.

The titles of the drawings are important, often an extension of the visual representation.

A process of receptive thought is demanded on the part of the observer. Evocative themes provoke re-flection. Plain titles like *Seaside villa* or *Livingroom* arouse reactions and emotions as others like *Planet like a festival,* *"Temple for erotic experiences"*, or *"Architectural nonsense"*.

The innate poetry of an image is extended by titles like *"Architecture to house the shadow of my death"* or *"Schattenarchitektur"*. Ironic and critical designs like *"Ergonomic chair"*, *"Radar for ladybugs"*, or *"Barbaric interiors"* become poems. Designed poetry is emphasized by design-action.

A common attitude runs through these 700 drawings, done between 1938 and 2004. New ideas strengthen the continuity of his thinking.

Sottsass is master of the unquantifiable in architecture. Mood and atmosphere are conveyed not only by the color and shape of elements such as cubes, vaults and oblique planes, but also by the ensemble. Recurrent features are gates, courtyards, gardens with trees enclosed by walls — and the sea. Self-contained paradises.

These fundamental themes are continually probed in depth. The path — the entry, and the exit — into nothingness, into death.

Whereas initially the objects — furniture, jewellery, ceramics — and their transformation are in the foreground, later thoughts are circling around architecture, which is becoming an ever growing importance for Sottsass.

In the 90s, the conceptual sketches are replaced by precise large-scale drawings. For Sottsass the transition between artistic expressions is fluid, there are no borderlines between sculpture, painting, architecture and design.
Sottsass transgressed these borders long time ago — today this is called crossover — despite the resistance to and the criticism of an attitude that also led to a unilateral perception as designer. He is present worldwide with his products and his name is a household word, while his creative architectural potential has not been sufficiently perceived.

Sottsass is a magician.

Without Sottsass our world would lack color.

Hans Hollein, Vienna, January 16, 2005

Sottsass **700** drawings

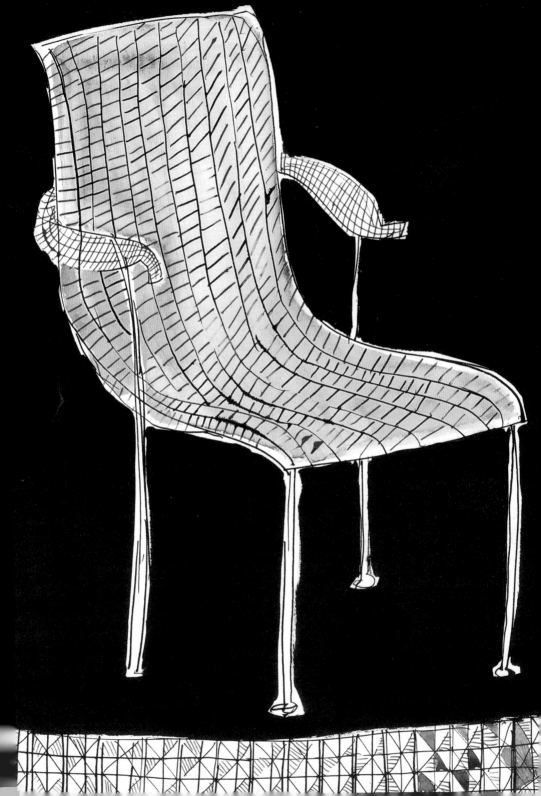

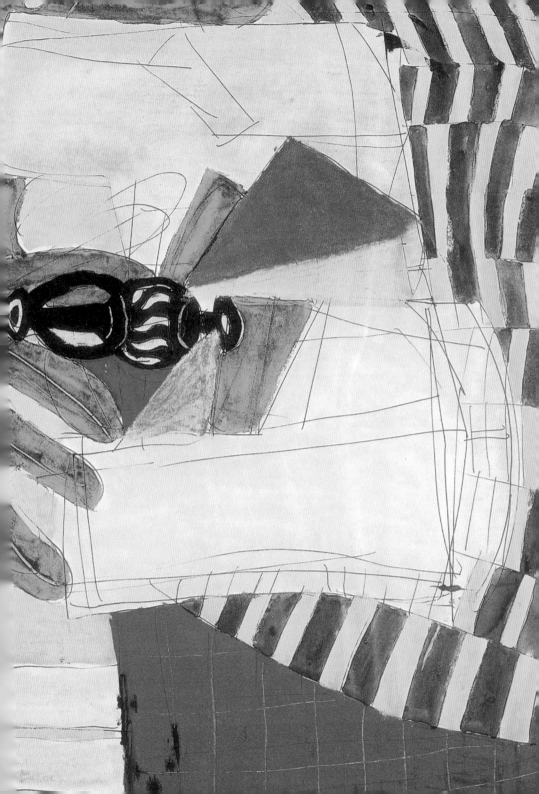

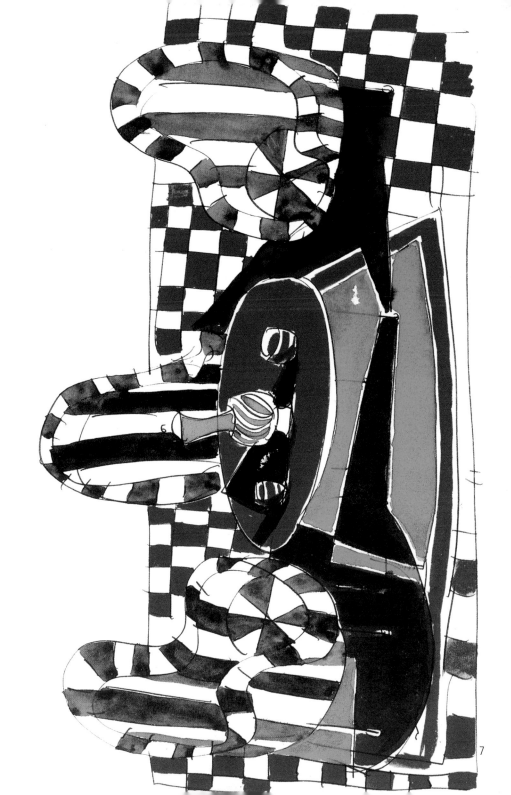

7

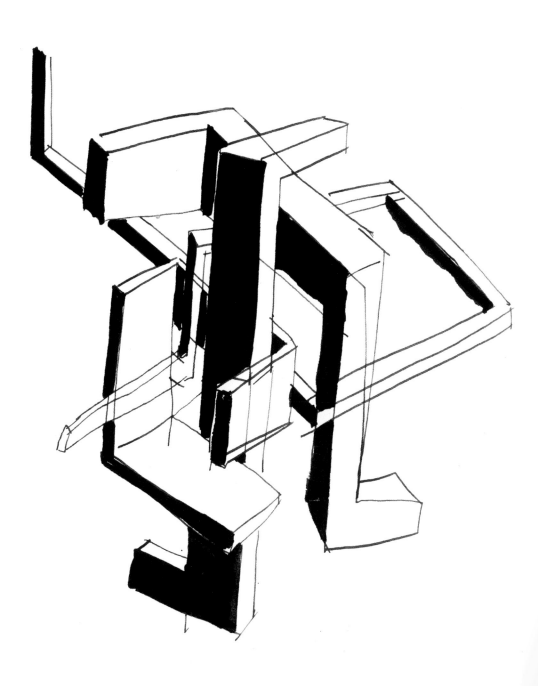

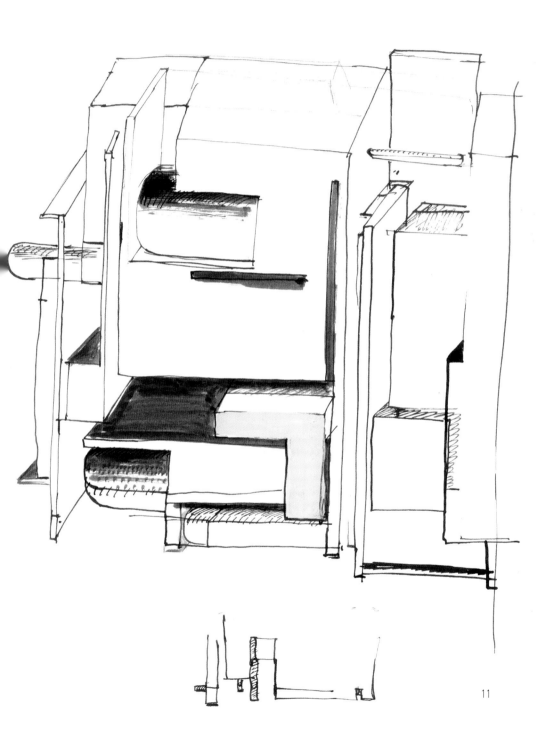

11

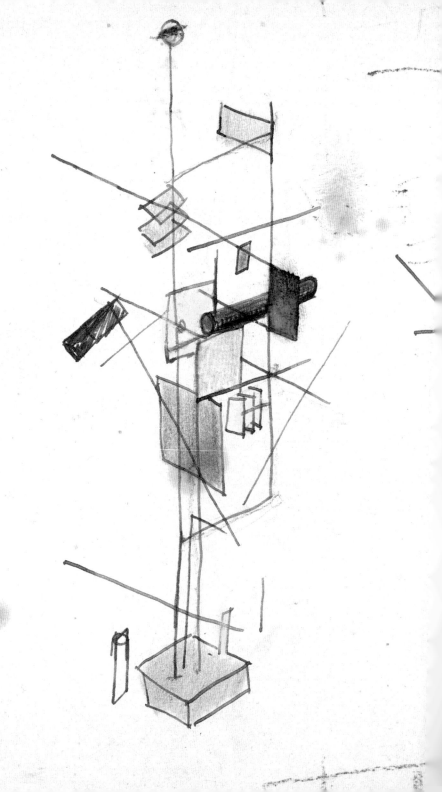

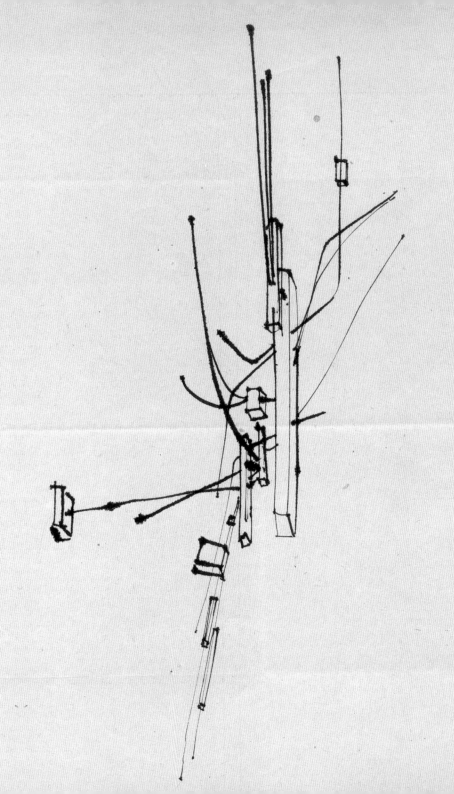

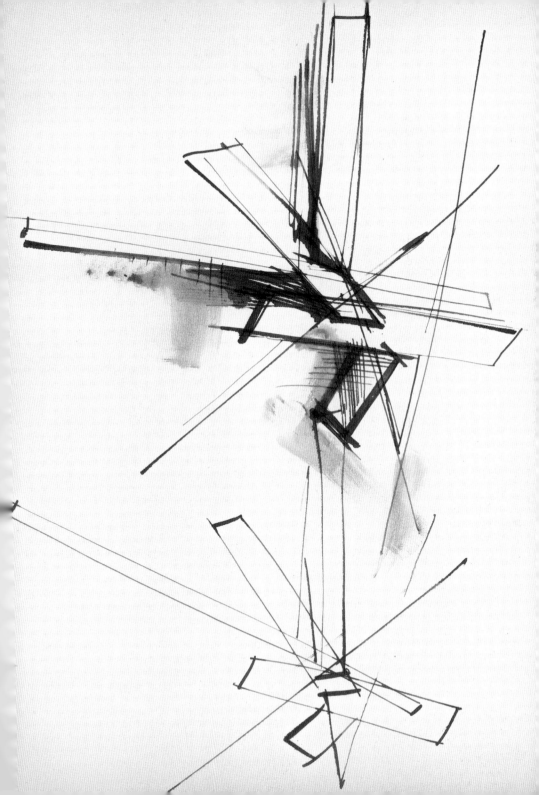

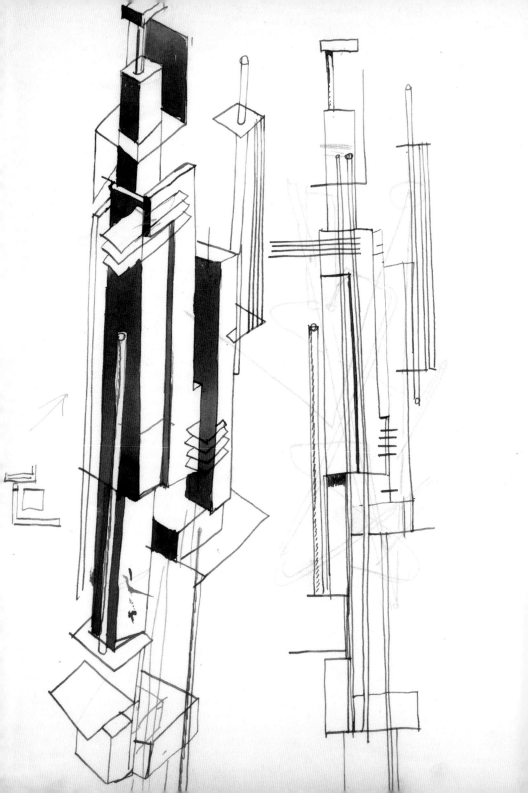

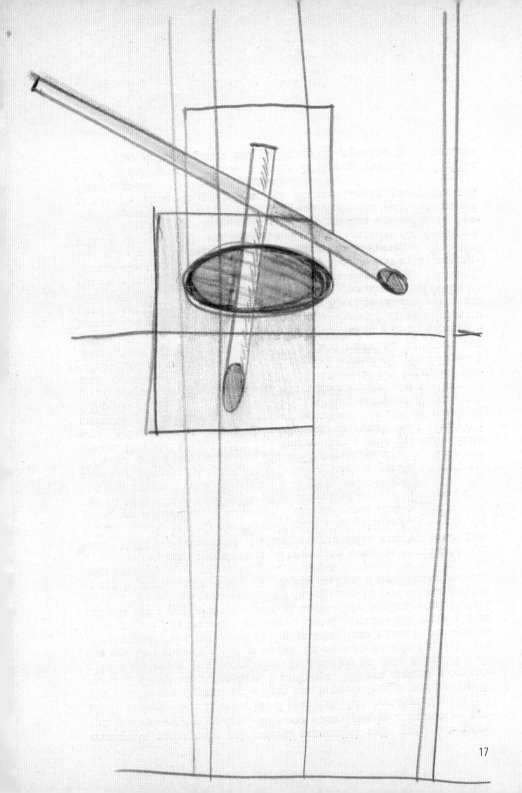

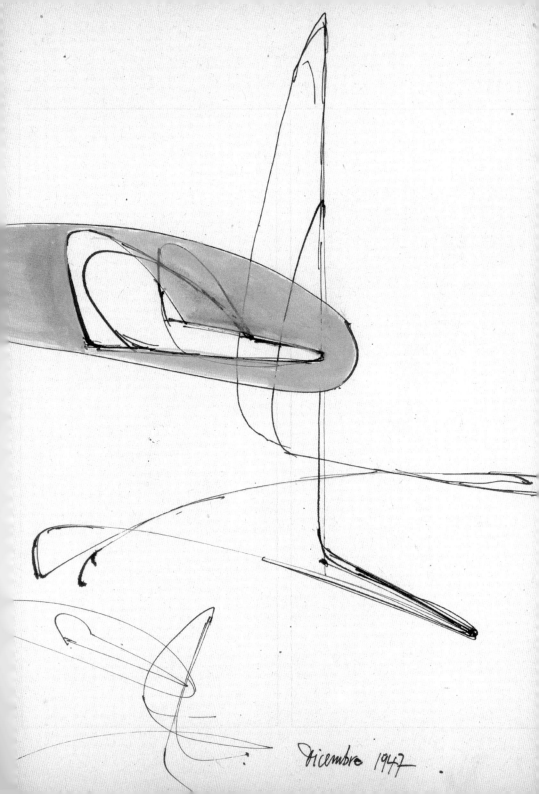

Dicembre 1947

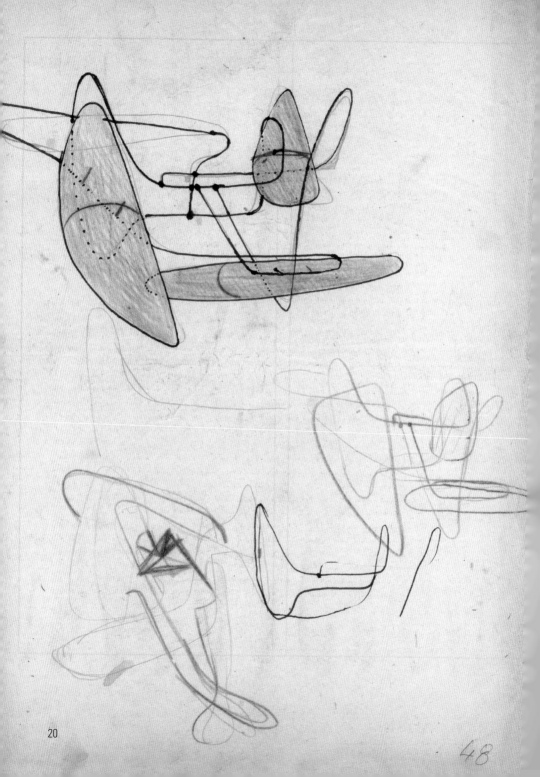

20

48

22

1.1.48

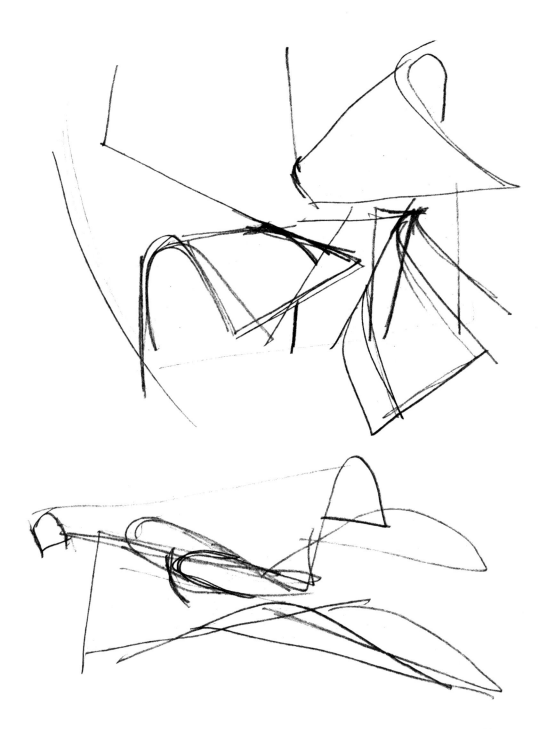

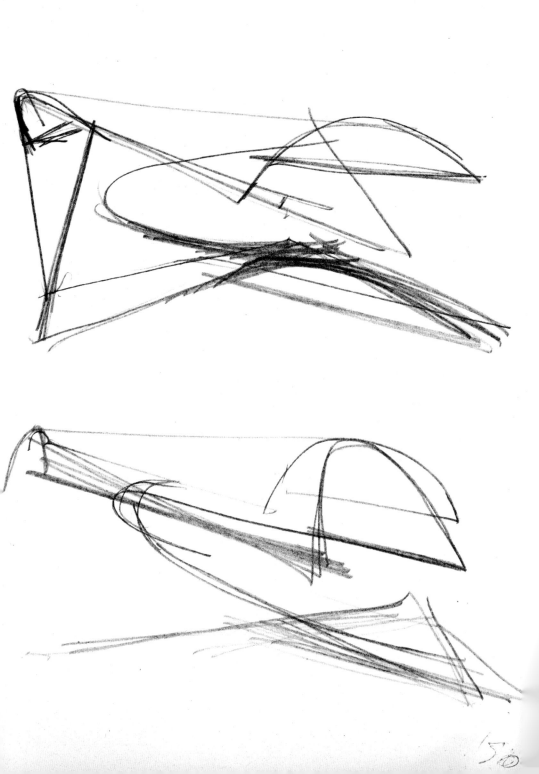

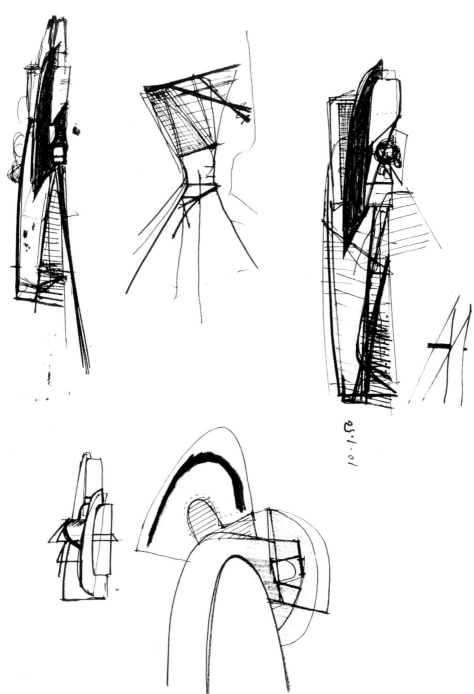

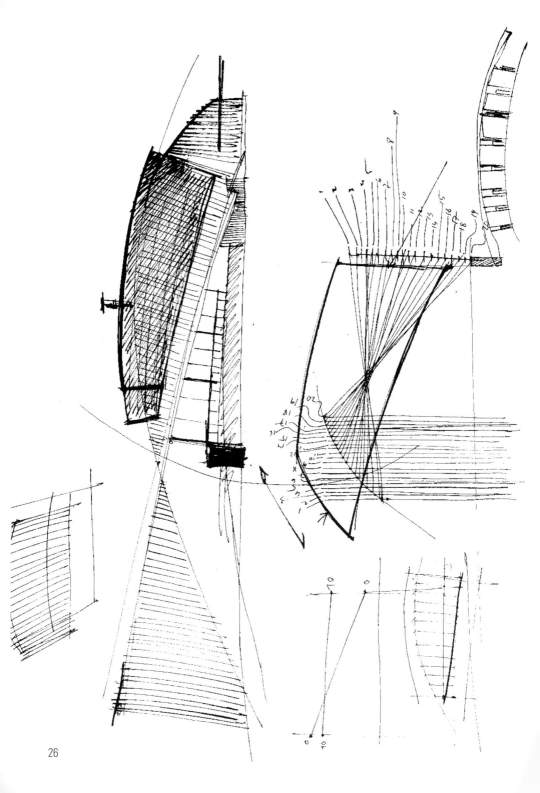

26

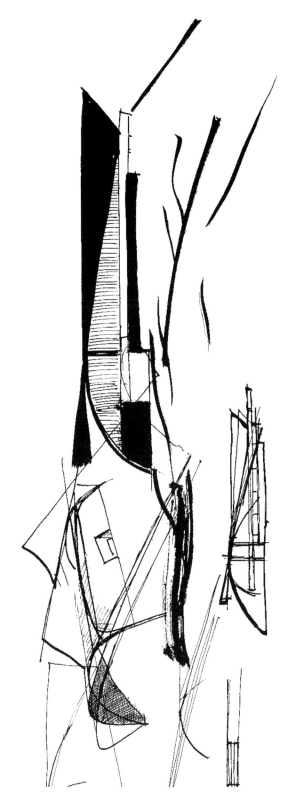

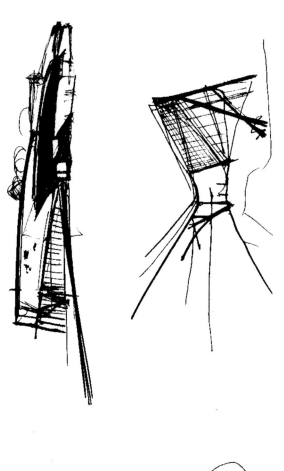

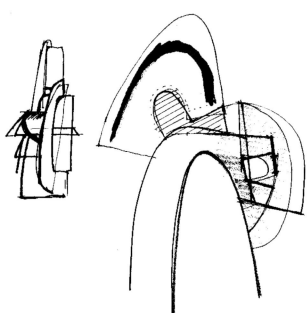

10. Gennaio 1953.

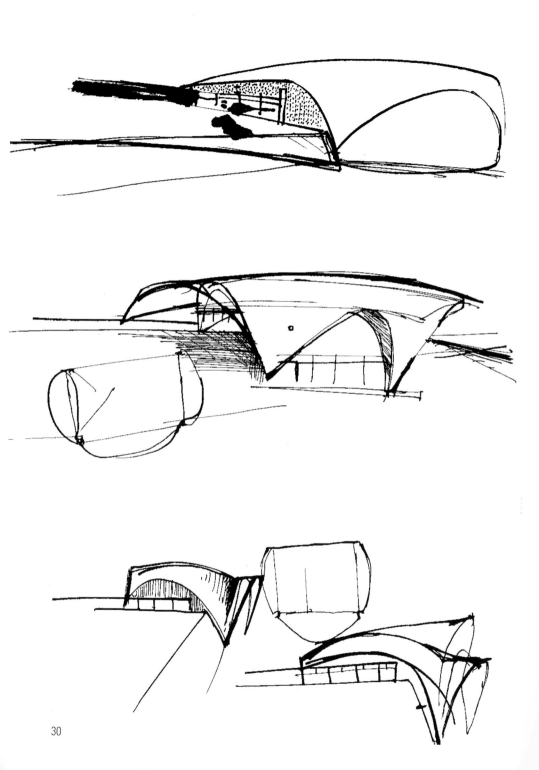

31

2

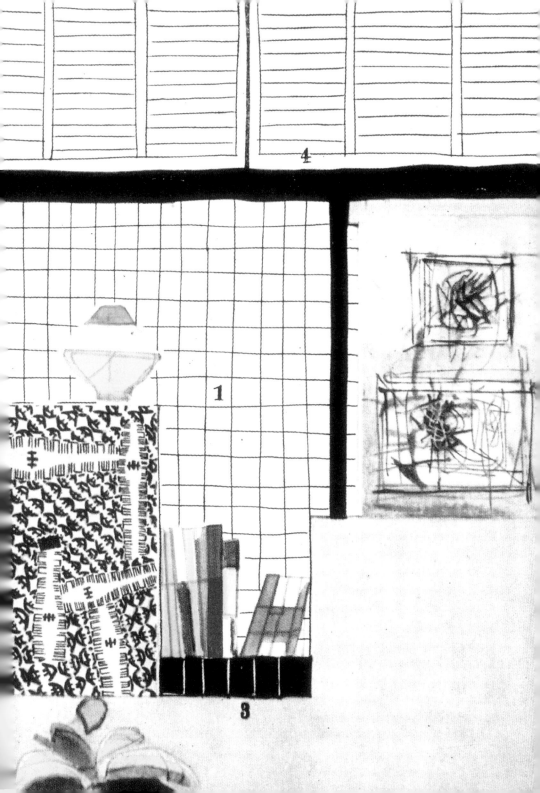

34

LA PORTA

TERRA
ROSSA
e
CERA.

36

DENTRO BIANCO

TERRA ROSSA

37

Eugolino

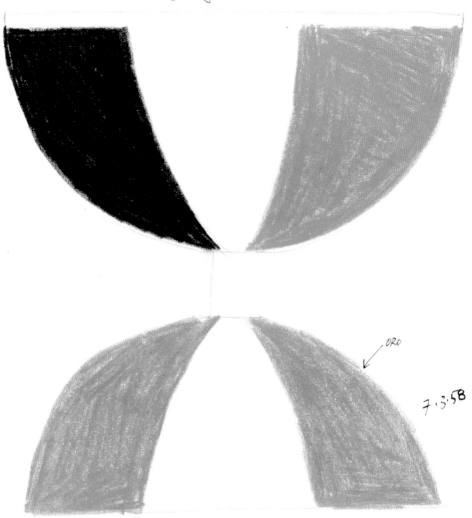

ORO

7·3·58

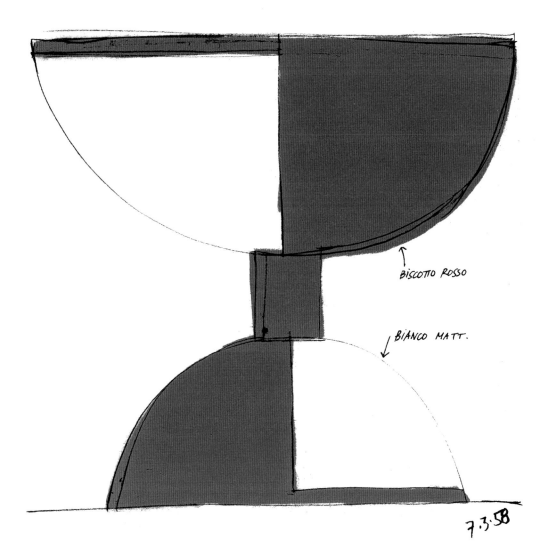

BISCOTTO ROSSO

BIANCO MATT.

7.3.58

39

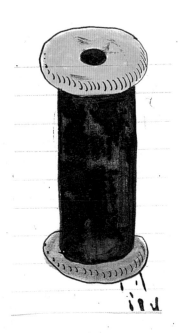

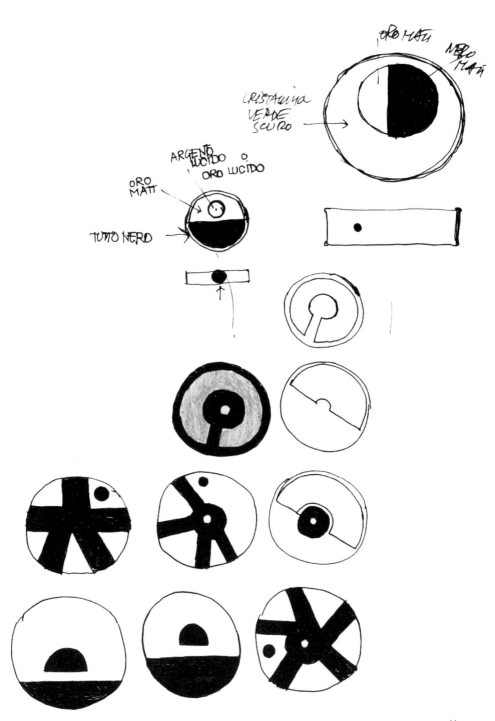

ORO MATT

NERO MATT

CRISTALLINA
VERDE
SCURO

ARGENTO
LUCIDO   O
ORO LUCIDO

ORO
MATT

TUTTO NERO

41

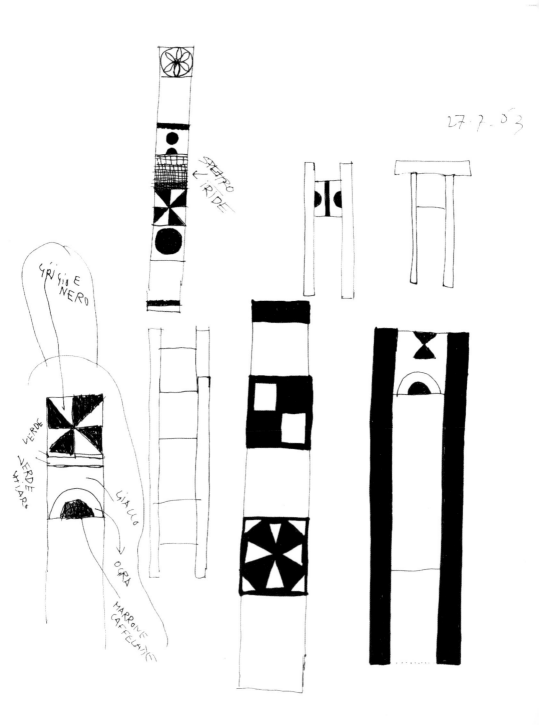

27·7·03

GRIGIO E NERO

SPECCHIO L'IRIDE

VERDE
VERDE CHIARO

GIALLO

OCRA

MARRONE CAFFELATTE

42

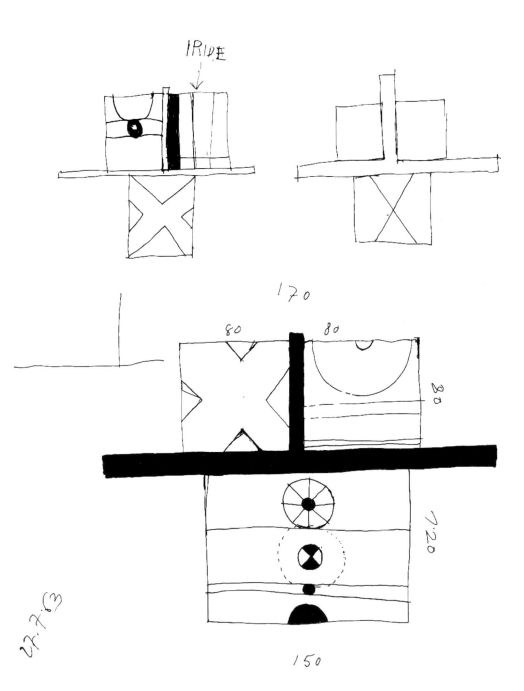

IRIDE

170

80   80

80

27.7.63

720

150

43

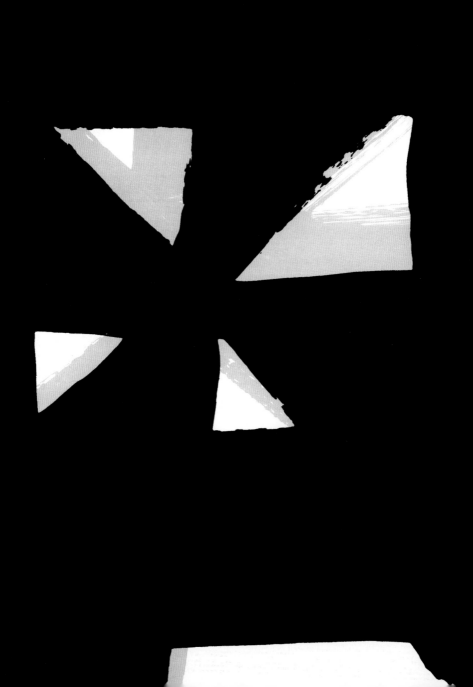

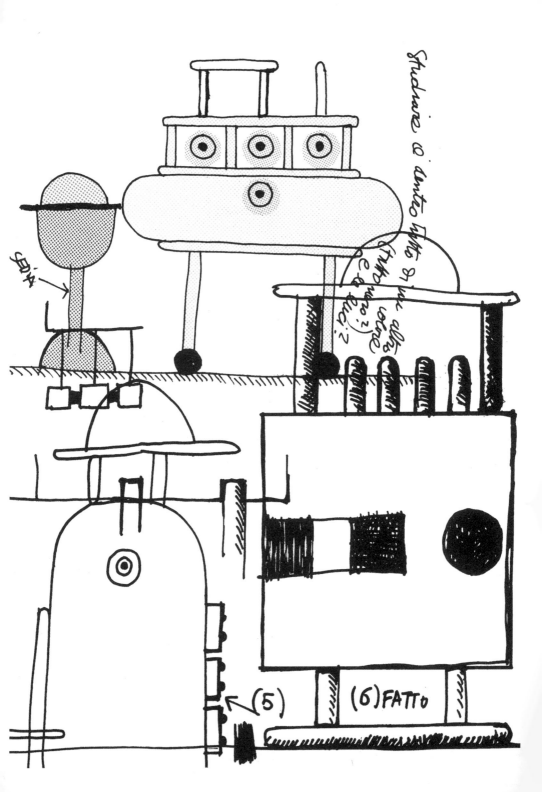

SEDIA

Studiare (o tanto futto) di un altro (ventilatore) e a aria? a che dei?

(5)

(6) FATTO

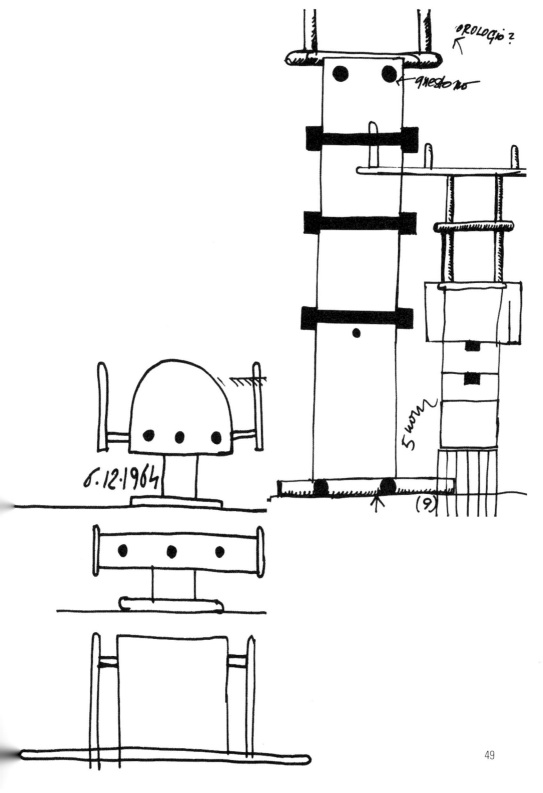

'OROLOGIO?

questo no

5 nov

6.12.1964

(9)

49

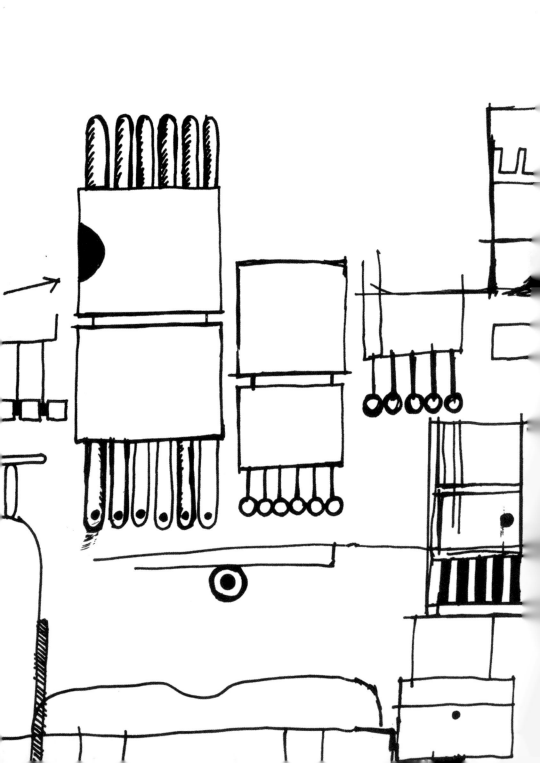

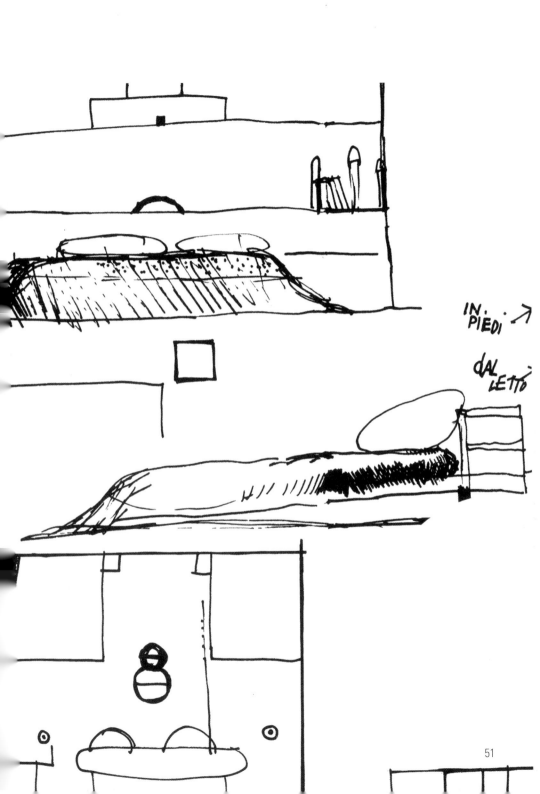

IN
PIEDI ↗

dAL
LETTO

51

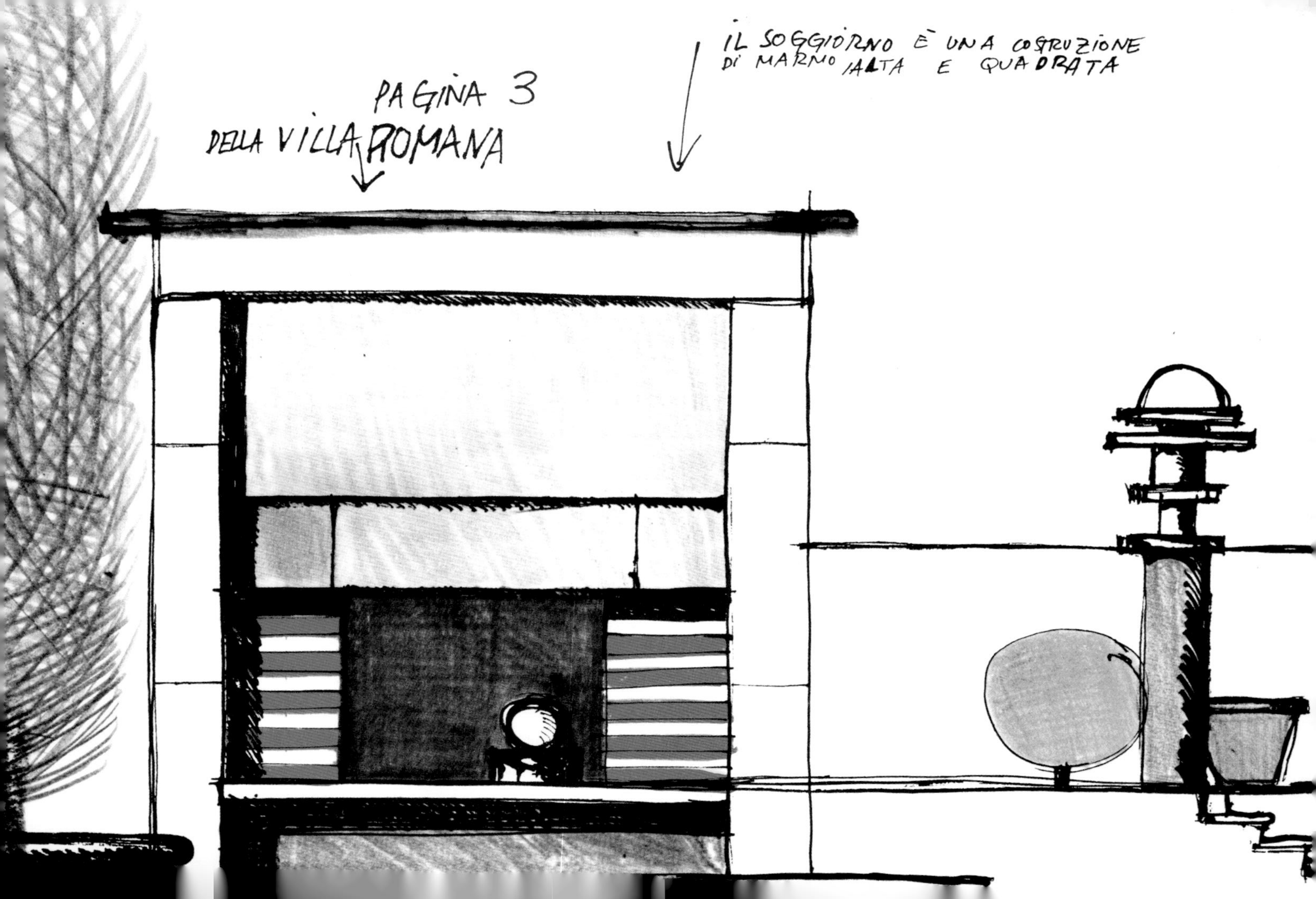

IL SOGGIORNO È UNA COSTRUZIONE
DI MARMO/ALTA E QUADRATA

PAGINA 3
↓
DELLA VILLA ROMANA

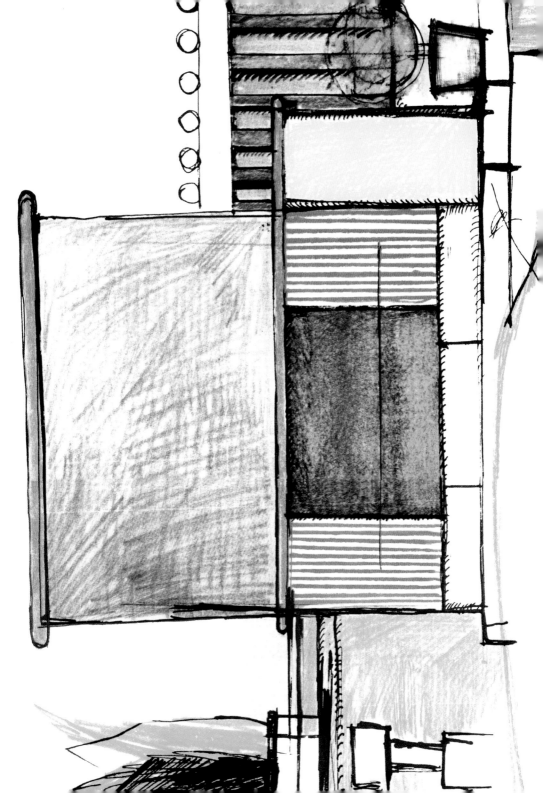

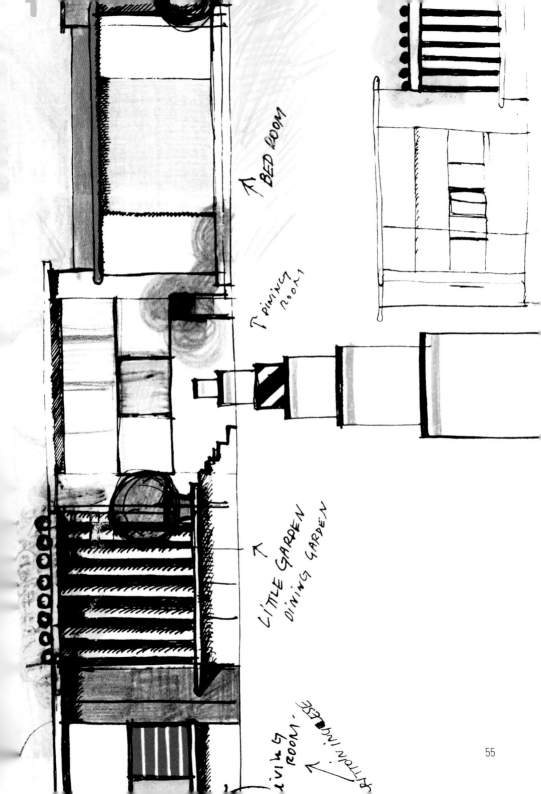

BED ROOM

DINING ROOM

LITTLE GARDEN

DINING GARDEN

LIVING ROOM

ENTRYN HALL

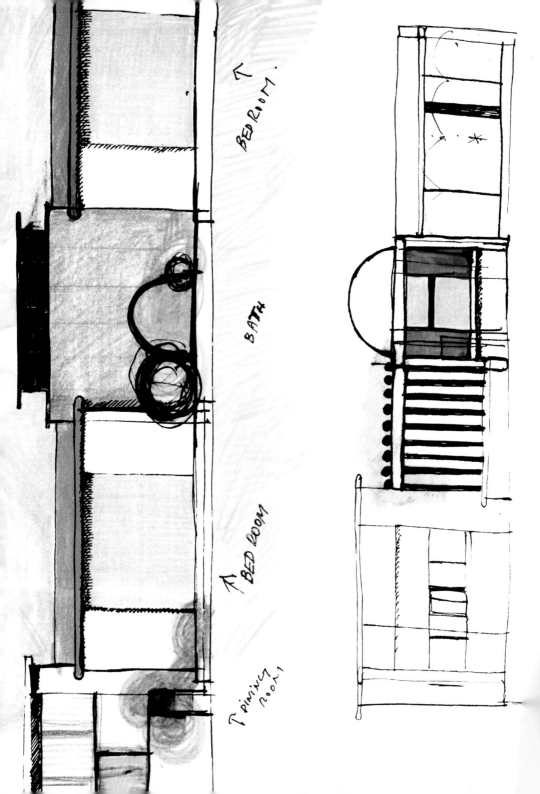

BED ROOM.

BATH

↑ BED ROOM

↑ DINING ROOM

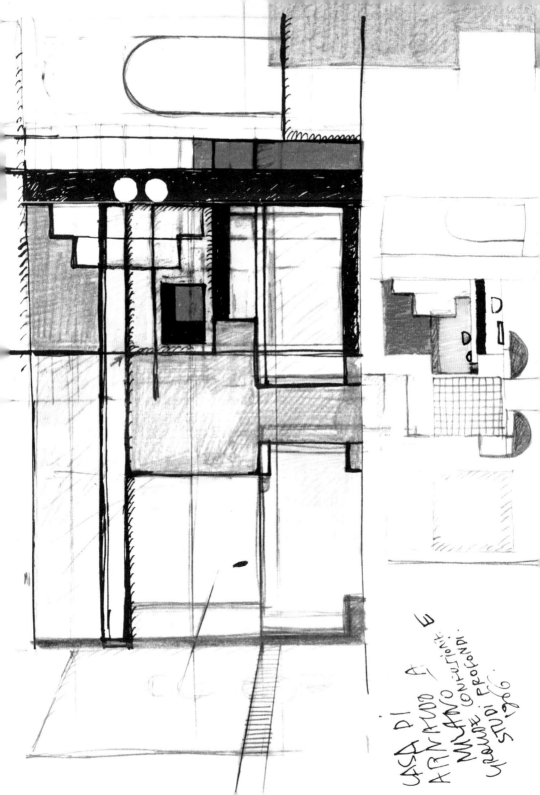

CASA DI
ARMANDO A
MILANO (CONFUSIONE E
GRANDE CONFUSIONE).
URANE PROFONDI.
STUDI 1996

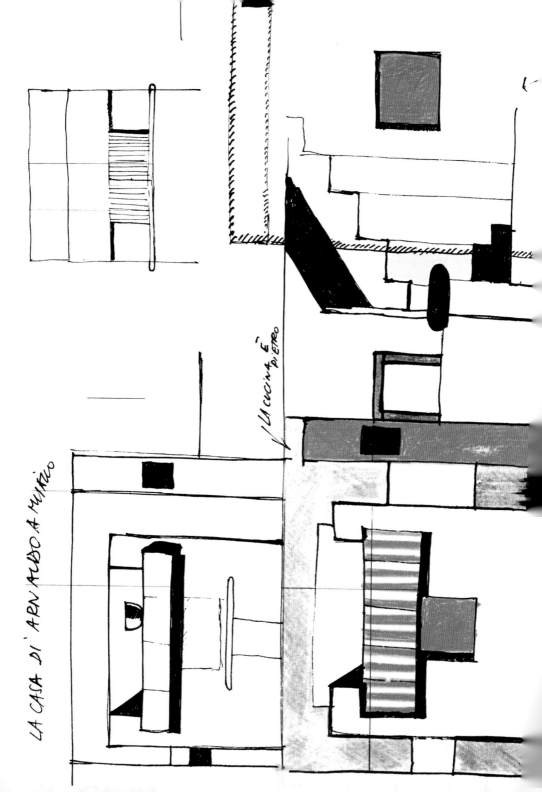

LA CASA DI ' ARN ALDO A MURANO

LA CUCINA È DIETRO

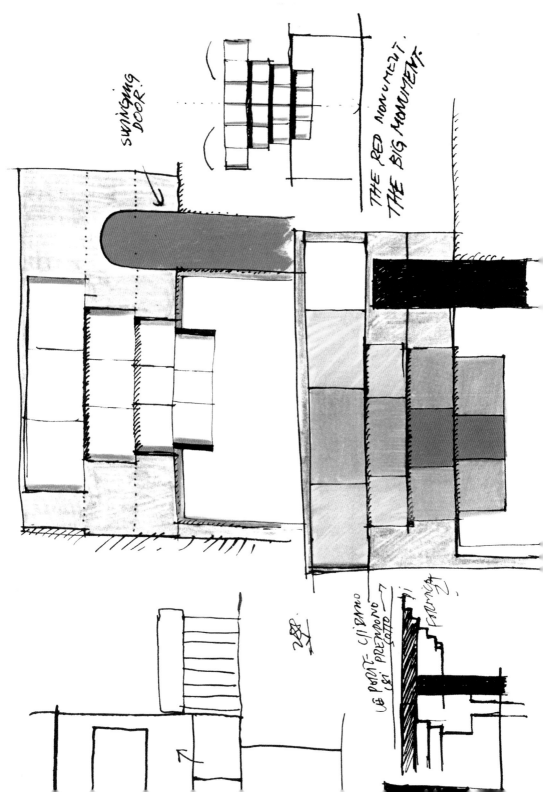

SWINGING DOOR.

THE RED MONUMENT.
THE BIG MONUMENT.

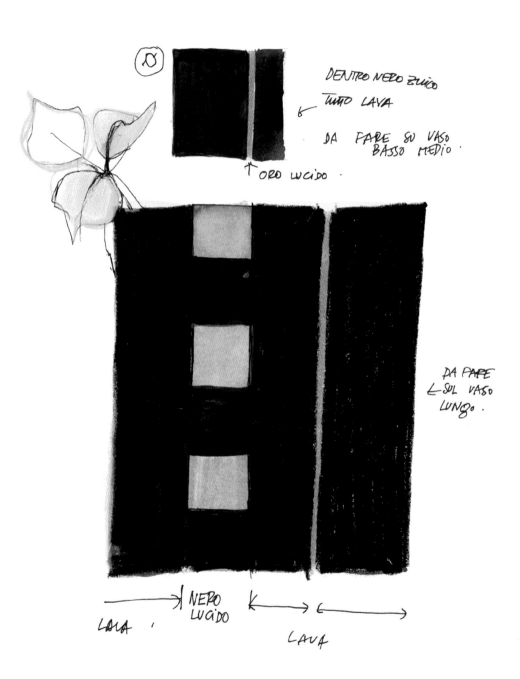

DENTRO NERO ZLúCo

TUTTO LAVA

DA FARE SU VASO
BASSO MEDIO .

ORO LUCIDO .

DA FARE
SUL VASO
LUNGO .

NERO
LUCIDO

LAVA

LAVA

60

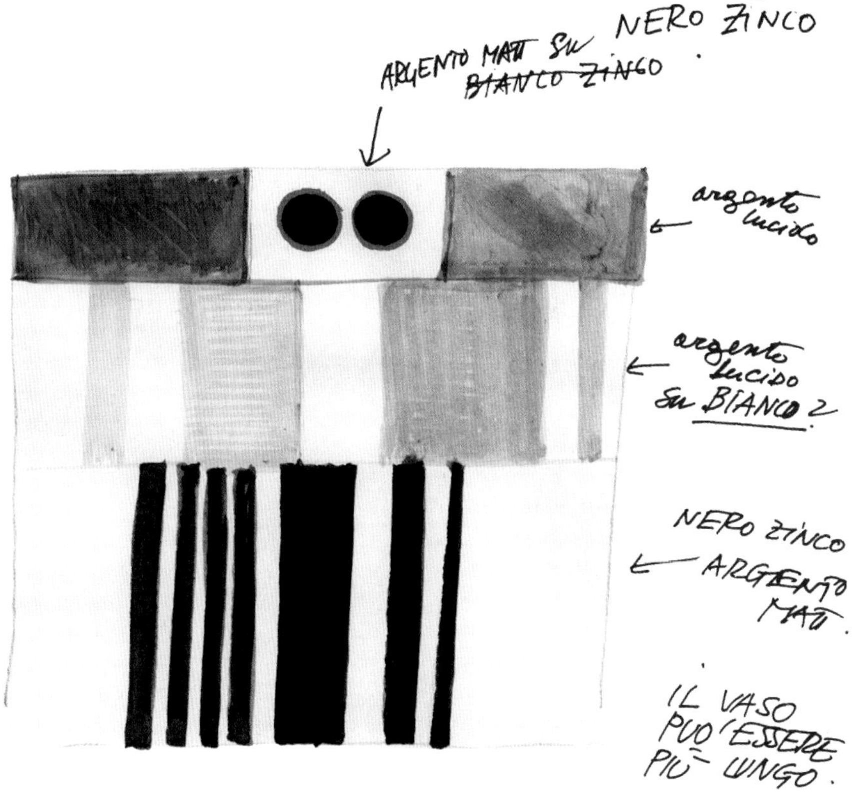

ARGENTO MATT su NERO ZINCO .
BIANCO ZINCO .

argento
lucido

argento
lucido
su BIANCO ?

NERO ZINCO
← ARGENTO
MATT.

IL VASO
PUÓ ESSERE
PIÚ LUNGO.

argento
matt

argento lucido

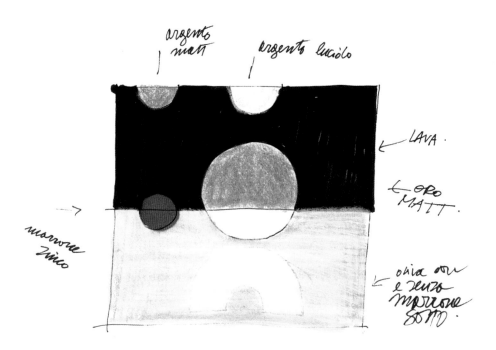

LAVA.

ORO
MATT.

marrone
zinco

chia on
e senza
marrone
sotto.

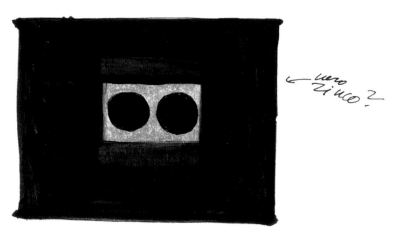

nero
zinco ?

Bolli lucioli
ORO Lucido

quadrato lucido - il resto
appura e contorno lava ?

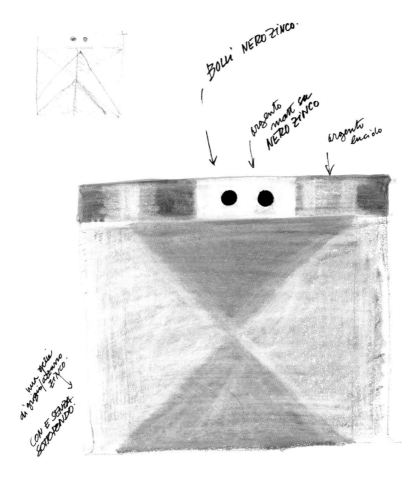

BOLLi NERO ZINCO.

argento matt con NERO ZINCO

argento lucido

una griglia di grigio/platino ZINCO.
CON E SENZA SOTTOFONDO.

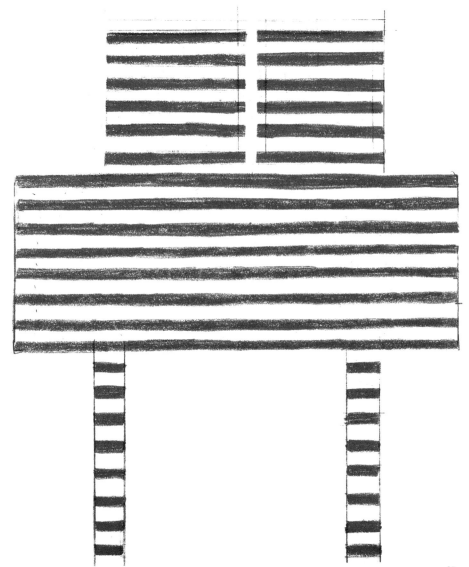

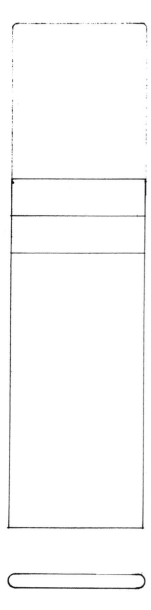

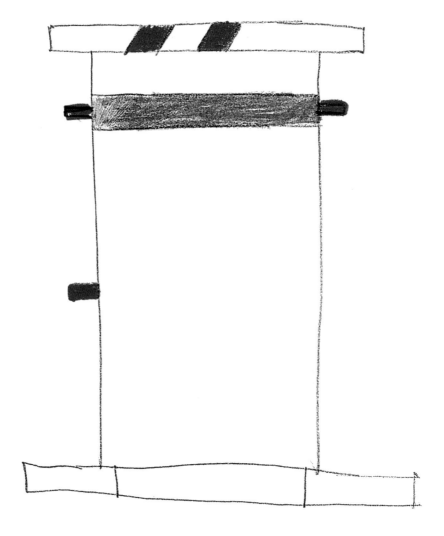

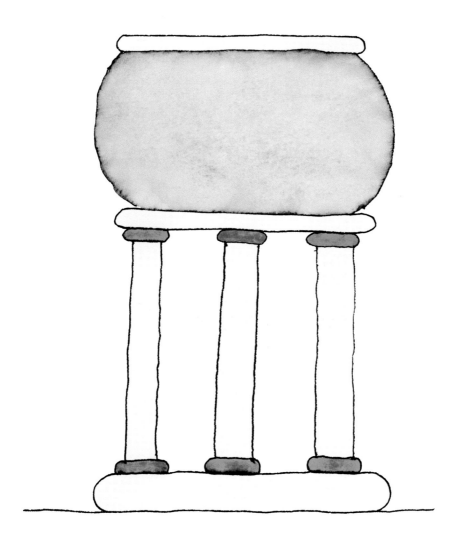

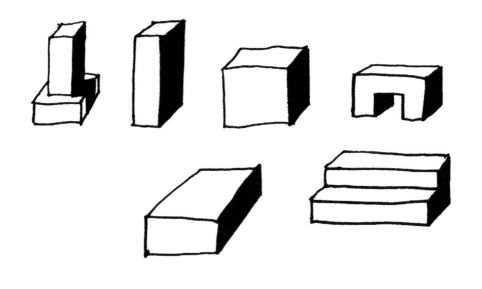

Mausoleum på torget: att rymma välstån-
dets aska.

MAUSOLEO SULLA PIAZZA :
PER CONTENERE LE CENERI
↓ DEL BENESSERE .

uppslag, kanske fortfarande alltför oord-
nade för att visas i konkret form. Utställningen skulle dock behandla en miljö
som delvis byggde på hippiekulturens er-
farenheter, en känslomässig och odog-
matisk uppställning som samtidigt hade
ett direkt program och ett budskap. Just
då, i december 1967, kom alla som be-
sökte det sottsaska hemmet vid Via
Manzoni i Milano, och det var en rad
konstnärer, arkitekter och författare, att

bli inbegripna i diskussioner om utställningen och att i viss mån deltaga i ut-
formningen av programmet.
I början av sommaren 1968 fortsatte vi
diskussionerna om utställningen och det
blev ännu mer väsentligt att föra projek-
tet i land, därför att den del av Biennalen
i Venedig där Sottsass skulle ha deltagit
med objekt aldrig kom till stånd genom
oroligheterna i juni. Att utställningen
skulle äga rum just i Sverige blev på sätt

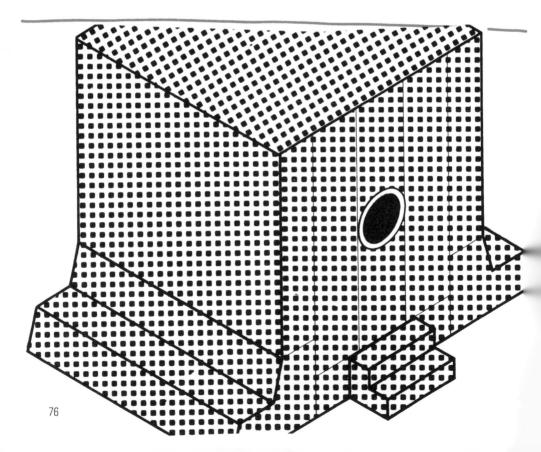

GRANDE ALTARE:
PER UN COSMICO SACRIFICIO DEL SANGUE UMANO (PRIMA CHE SIA BEVUTO DAI KSATRIJA, DALLE CASTE DEI MILITARI)

Stort altare:
för ett kosmiskt offer av människoblod
(innan det druckits av KSATRIYA, av mi-
litärernas kast).

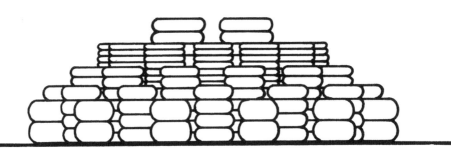

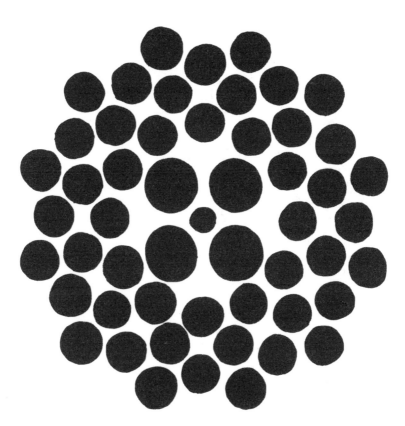

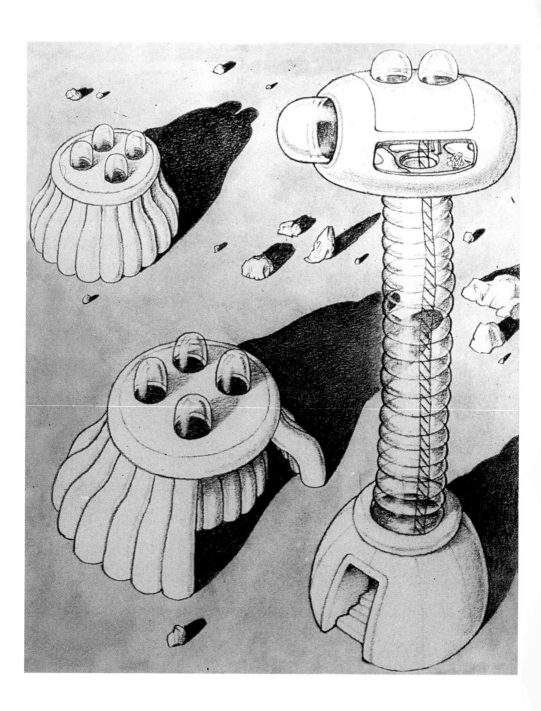

PLANS OF TEMPLES I

SCALE OF FEET

50 40 30 20 10   50   100   150

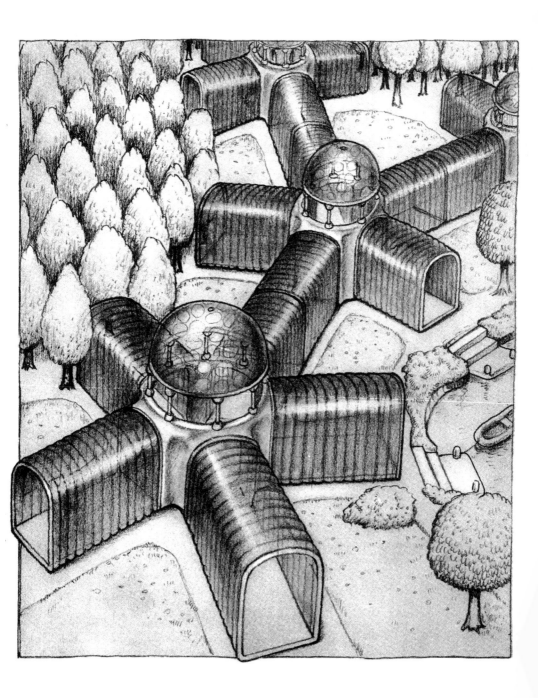

IRRAWADD

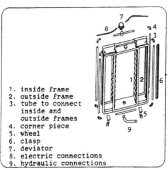

1. inside frame
2. outside frame
3. tube to connect inside and outside frames
4. corner piece
5. wheel
6. clasp
7. deviator
8. electric connections
9. hydraulic connections

single frame

double frame

triple frame

gallery

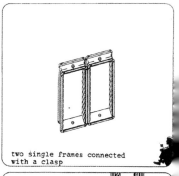

two single frames connected with a clasp

two single frames closing one to another

two single frames closed one to another

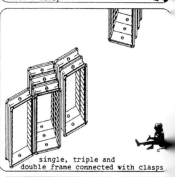

single, triple and double frame connected with clasps

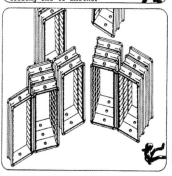

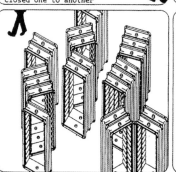

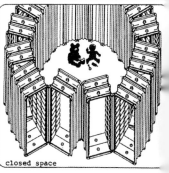

closed space

84

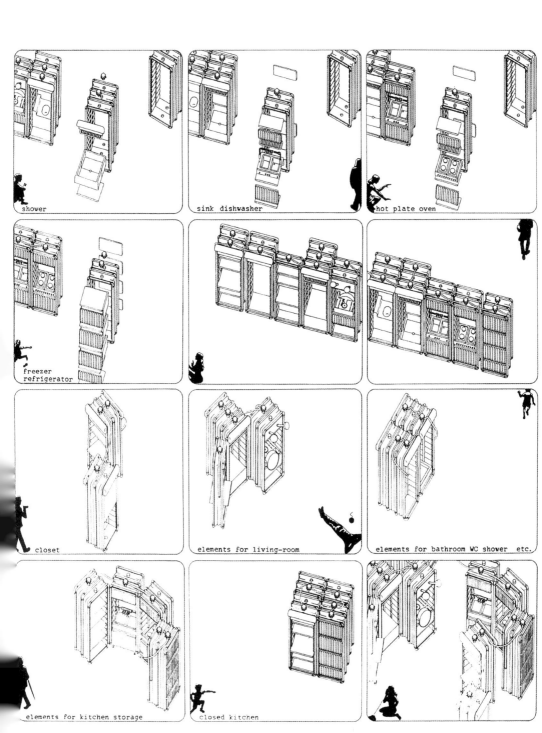

shower

sink dishwasher

hot plate oven

freezer
refrigerator

closet

elements for living-room

elements for bathroom WC shower etc.

elements for kitchen storage

closed kitchen

85

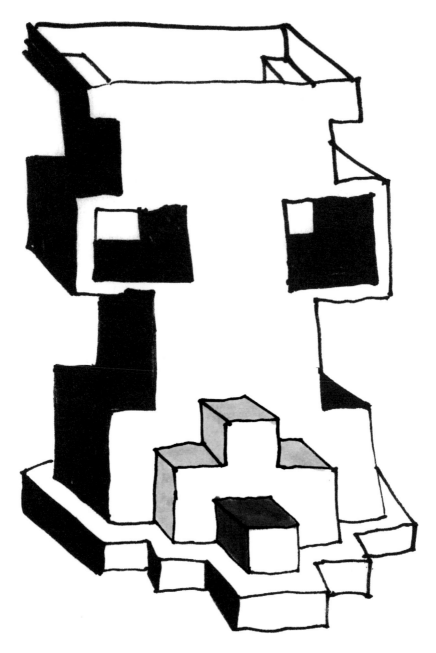

DOMENICA SERA
23 - 1 - 1972

Type A Capsule: basic unit for important buildings such as capitol buildings, banks, insurance buildings, newspaper headquarters etc.

ETTORE SOTTSASS JR.

PER RITARDATO ARRIVO DELL'AEROMOBILE
BECAUSE OF LATE ARRIVAL OF THE AIRCRAFT

BLOCK
NOTES

I want to solve the world's architectural controversy once and for all

VOGLIO RISOLVERE
PER SIEMPRE
IL PROBLEMA MONDIALE
DELL'ARCHITETTURA

Type B Capsule (rational): basic unit for cheap low-cost housing, prefabricated, easy-to-build etc. Just to store the working class

CELLULA
TIPO "A"
ELEMENTO BASE
PER EDIFICI
IMPORTANTI:
TIPO PALAZZI DI
GOVERNO, BANCHE,
ASSICURAZIONI,
GIORNALI
ETC.

CELLULA (RAZIONALE)
TIPO "B"
ELEMENTO BASE
PER EDIFICI
POPOLARI, A
BUON MERCATO,
PREFABBRICATO,
FATTO IN FRETTA
ETC.
TANTO PER
IMMAGAZZINARE LA
CLASSE CHE
PRODUCE.

Unsymmetrical unit (somewhat romantic): I can't see what's so funny

ELEMENTO
DISSIMETRICO
(UN PO' ROMANTICO,
PER LA VERITÀ)

NON VEDO CHE COSA C'È DA RIDERE

brick *MATTONE*   window *FINESTRA*   door *PORTA*   toilet *GABINETTO*

GRUPPO DI ELEMENTI "C" PER LE CLASSI
PIÙ POVERE (SLUMS SUD AMERICANI)
LE CASE SE LE FACCIANO DA SÉ E NON
ROMPANO

Group of unit C's for the poorest class (South American slums): let them build their houses themselves and leave us alone

ECCEZIONE ARCHITETTONICA
FANTASIOSA (CON TESTO
CRITICO SULL'ESPRESSO)
PERMESSA SOLTANTO A
QUALCHE ALTO FUNZIONARIO.

Exceptionally imaginative architecture (with review from "Espresso") only for important officials

87

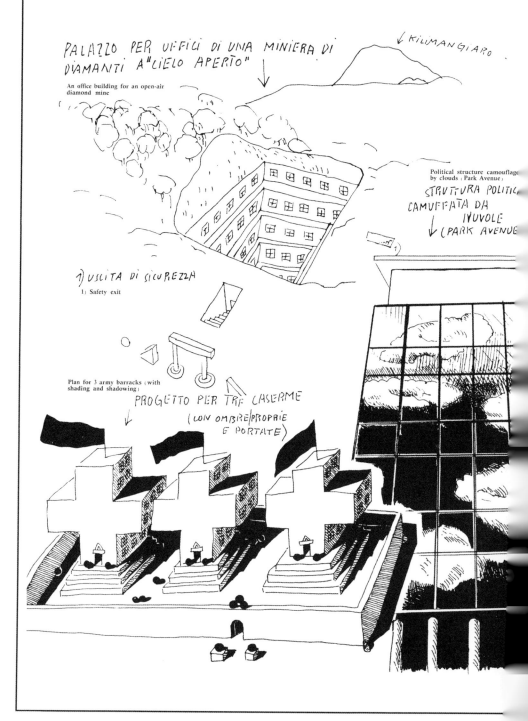

PALAZZO PER UFFICI DI UNA MINIERA DI
DIAMANTI A "CIELO APERTO"

An office building for an open-air
diamond mine

↓ KILIMANGIARO

Political structure camouflage
by clouds (Park Avenue)

STRUTTURA POLITIC
CAMUFFATA DA
IVUVOLE
↓ (PARK AVENUE

1) USCITA DI SICUREZZA

1) Safety exit

Plan for 3 army barracks (with
shading and shadowing)

PROGETTO PER TRE CASERME
(CON OMBRE PROPRIE
E PORTATE)

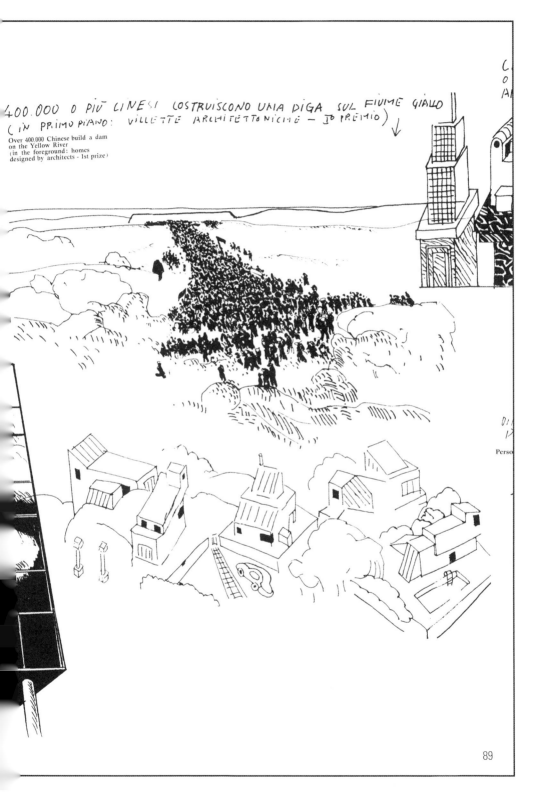

400.000 O PIÙ CINESI COSTRUISCONO UNA DIGA SUL FIUME GIALLO
(IN PRIMO PIANO: VILLETTE ARCHITETTONICHE — 1° PREMIO)

Over 400.000 Chinese build a dam
on the Yellow River
(in the foreground: homes
designed by architects - 1st prize)

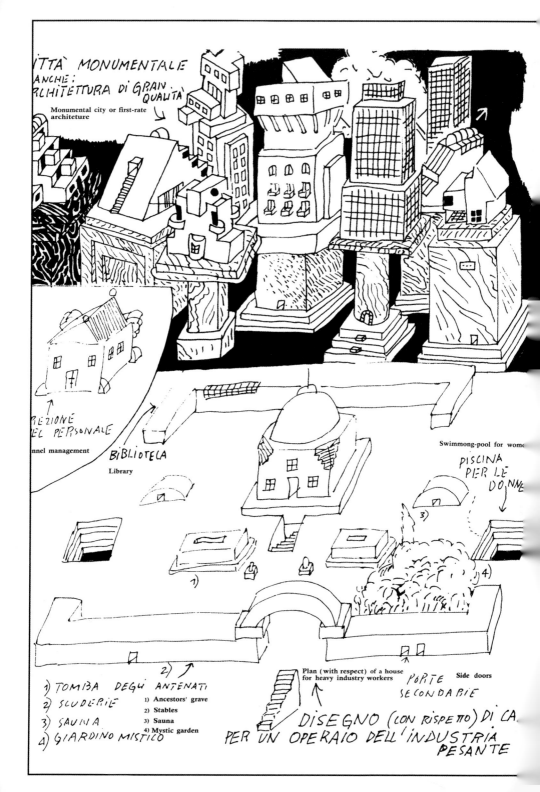

CITTÀ MONUMENTALE
ANCHE:
ARCHITETTURA DI GRAN QUALITÀ

Monumental city or first-rate architecture

ISPEZIONE DEL PERSONALE

Personnel management

BIBLIOTECA
Library

Swimmong-pool for wome

PISCINA PER LE DONNE

3)

4)

1)

2)

Plan (with respect) of a house for heavy industry workers

PORTE SECONDARIE   Side doors

1) TOMBA DEGLI ANTENATI
2) SCUDERIE
3) SAUNA
4) GIARDINO MISTICO

1) Ancestors' grave
2) Stables
3) Sauna
4) Mystic garden

DISEGNO (CON RISPETTO) DI CA.
PER UN OPERAIO DELL'INDUSTRIA PESANTE

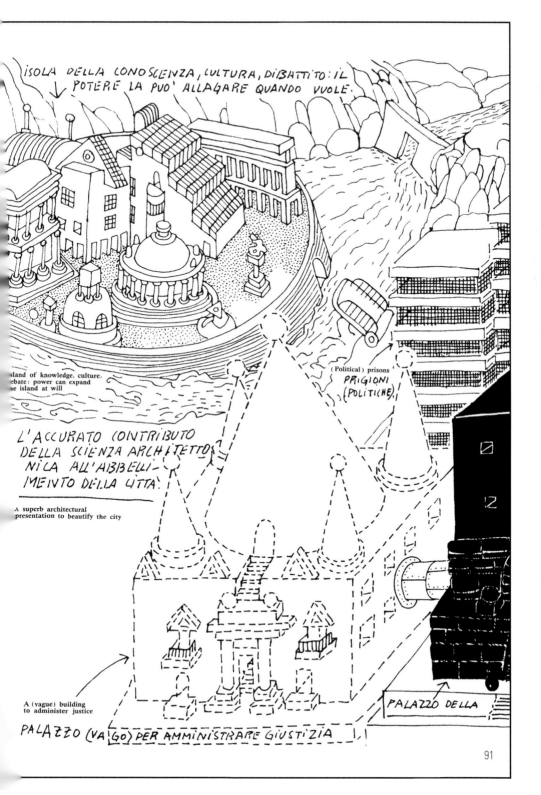

ISOLA DELLA CONOSCENZA, CULTURA, DIBATTITO: IL
POTERE LA PUO' ALLAGARE QUANDO VUOLE.

sland of knowledge, culture,
ebate: power can expand
ne island at will

L'ACCURATO CONTRIBUTO
DELLA SCIENZA ARCHITETTO
NICA ALL'ABBELLI-
MENTO DELLA CITTA.

A superb architectural
presentation to beautify the city

(Political) prisons
PRIGIONI
(POLITICHE)

12

A (vague) building
to administer justice

PALAZZO (VA GO) PER AMMINISTRARE GIUSTIZIA

PALAZZO DELLA

91

(Political) prisons

PRIGIONI (POLITICHE)

POLIZIA (POLITICA)

Court house (politics)

PALAZZO DEL GOVERNO Capitohouse

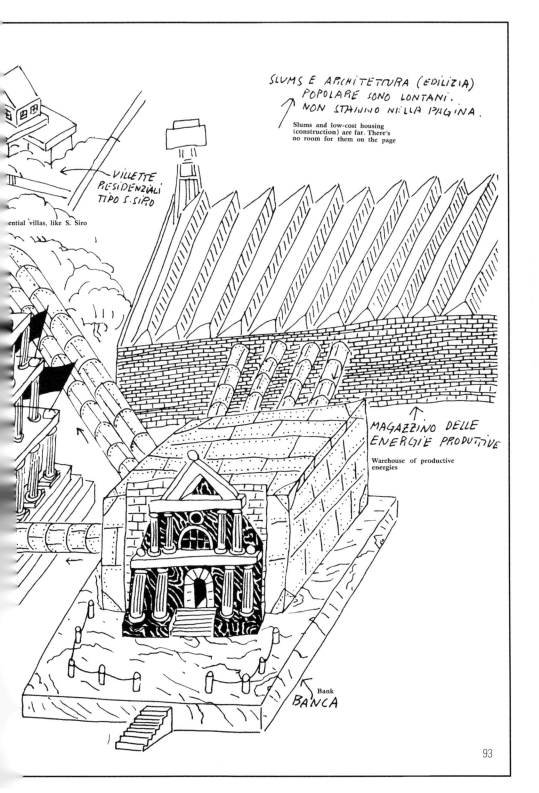

SLUMS E ARCHITETTURA (EDILIZIA)
POPOLARE SONO LONTANI.
NON STANNO NELLA PAGINA.

Slums and low-cost housing
(construction) are far. There's
no room for them on the page

VILLETTE
RESIDENZIALI
TIPO S. SIRO

ential villas, like S. Siro

MAGAZZINO DELLE
ENERGIE PRODUTTIVE

Warehouse of productive
energies

Bank
BANCA

93

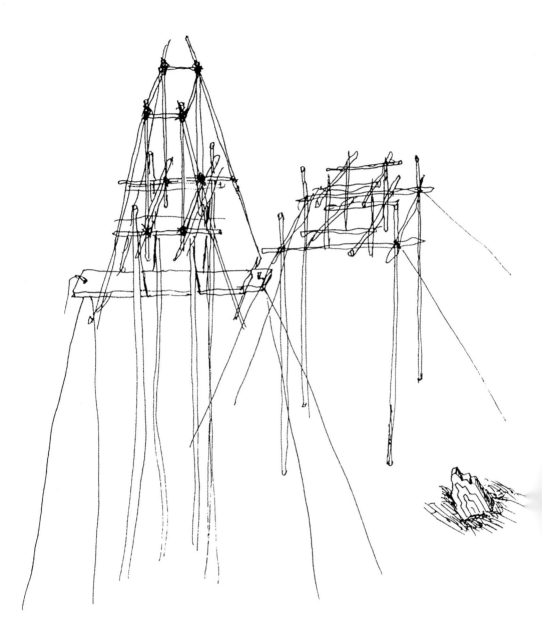

GRANDE COSTRUZIONE

PSEUDO ARCHITETTURA
(TANTO il canno sta con lo stesso)

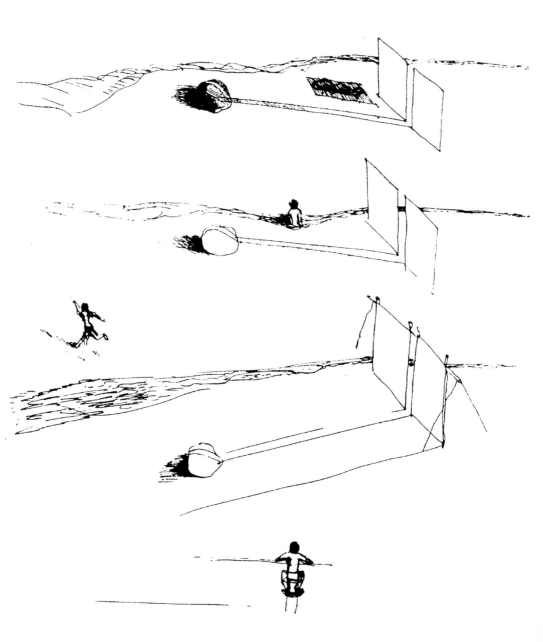

MÍ SVEGLIO, MÍ LAVO...CORRO AL BAR

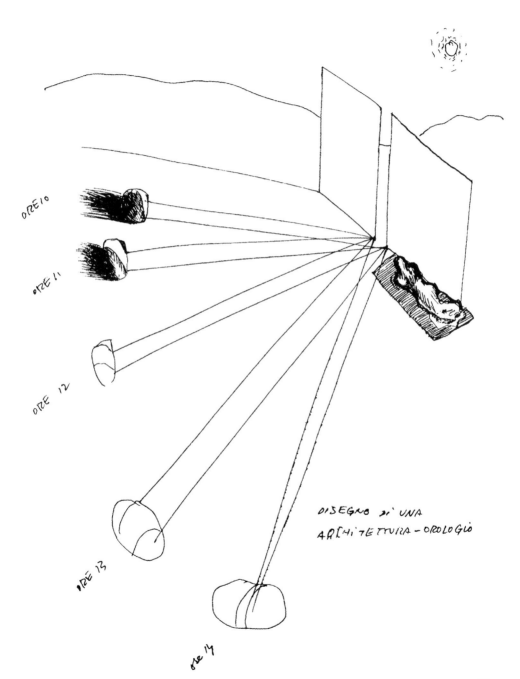

ORE 10

ORE 11

ORE 12

ORE 13

DISEGNO DI UNA
ARCHITETTURA - OROLOGIO

ORE 14

97

1) RIVISITARE L'ERGONOMIA (COSTUME - DINAMICA...)
2) LAVORO MANUALE (COME) TERAPIA — 2000 PALI —
3) RIVISITARE LA COSTRUZIONE
4) (L'ARCHITETTURA COME AZIONE SLEGATA
   (NON MEDIA TRA UOMO E DA~~~~~~PAESAGGIO
                   NATURA) FULLER
                             CONTAINERS ⊕ ETC.)

FARLO CON MINIATURE

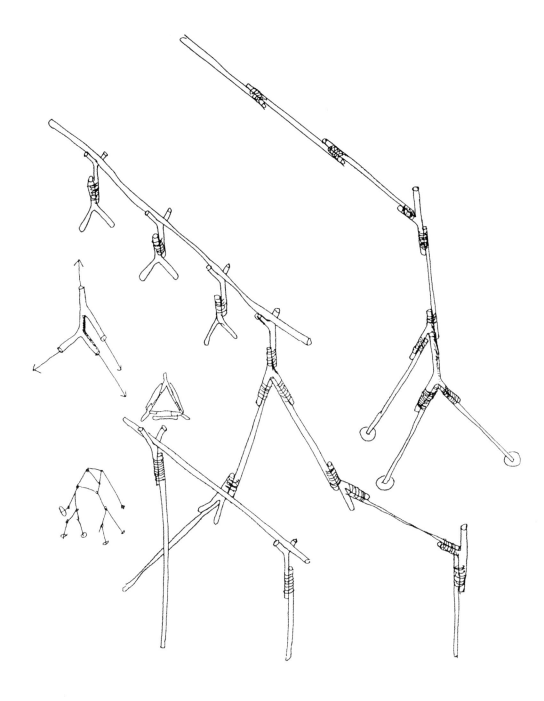

STRUTTURA
DA INGEGNERE POVERO

CASA AL VENTO

L'OMBRA DI UNA FINESTRA

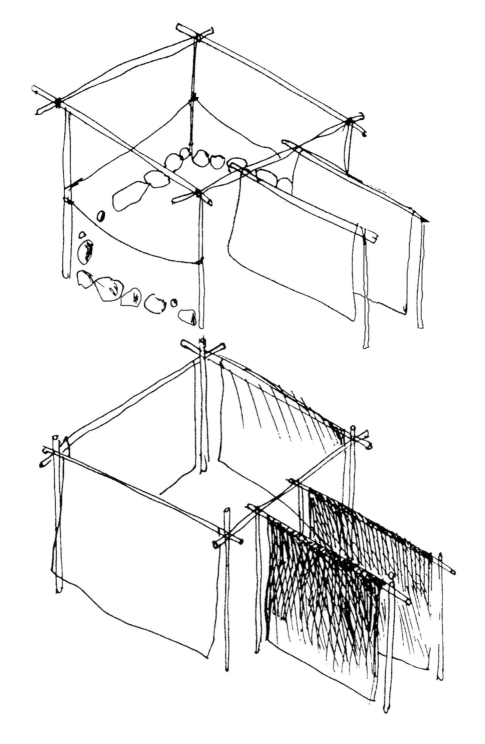

CORTILE SACRO

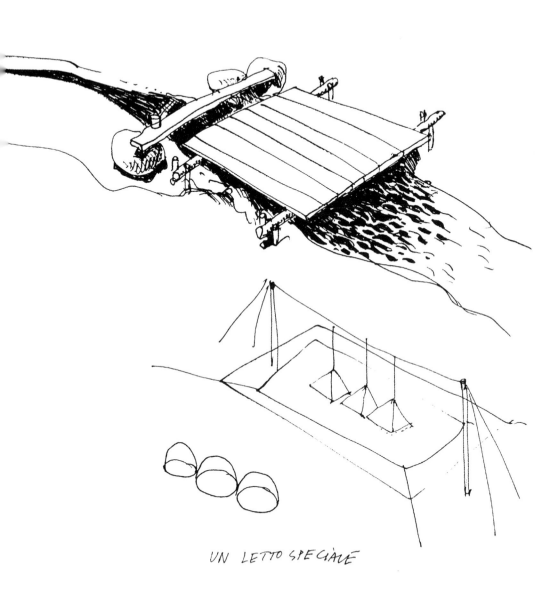

UN LETTO SPECIALE

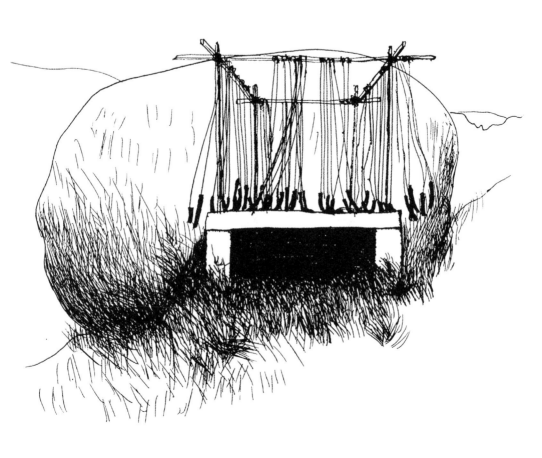

ARCHITETTURA ROMANTICA

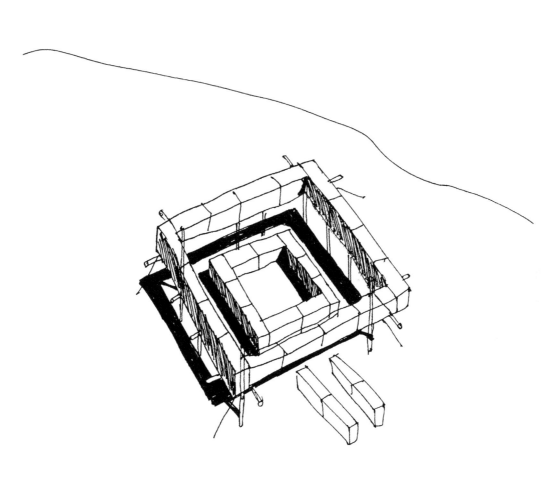

CHIOSTRO APERTO

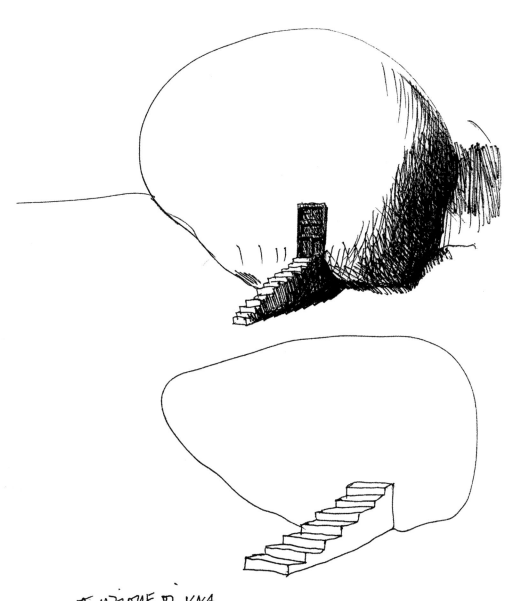

COSTRUZIONE DI UNA
SCALA ~~XXXXX~~ DI ACCESSO
AD UN POSTO INACESSIBICE.
(IN MARMO CIPOLLINO)

ORNAMENTO

STOCCADDA
Giugno .74

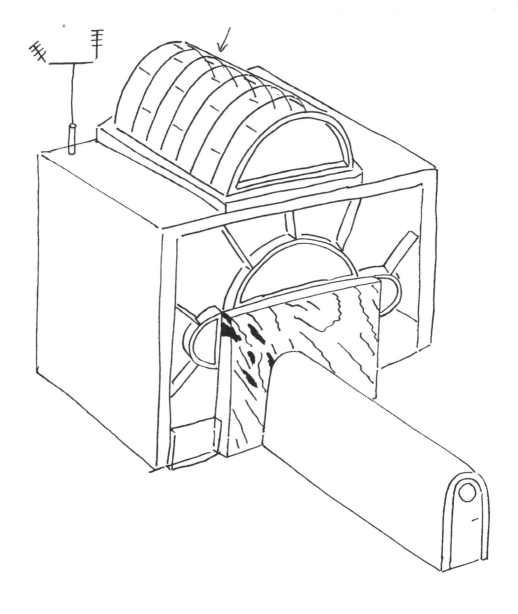

PARTICOLARE ARCHITETTONICO
CON PREZIOSITÀ MARMOREE

PROFESSIONALE ARCHITETTONICO DI
PROGETTO STILE RAZIONAL - POPULISTA
PER CASA POPOLORE, A SCHIERA.

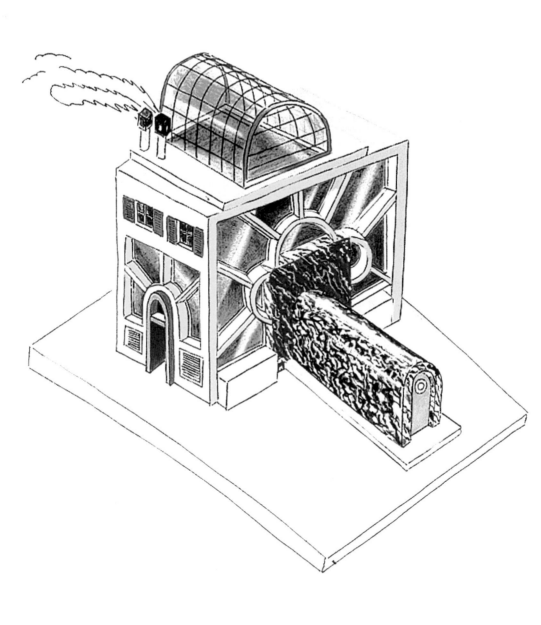

PROGETTO DI VILLA CON PREZIOSITÀ MARMOREE

LA SCELTA LINGUISTICA DI PARTENZA FU CATEGORICA:
RIALLACCIARSI AD UNA CULTURA SCHIETTAMENTE RAZIONALISTA,
IMMUNE DA COMPROMESSI VERNACOLARI O FALSAMENTE MIMETICI.

BRUNO ZEVI

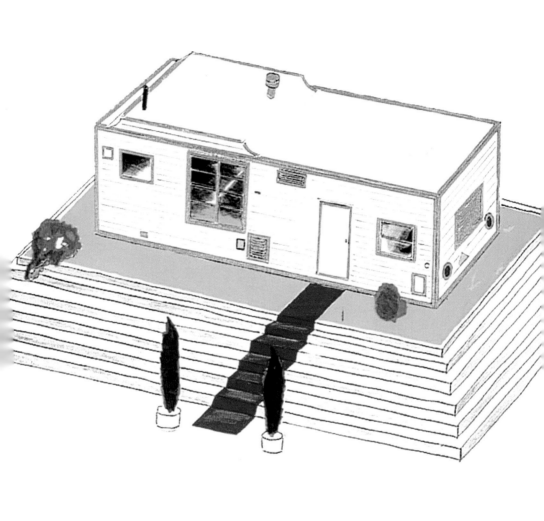

CHI HA PAURA DI FRANK LLOYD WRIGHT ?

NONSENSE ARCHITETTONICO

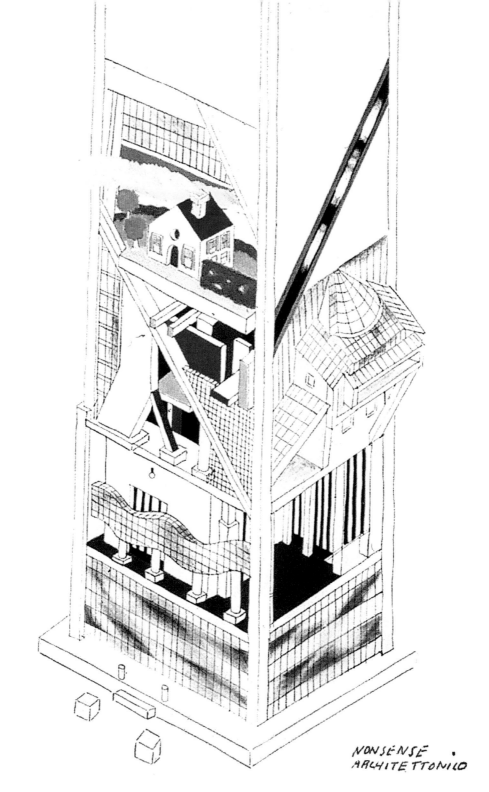

NONSENSE
ARCHITETTONICO

PROGETTO PER GLI UFFICI IBM

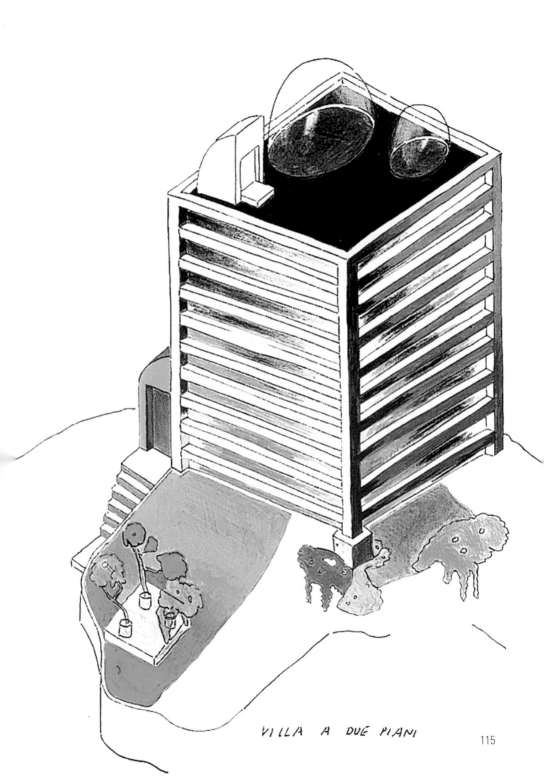

VILLA A DUE PIANI

115

PROGETTO PROFESSIONALE ARCHITETTONICO
DI CASA POPOLARE A SCHIERA
STILE / RAZIONAL-POPULISTA

PROGETTO DI ARCHITETTURA MONUMENTALE PER
LA CONSERVAZIONE DELLE MEMORIE NAZIONAL-POPOLARI

117

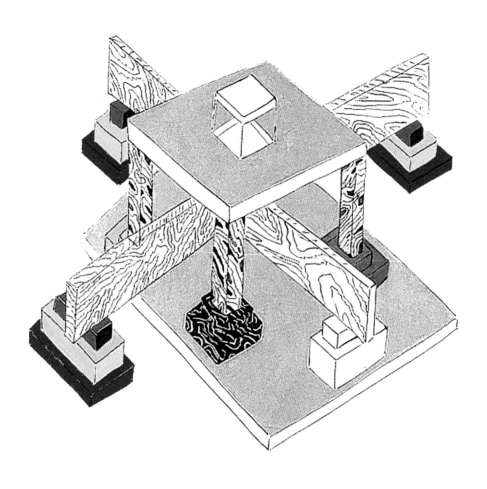

ARCHITETTURA PER RICONOSCERE I PUNTI CARDINALI

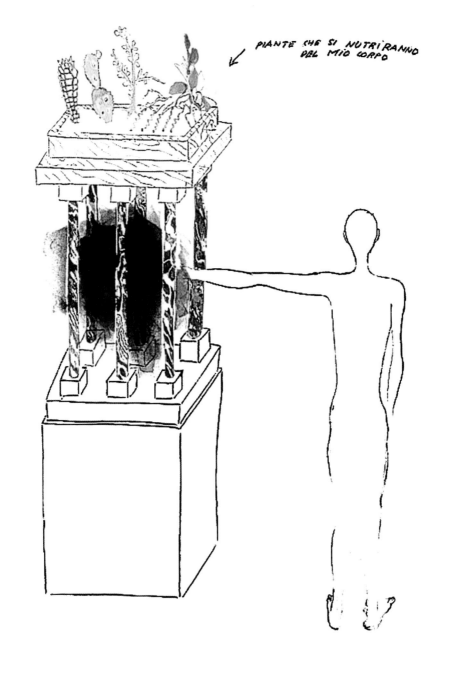

PIANTE CHE SI NUTRIRANNO
DEL MIO CORPO

ARCHITETTURA PER OSPITARE L'OMBRA DELLA MIA MORTE
(SECONDO DON JUAN)

SE FOSSI RICCO, MOLTO RICCO,
MI CONFRONTERÉI CON I MIEI COMPLESSI

PROGETTO DI PIAZZA MONUMENTALE

121

PROGETTO ROMANO-ARABO

APPARTAMENTO

123

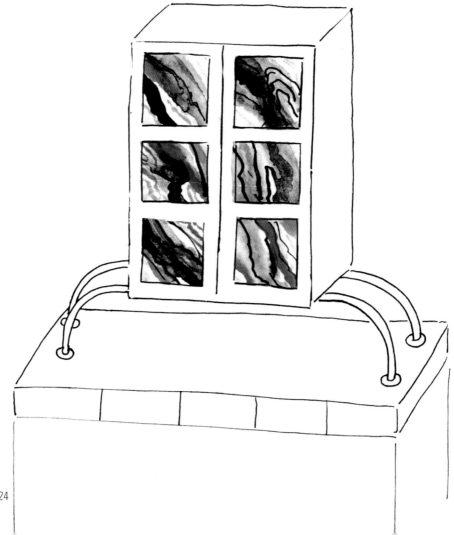

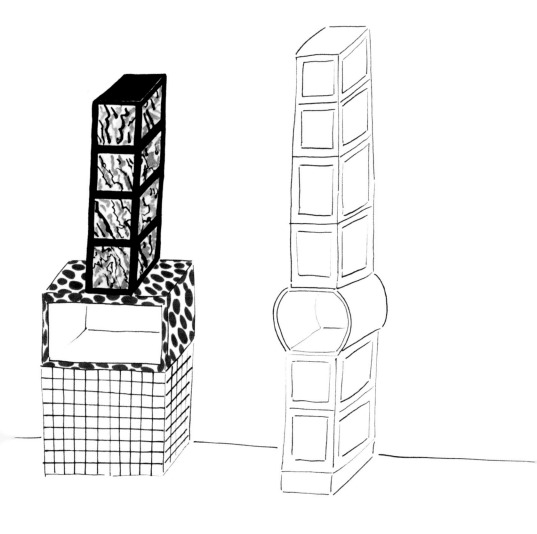

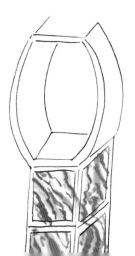

125

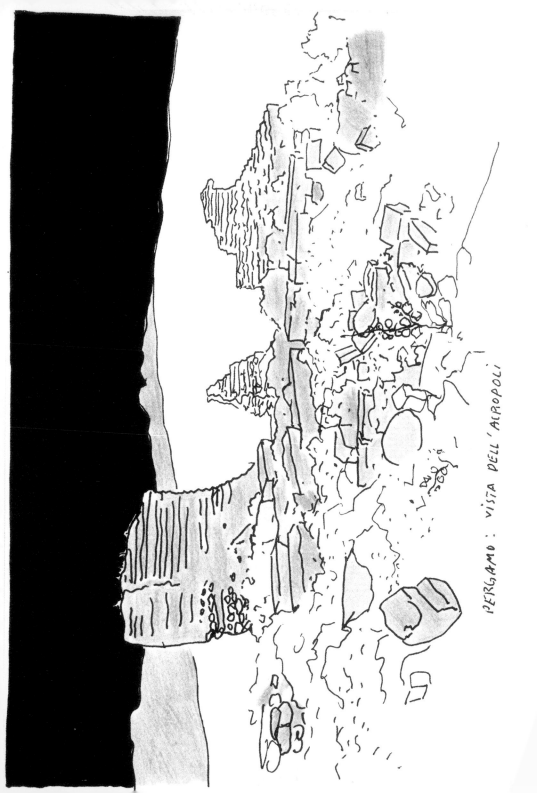

PERGAMO : VISTA DELL'ACROPOLI

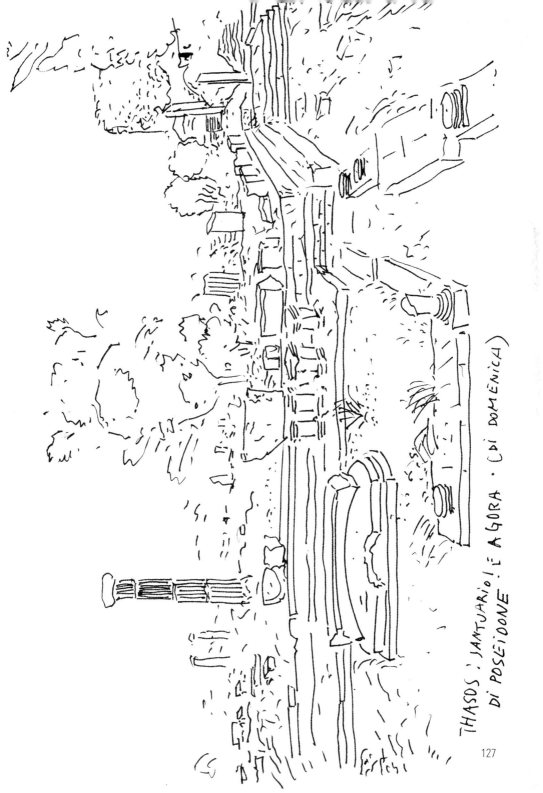

THASOS : SANTUARIO : LE AGORA · (DI DOMENICA)
DI POSEIDONE

127

L'AMICO AMERICANO-INGLESE-FRANCESE
GIRA LA GRECIA CON REGISTRATORE
CASSETTE E AURICOLARI
DA AEREO, ARANCIONI.
CASSETTE VARIE, KAFKA
TOLSTOI, LEZIONI DI MATE-
MATICA E FISICA,
DIALOGHI DA FILM,
FUMETTI E VARIE.
CASSETTA DEI RUMORI
DELL'ORRORE. PUNK.
"MORE DEATH AND HORROR
SOUND EFFECTS. N° 2!

SIDE ONE :
DEATH OF THE FLY
VAMPIRE FEEDING
DEATH BY HARAKIRI
SWEENEY TODD THE
            BARBER
WIND THROUGH CRACKIN
DOOR
WIND IN THE TREES
SINTETIZED WIND
(ELECTRONIC)
SEA MONSTER
SHARPENING
THE KNIFE
FALLING SCREAM
PREMATURAL BURIAL
WILD DOGS
THE IRON MAIDEN
DEATH IN THE SWAMP
THE POISONED DRINK
THE RACK
MIDNIGHT STRANGLER
ASSORTED GUN SHOTS
AT THE DENTIST

PERGE - (ANTALYA) LA PORTA VECCHIA.

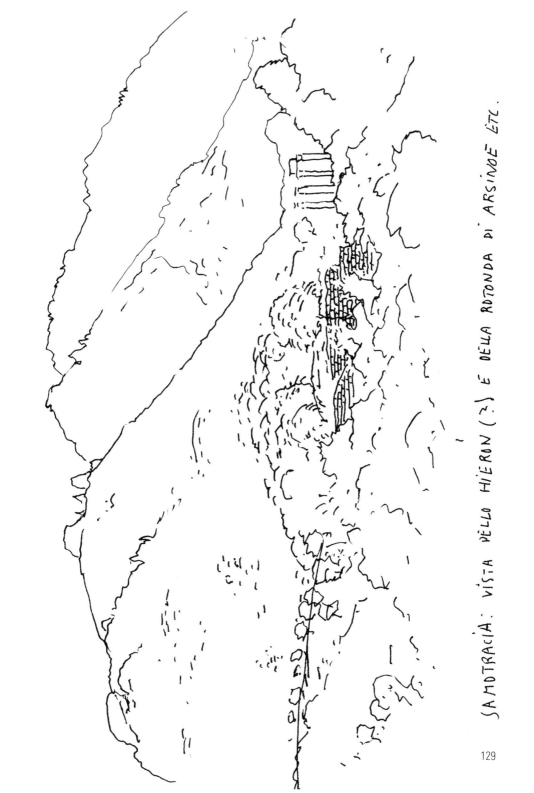

SAMOTRACIA: VISTA DELLO HIERON (?) E DELLA ROTONDA DI ARSINOE ETC.

129

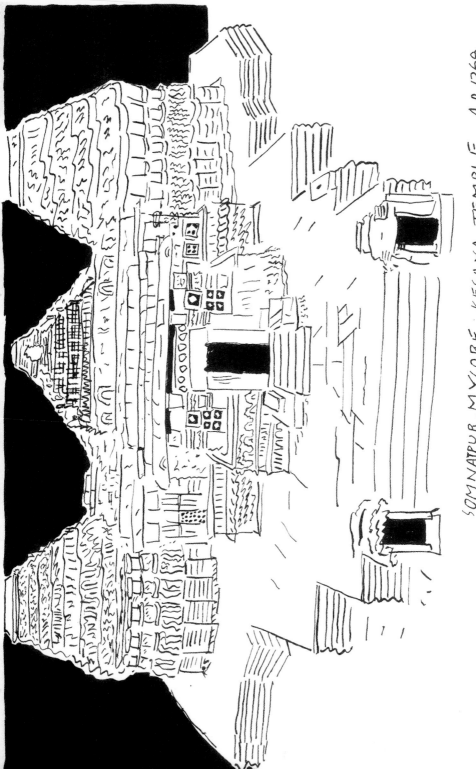

SOMNATPUR, MYSORE : KESAVA TEMPLE A.D. 1268

"L'OMBRA PRODOTTA DALLO GNOMON - MERIDIANA, DEV'ESSERE SEGNATA ALLE 5 DELLA MATTINA E SI TIRA UN CERCHIO CON QUELLA DISTANZA (CON IL GNOMON COME CENTRO). POI SI GUARDA L'OMBRA CHE IL GNOMON CONTINUA A FARE E SI SEGNA IL PUNTO DOVE L'ESTREMITÀ DI QUELL'OMBRA TOCCA IL CERCHIO DESCRITTO PRIMA. DAI DUE PUNTI SEGNATI SULLA CIRCONFERENZA, TRACCIARE DUE ARCHI UGUALI CHE S'INTERSECANO E POI TRACCIARE UNA LINEA TRA IL CENTRO E L'INTERSEZIONE. QUELLA È LA DIREZIONE NORD-SUD "

" I DISEGNATORI INDIANI DI ARCHITETTURE DISEGNAVANO I PIANI IN MODO CHE LE COSTRUZIONI GODESSERO IL MASSIMO BENEFICIO DALLA RADIAZIONE SOLARE (AUTOMATICAMENTE, PIACESSE O NO AGLI OCCUPANTI "

SCHEMA
" OMBRA IN SCATOLA "
SCATOLA DI OMBRA NEL DESERTO

AMBARNATH : MAHADEVA TEMPLE
11° SECOLO

GRANDE TEMPIO DI MADURAI

" SI MUOVE TUTTO A STRATI — NON SI VEDE NIENTE —
TUTTO È DIVERSO — TUTTO È UGUALE — SI COSTRUISCE
UNA MONTAGNA CHE NON HA FORMA — L'È SOLTANTO
L'ALTO E IL BASSO. L'È SOLTANTO PRIMA E DOPO.
CERTO NON SONO RIUSCITO A DISEGNARE CHE TUTTO GRONDA
GIÙ COME UN LIQUIDO DI PESCI ANSIOSI. "

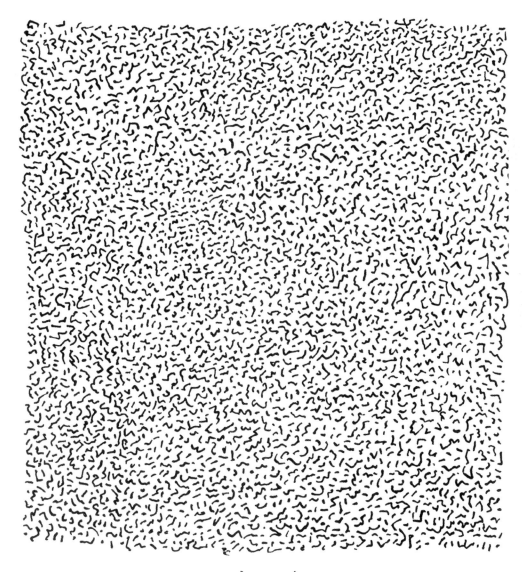

PROGETTO DI LAMINATO PLASTICO (15·10·78)

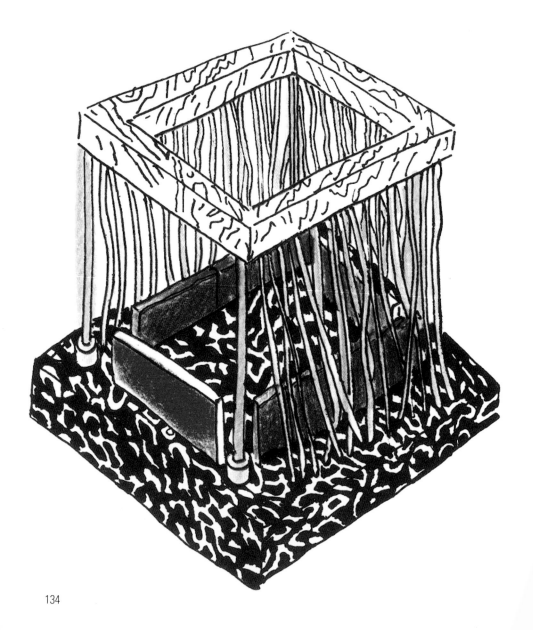

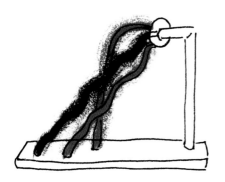

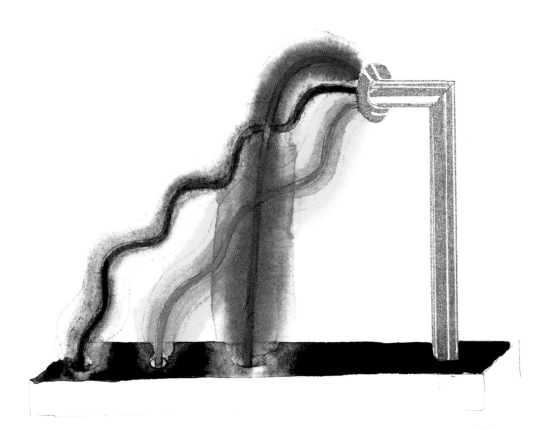

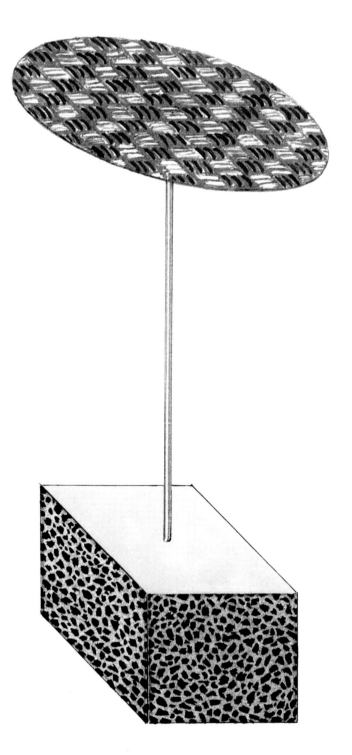

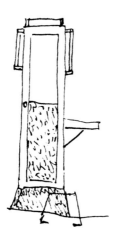

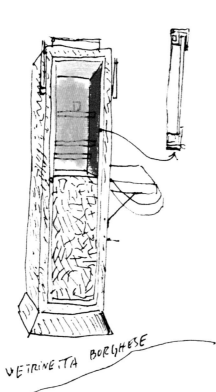

VETRINETTA BORGHESE

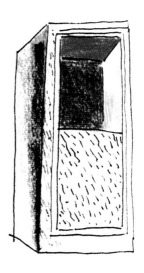

25·11·79

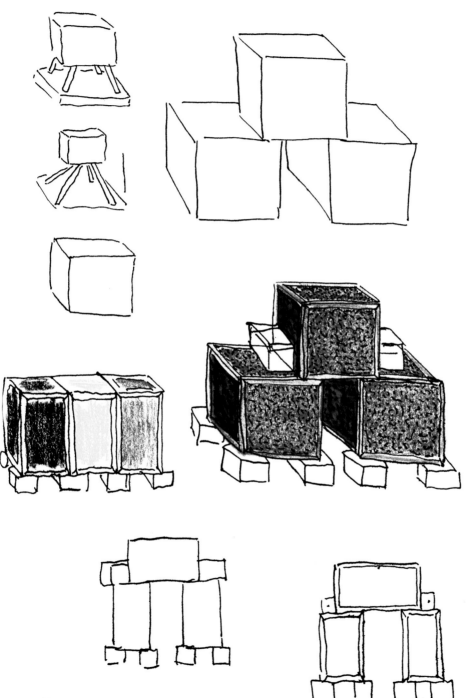

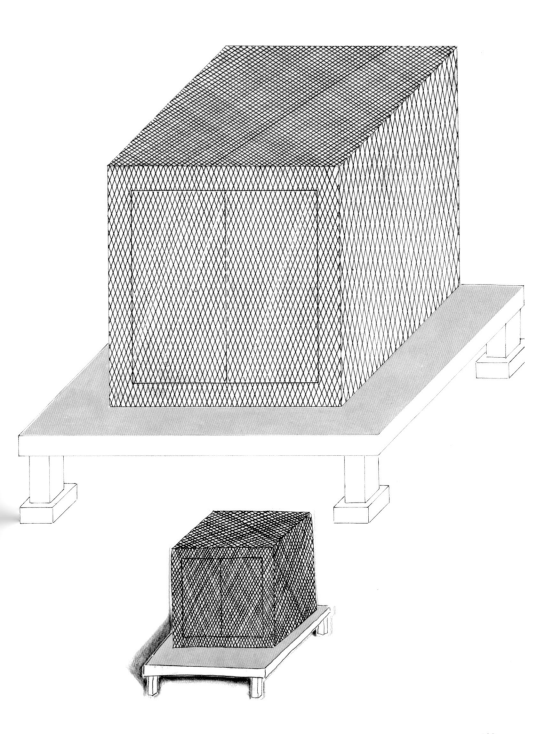

" FACTOTUM "

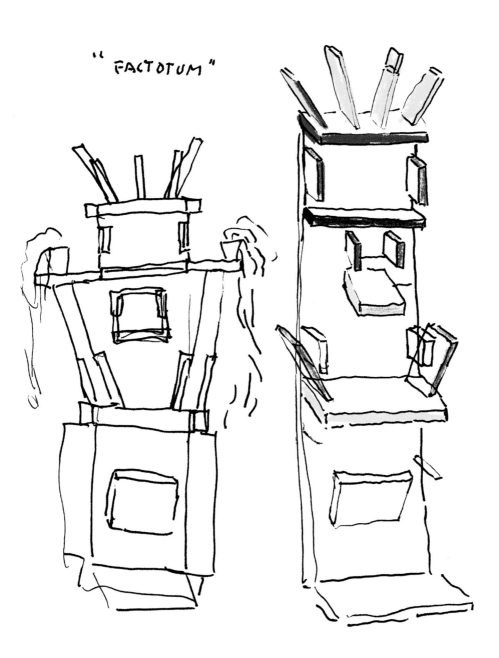

CARGO

LIBRERIA
DIVISORIO
SOGGIORNO

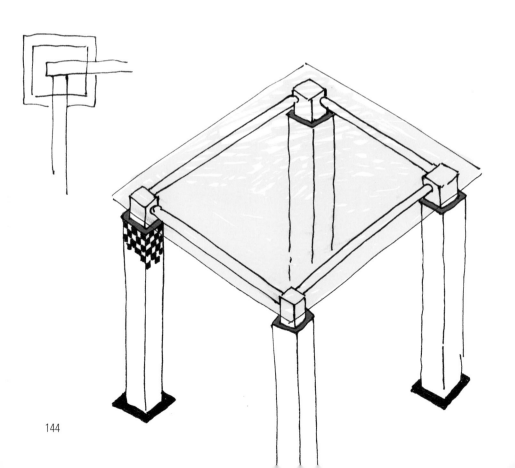

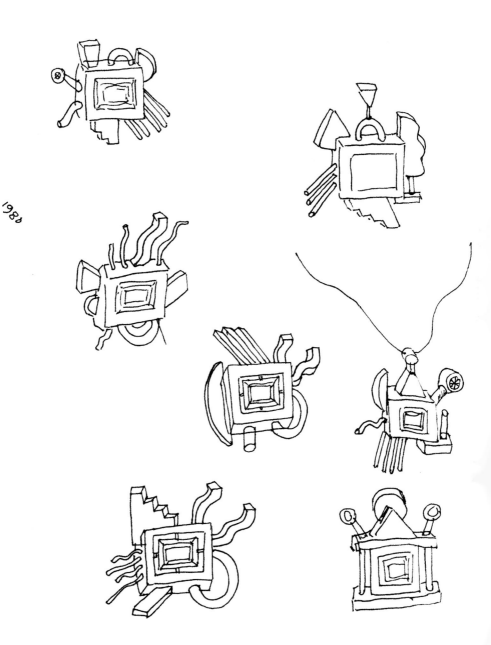

23.7.1980

146

*** ↗

20.6.81
JO... JA))

19.6.81
SOTTSASS

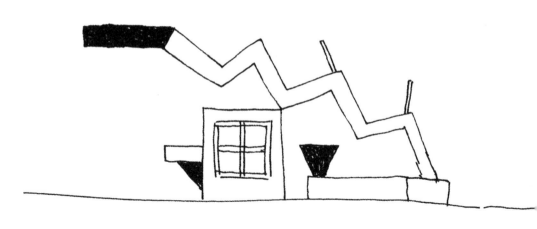

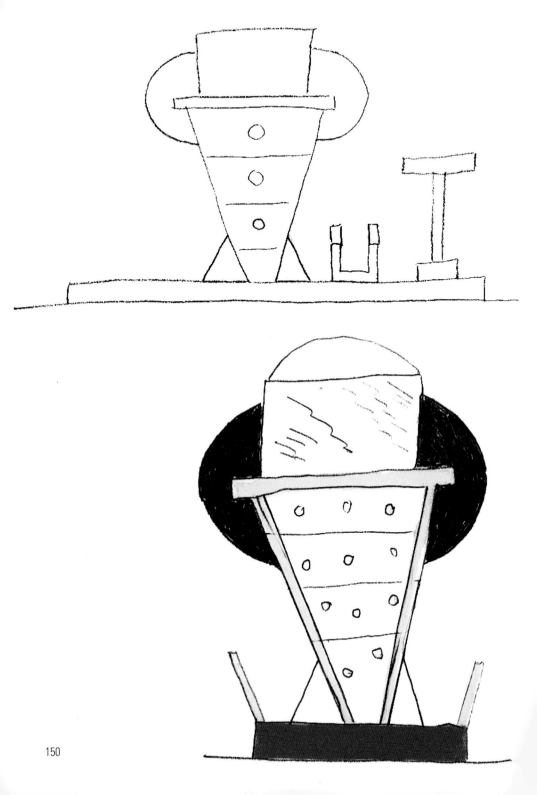

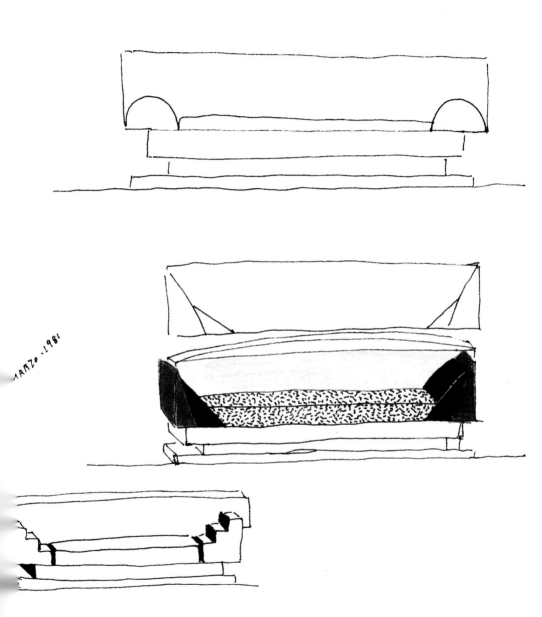

MARZO·1981

151

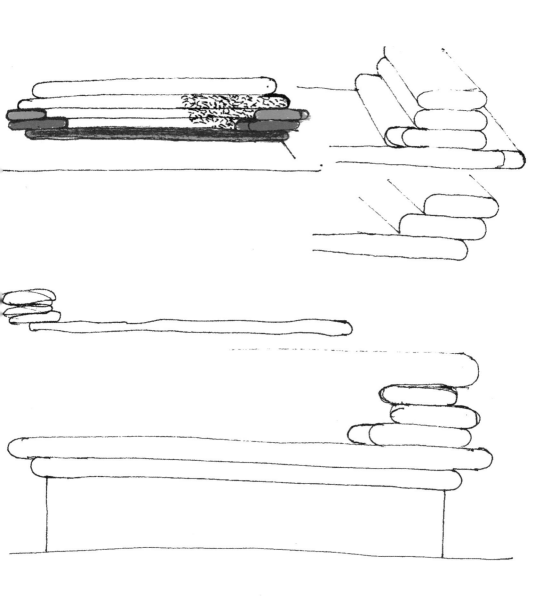

BIEDERMAYER 1820 ~

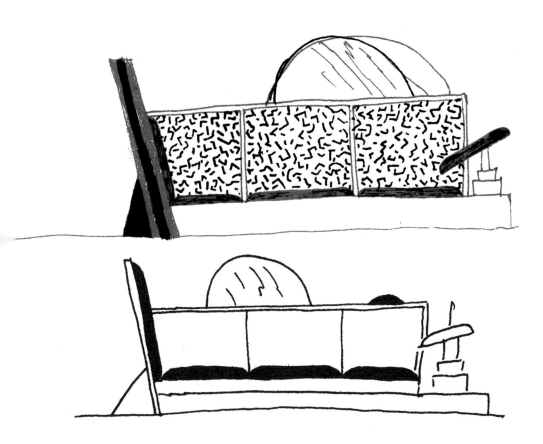

17.4.81
sarson

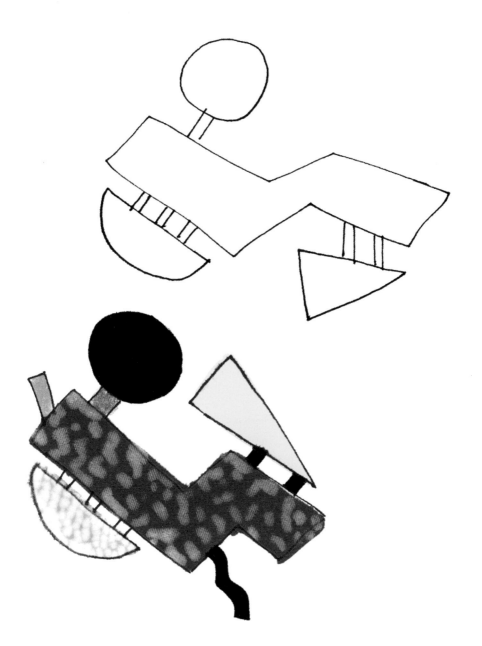

17.4.'81
Sottsass

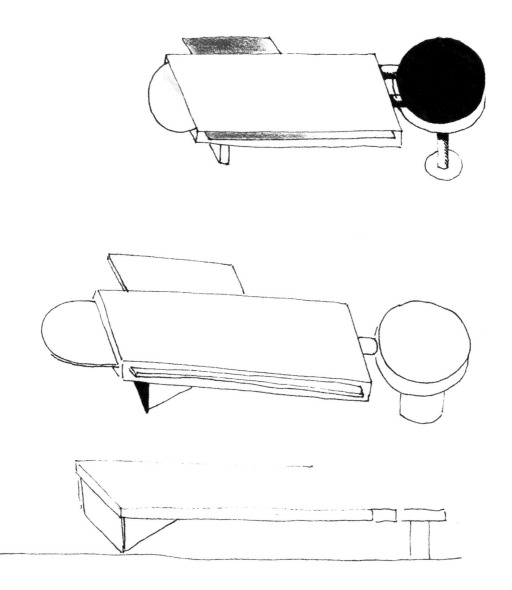

20.6.81
SOTTAS

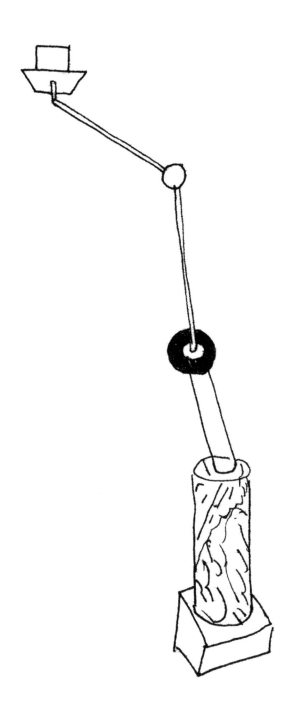

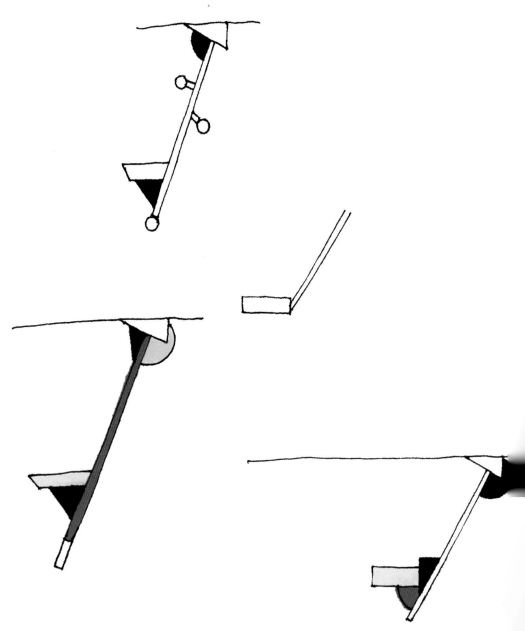

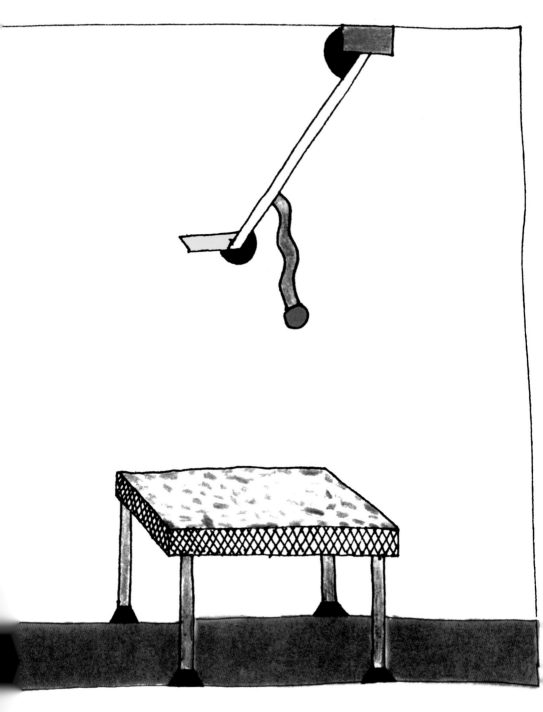

159

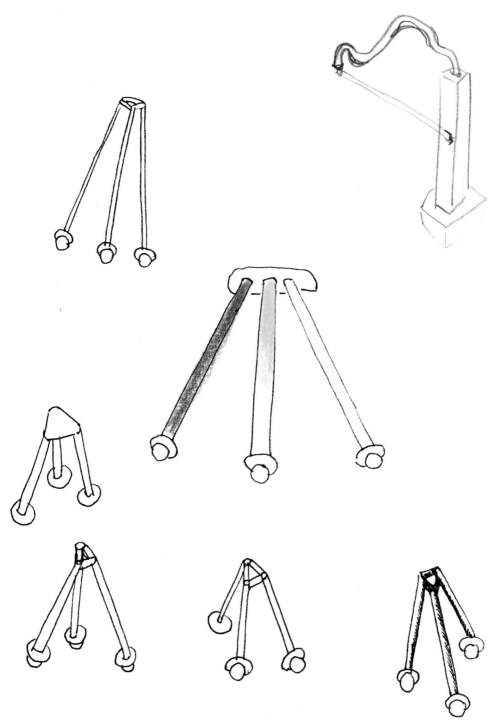

3 · 11 · 82

161

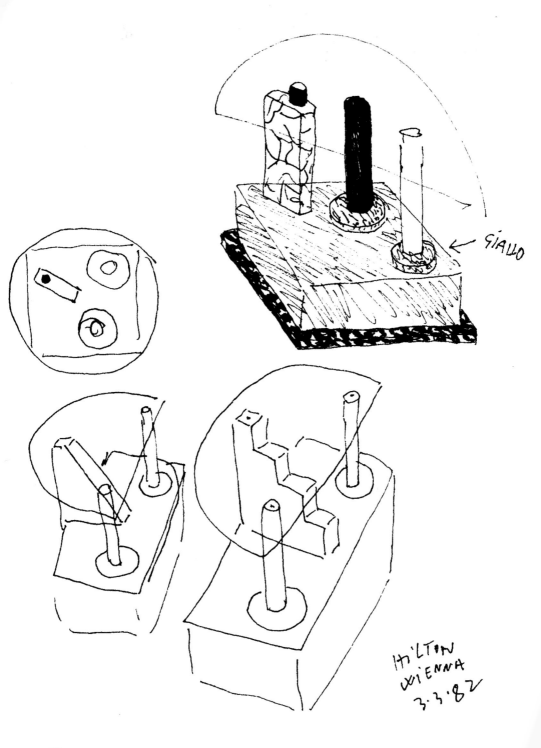

GIALLO

HILTON
WIENNA
3.3.'82

15 · 1 · 82

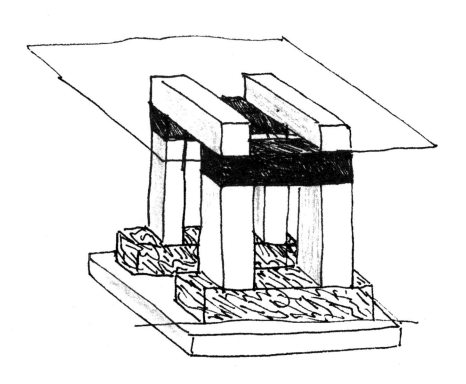

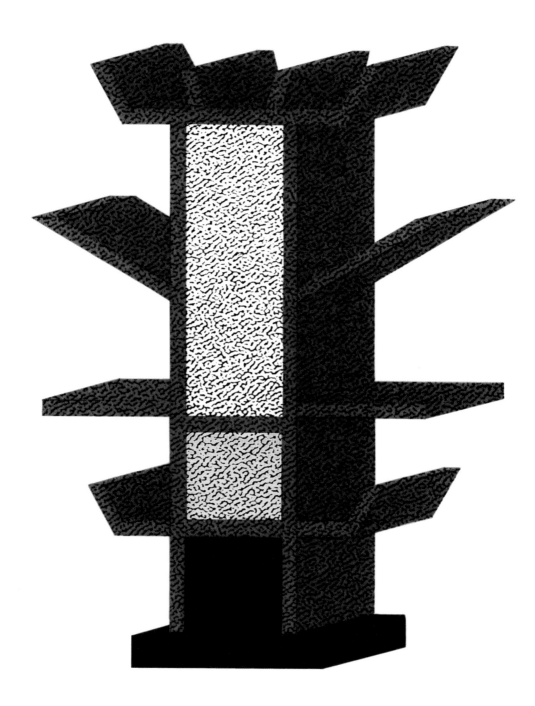

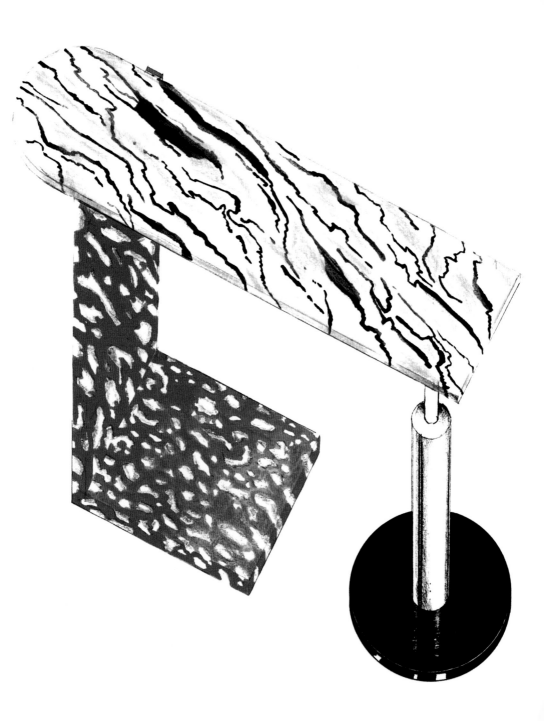

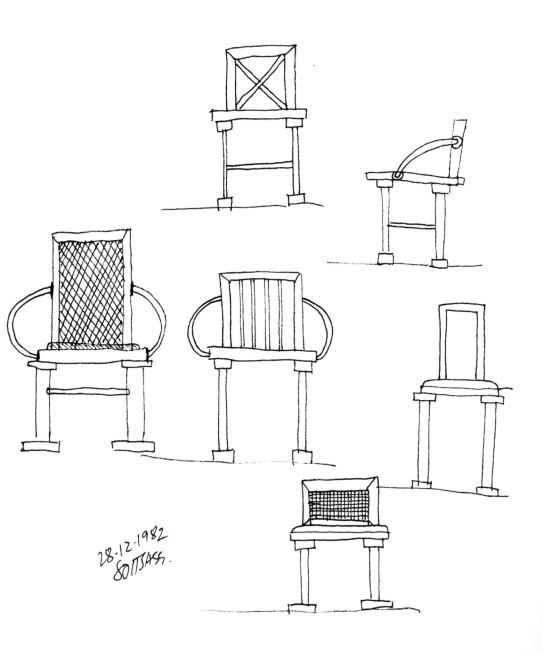

28.12.1982
SOTTSASS.

168

28-12-82
SOTTSASS

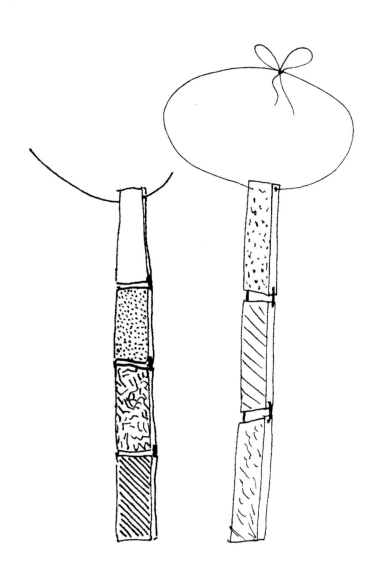

CRAVATTA DI LEGNO

18·3·82
MILANO

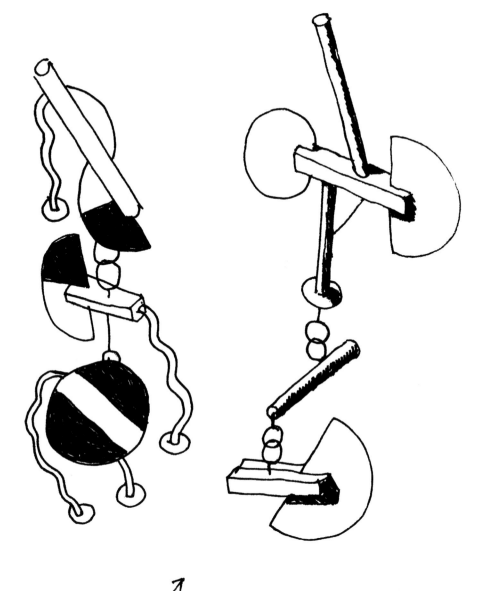

CAPRI
PER BARBARA

CAPRI
APRILE
1982

1982

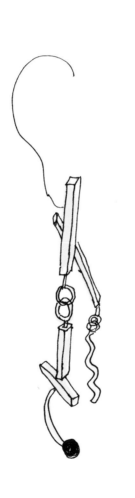

CAPRI 1982
APRILE.

172

22.2.82
PALERMO
1.30. P.M.
SOTTSASS

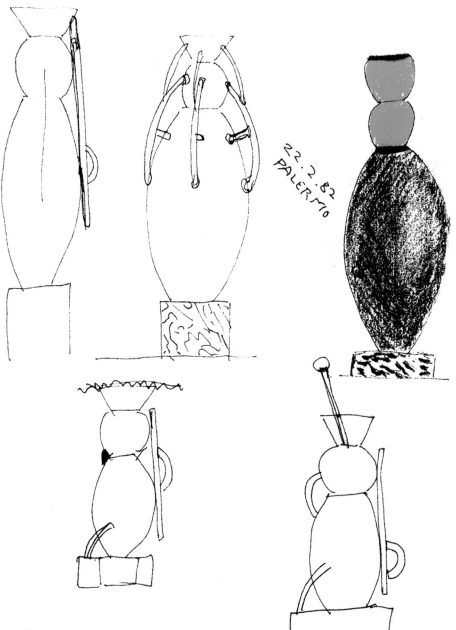

22.2.82
PALERMO

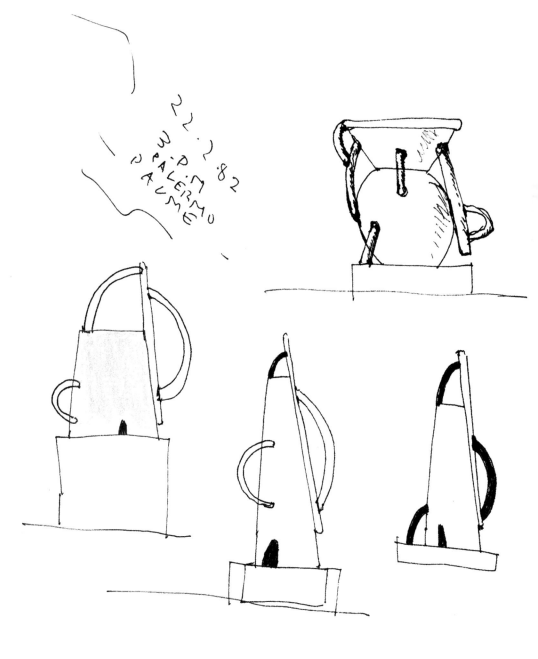

22.2.82
3.P.M
PALERMO
PAUME

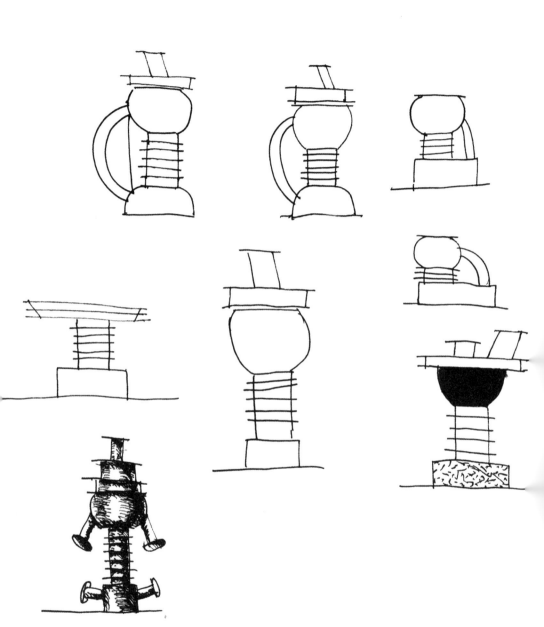

DUE PALME
PALERMO

19
2·82

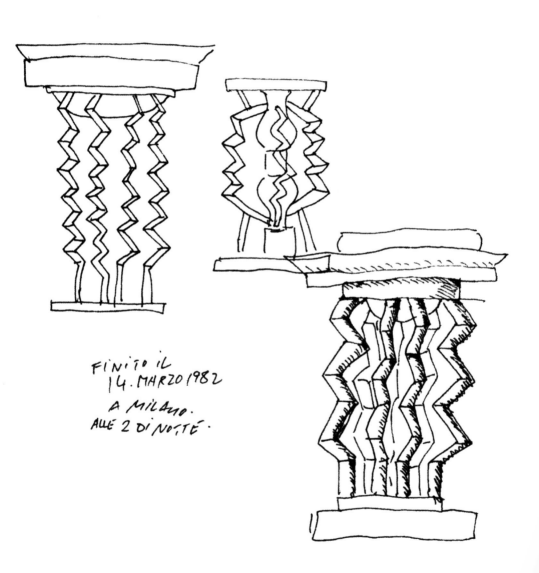

FINITO IL
14. MARZO 1982

A MILANO.
ALLE 2 DI NOTTE.

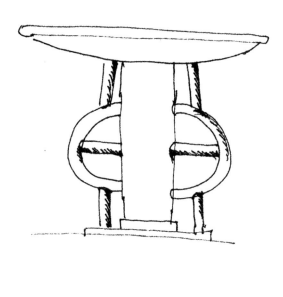

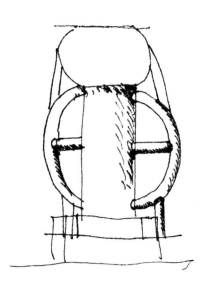

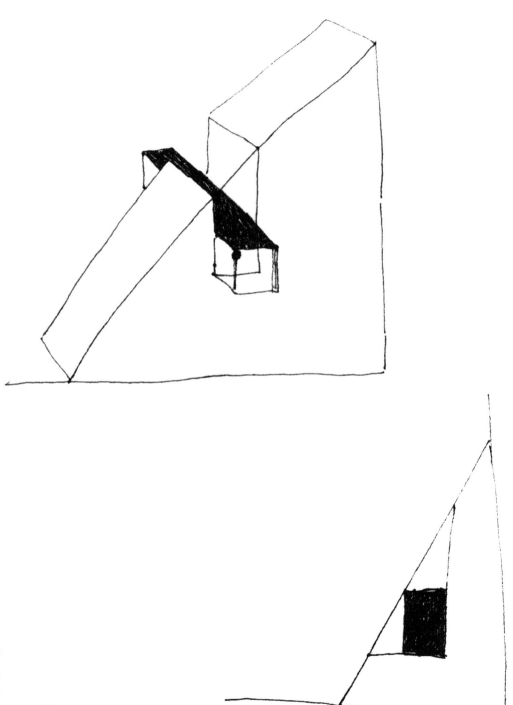

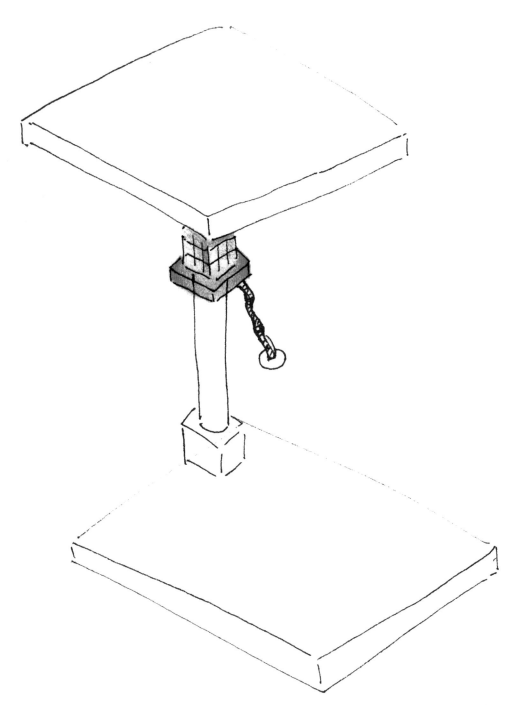

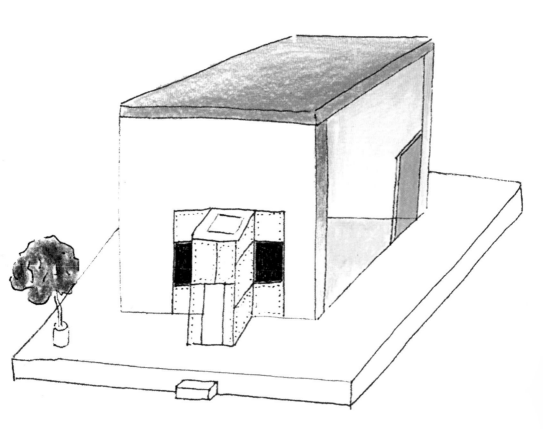

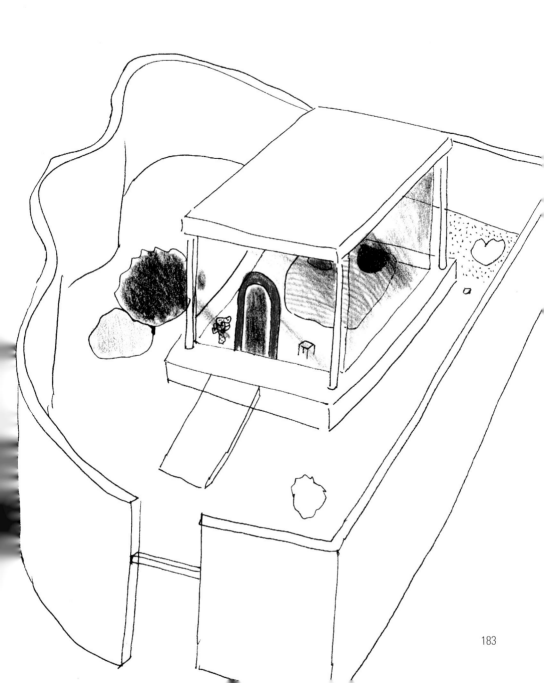

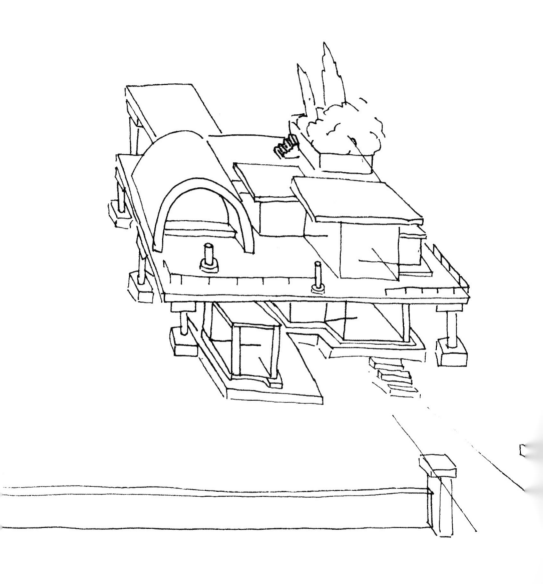

8·11·1982
SOTTSASS

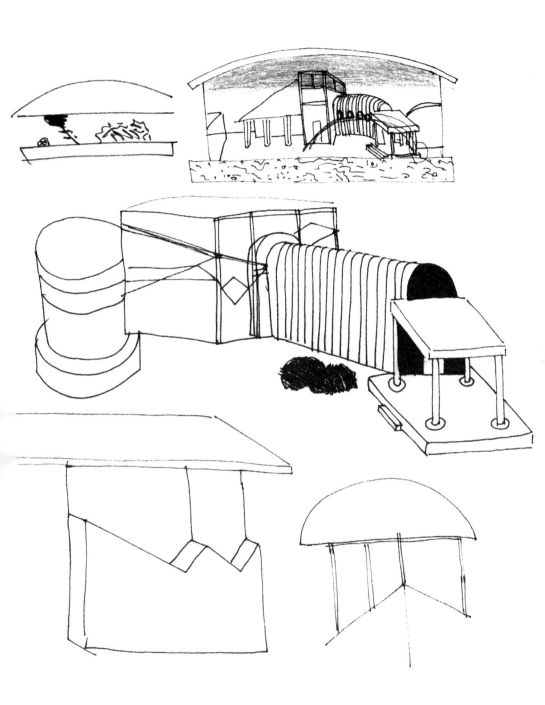

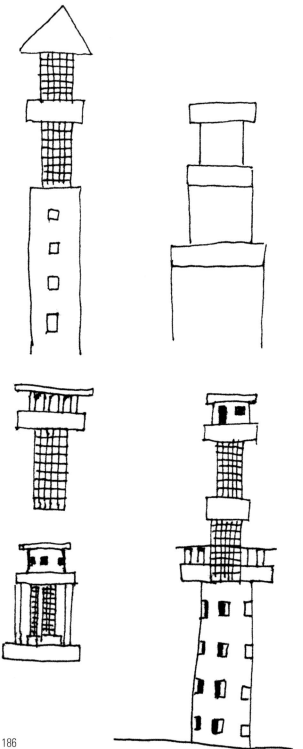
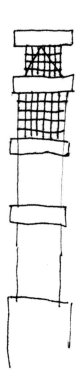

ARCHITETTURA
SOGNATA LA NOTTE DEL 2 APRILE 1983
IL FONDO NERO E LE RIGHE VERDI
NON C'ERANO FINESTRE.

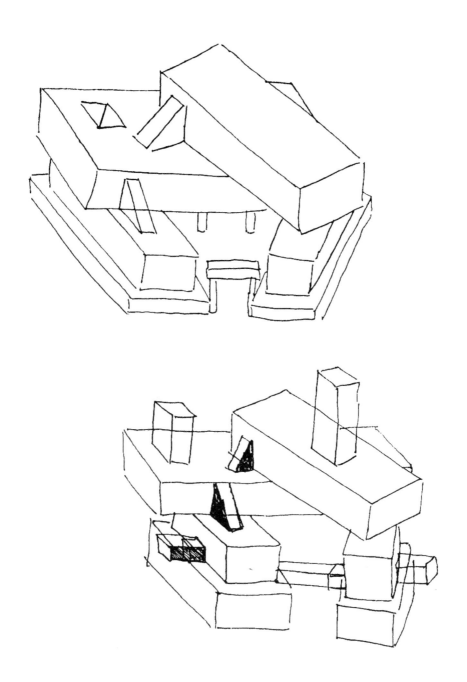

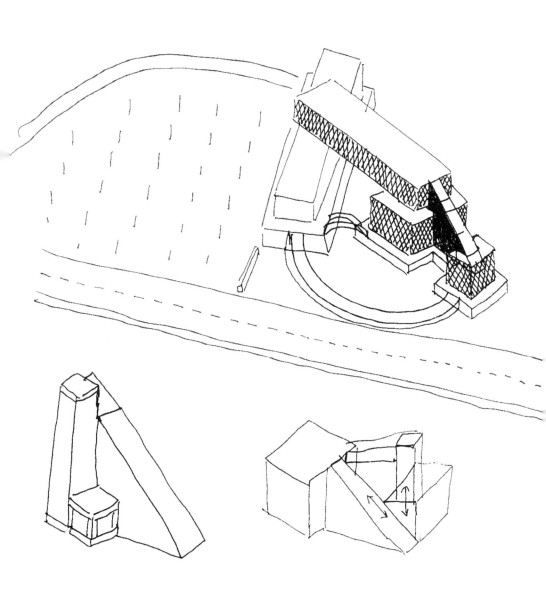

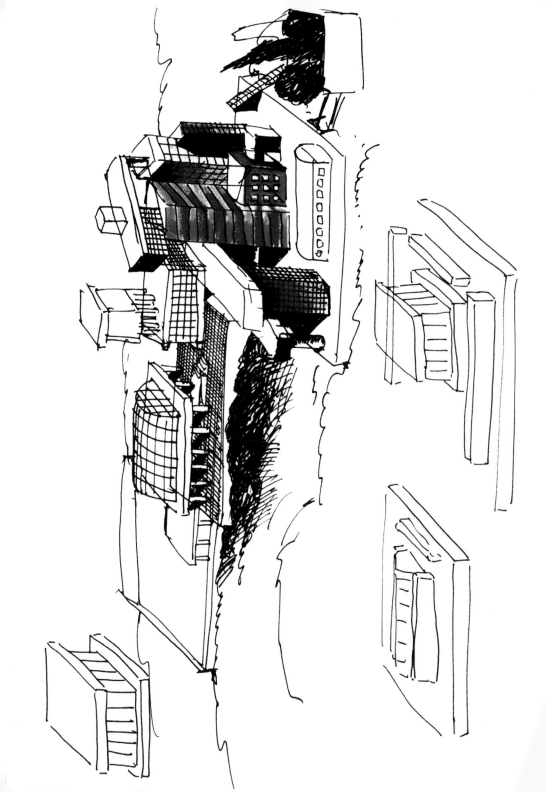

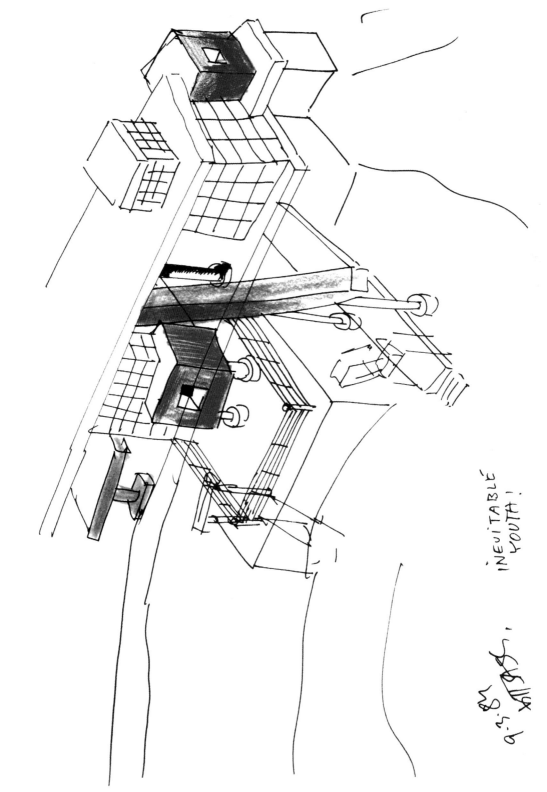

INEVITABLE
YOUTH!

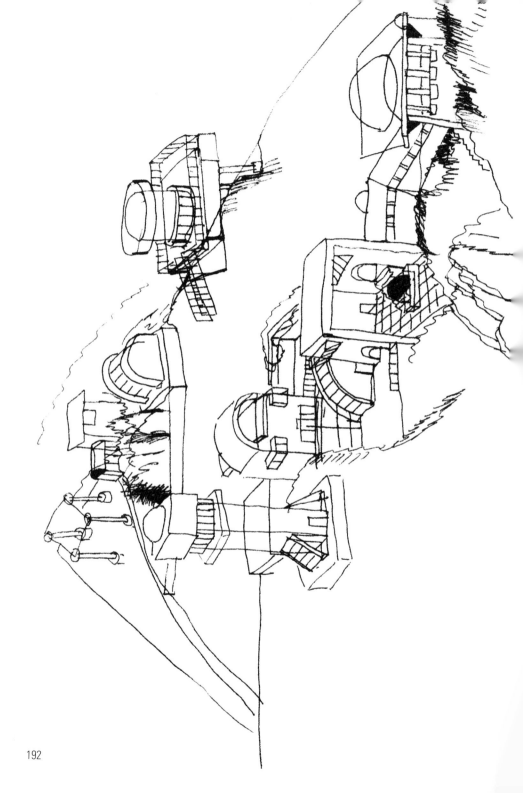

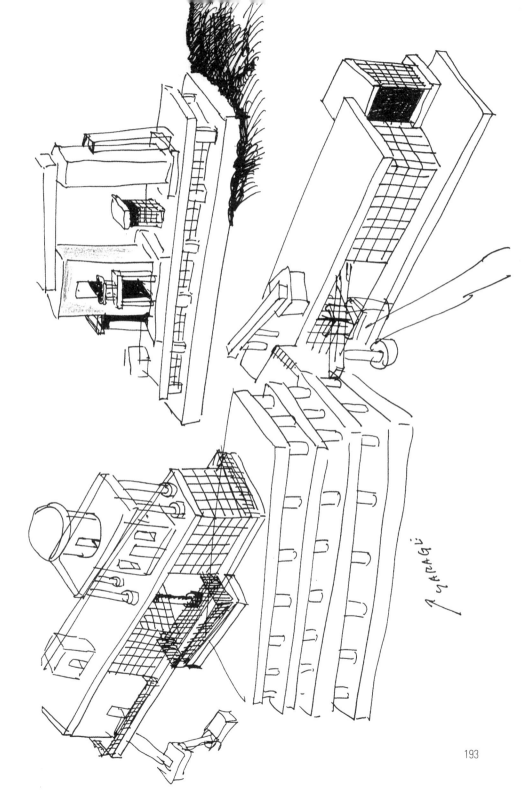

193

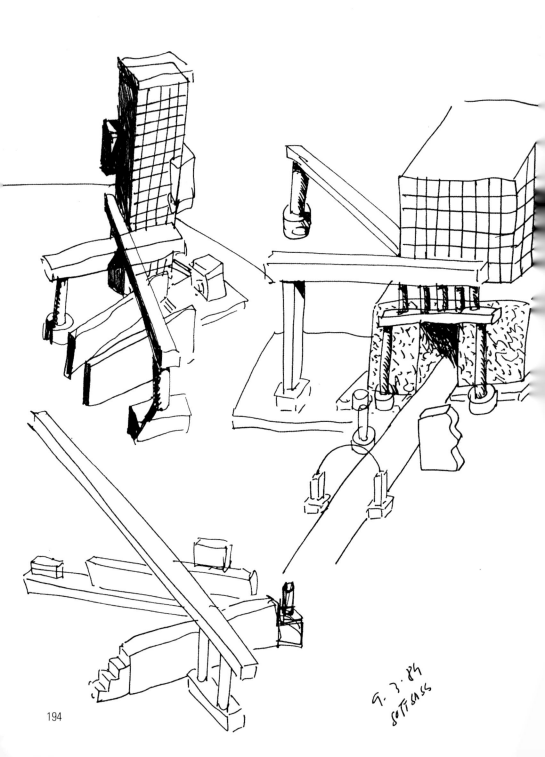

9.3.84
SOTTSASS

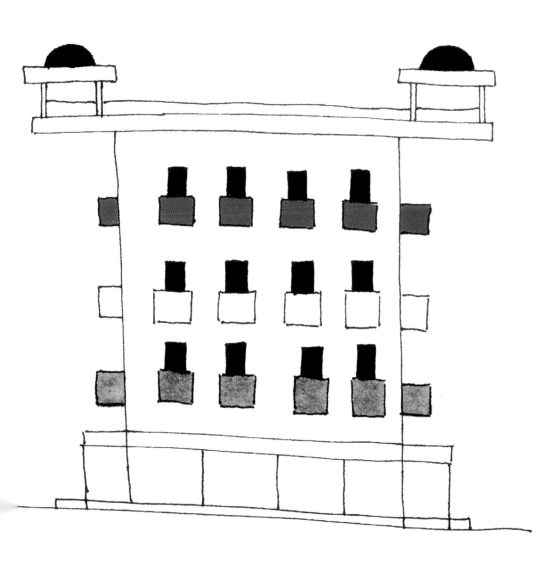

ALBERGO A RIMINI
PER TURISTI TEDESCHI . . . .

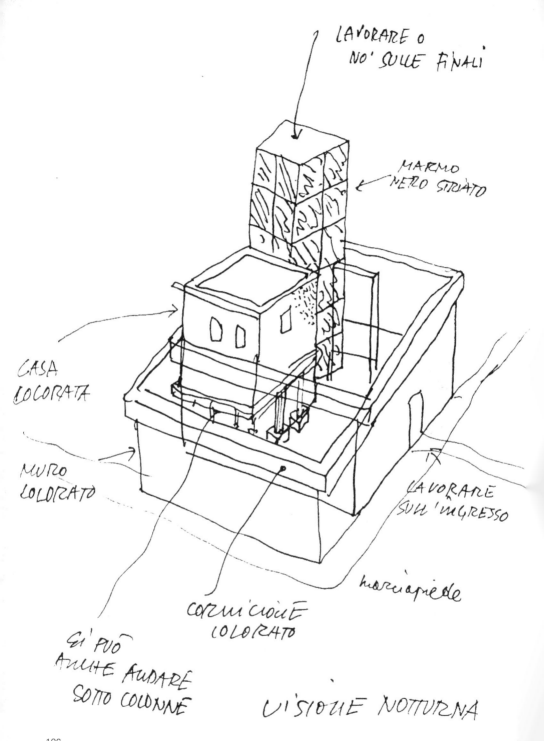

LAVORARE O
NO' SULLE FINALI

MARMO
NERO STRIATO

CASA
COLORATA

MURO
COLORATO

LAVORARE
SULL'INGRESSO

marciapiede

CORNICIONE
COLORATO

SI PUÒ
ANCHE ANDARE
SOTTO COLONNE

VISIONE NOTTURNA

196

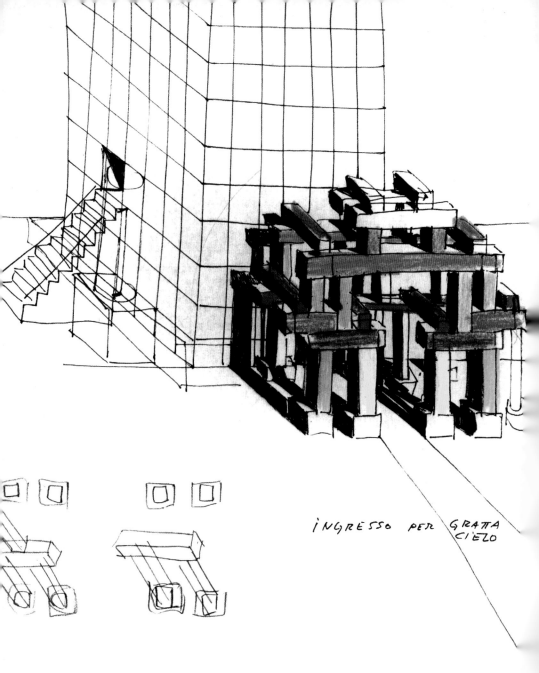

INGRESSO PER GRATTA
CIELO

SOTTSASS
9 · 1 · 84

198

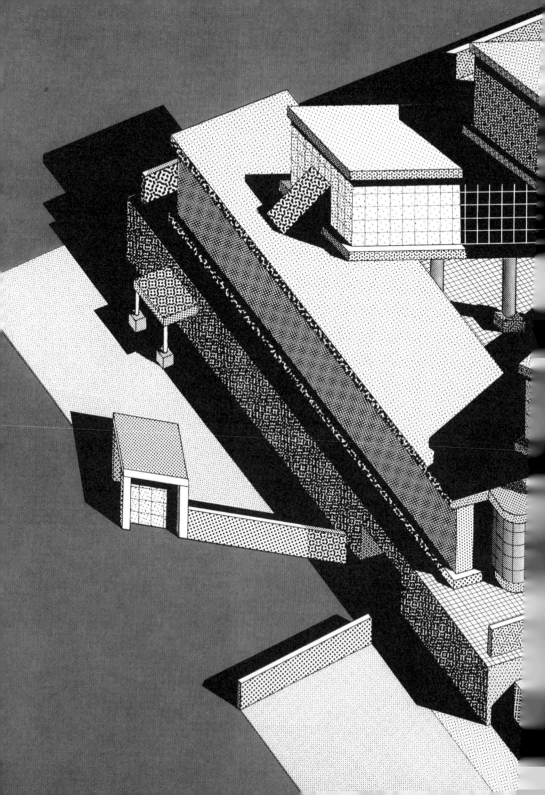

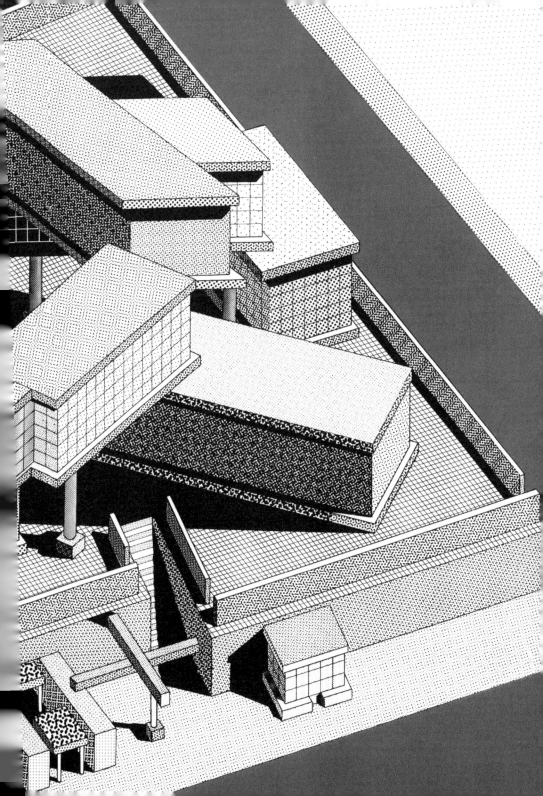

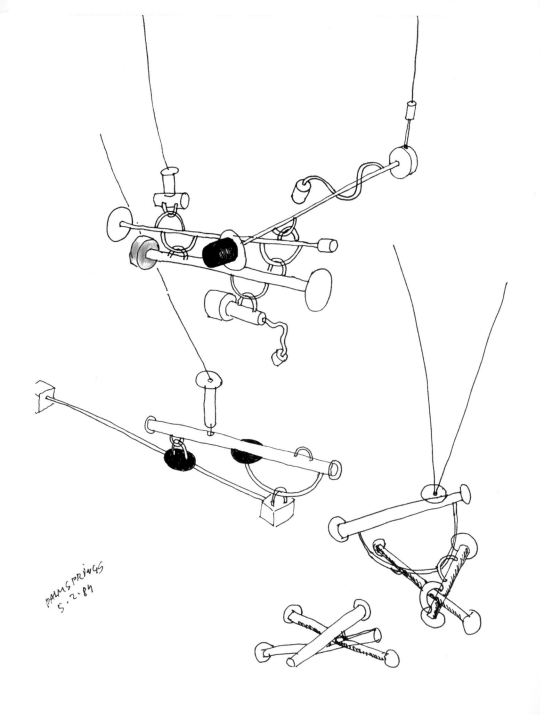

PALM SPRINGS
5.2.89

Scott

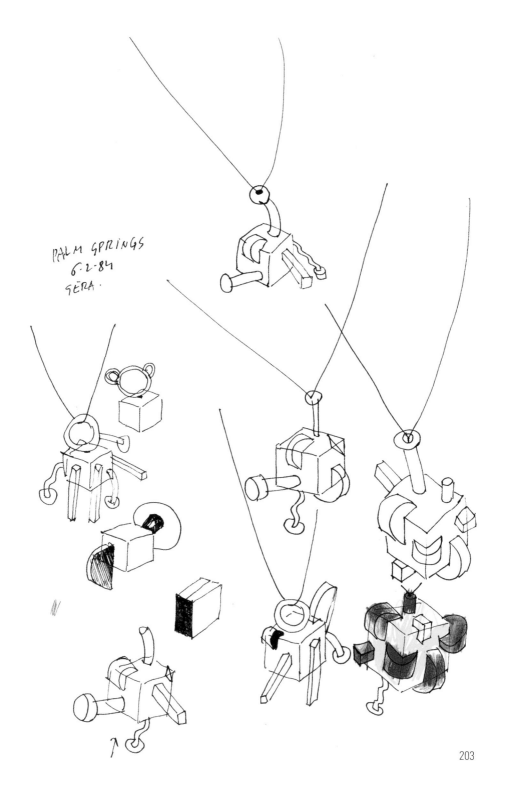

PALM SPRINGS
6·2·84
GERA·

4.7.83
16/18.5.

MILANO
83
5.2.83
SOTTSAS

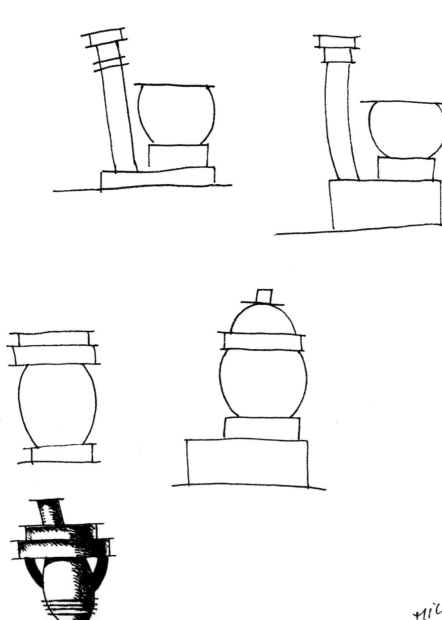

MILANO
4.2.83
SOTTSASS

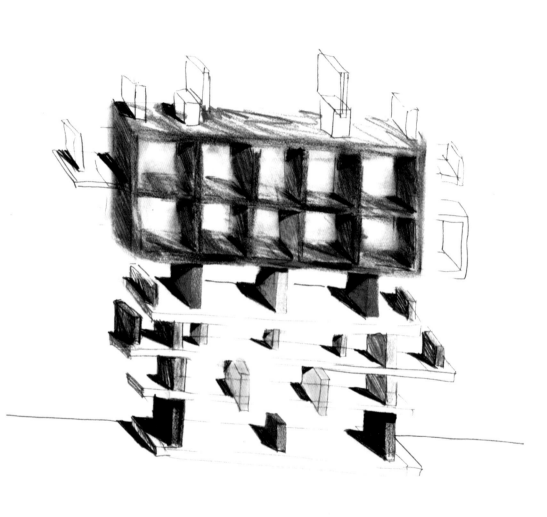

8.III.89
SOTTSASS

SOTT SASS
2·11·'84
MILANO

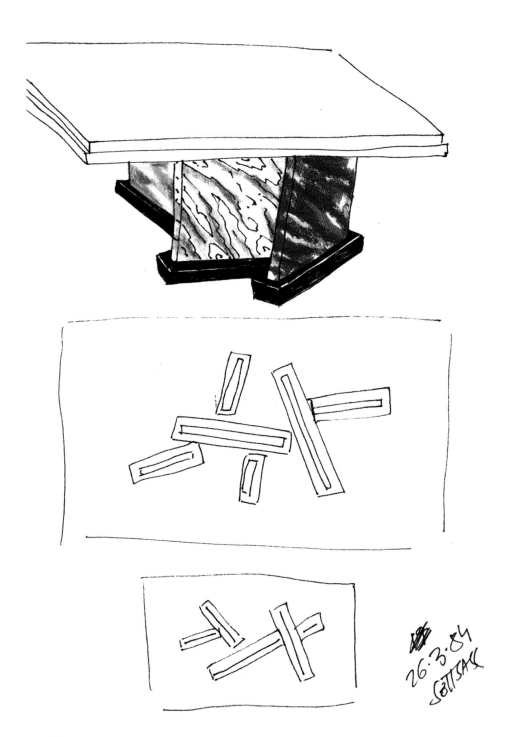

26.3.84
SOTTSASS

210

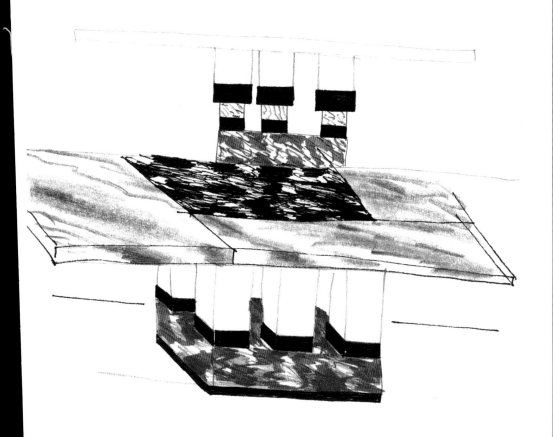

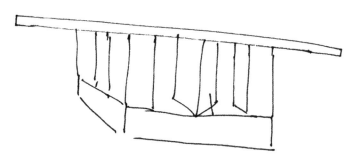

26.3.84
SOTSASS

211

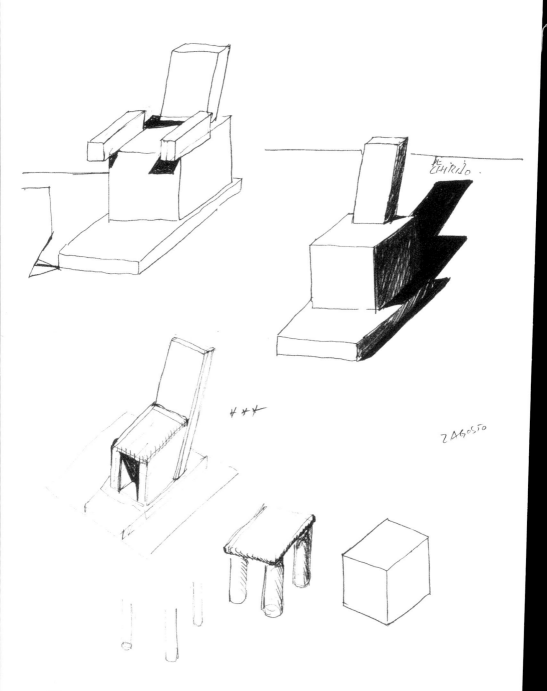

DE
CHIRICO .

ZAGOSTO

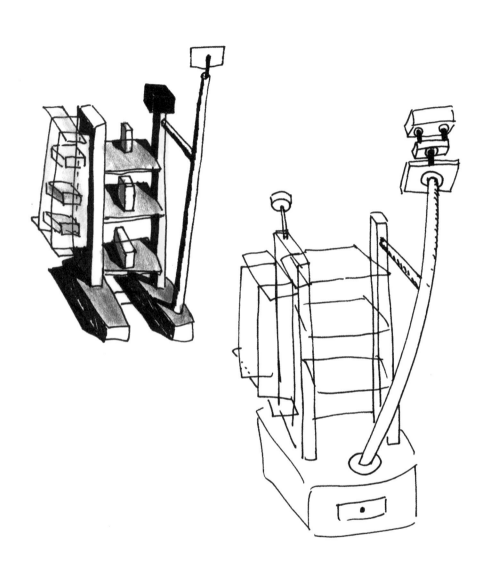

17.3.84

Sottsass

DISEGNO DA TELEFONO

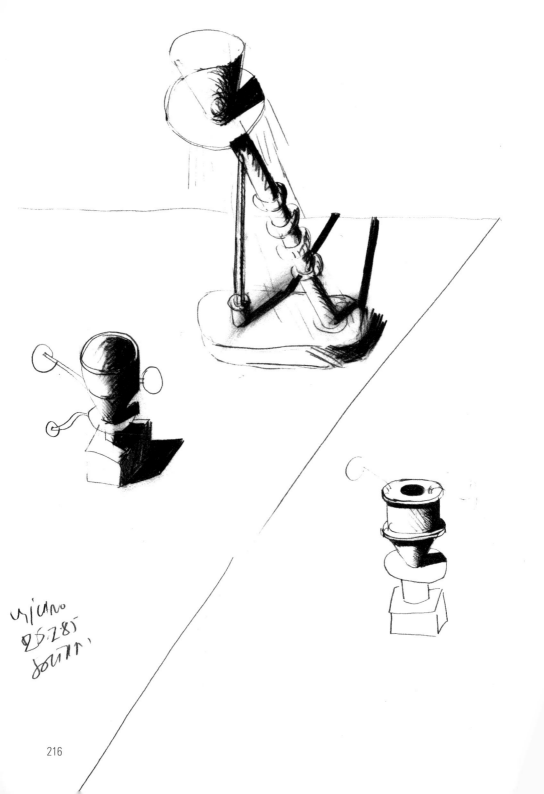

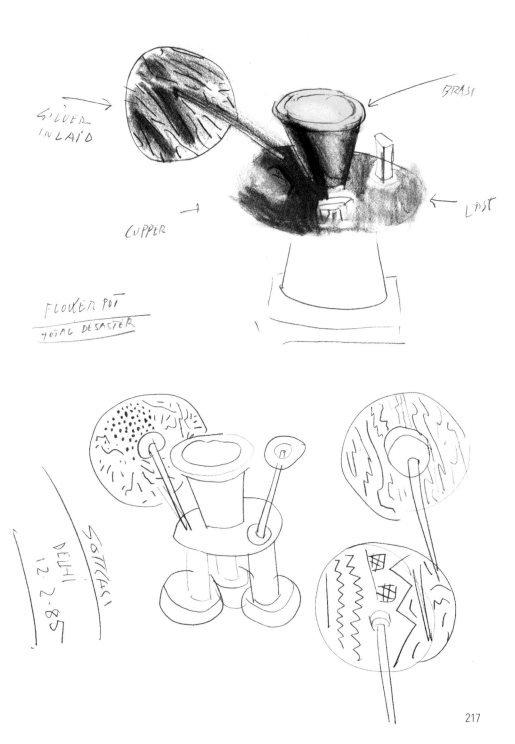

SILVER
INLAI'D

BRASI

CUPPER

LAST

FLOWER POT
TOTAL DESASTER

SUITCASE!
DELHI
12. 2. 85

218

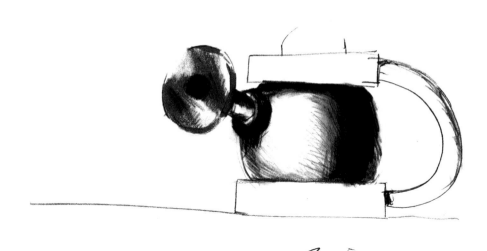

20.5.85.

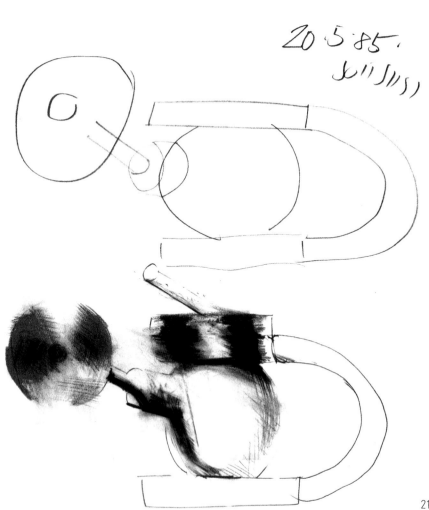

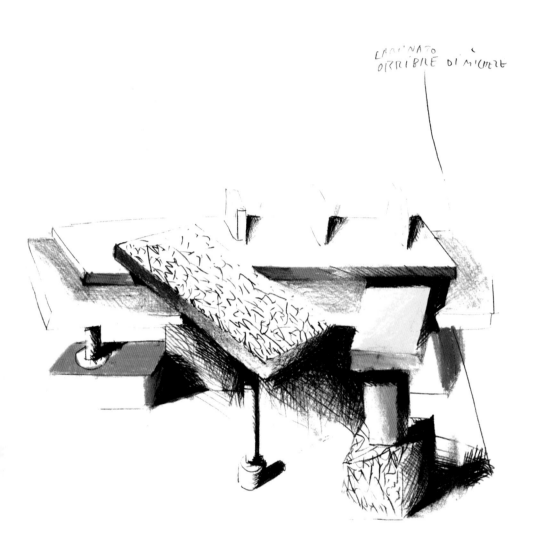

LAMINATO
ORRIBILE DI MICHELE

FORSÉ
CAMMINATO MICHELE

MILANO
80 13/23
1 APRILE
85.

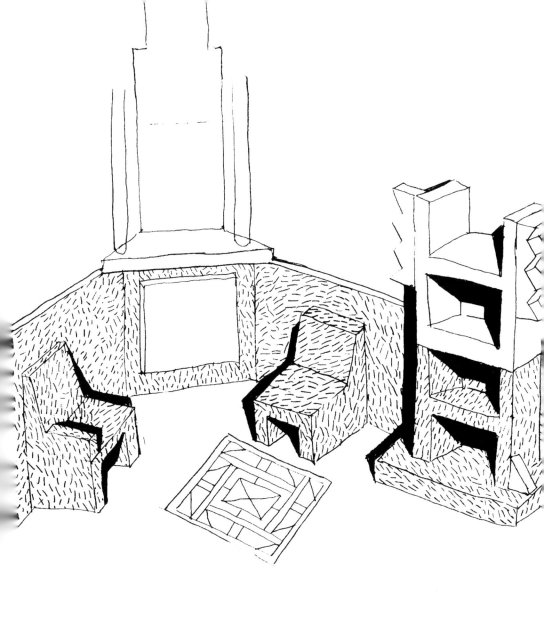

BARBARIC INTERIOR"

SOTTSASS 82

"BARBARIC FURNITURE"

SITTSASS '85

226

325

26 MAGGIO
1985

LESS THAN 150.000$

ARCHITETTURA
DI LISSONE
6.6.85
SOTTSASS

" ARCHI TETTURA "

b.G 85 (H4)
80 ? 9.9
MILANO

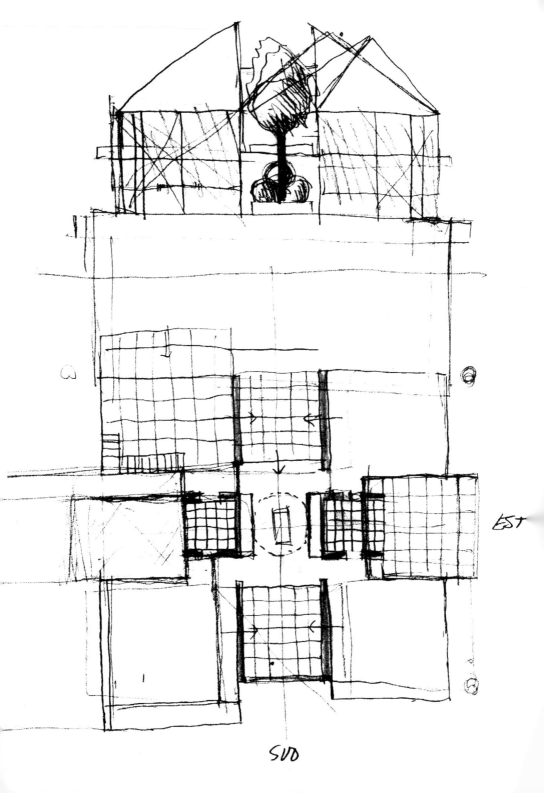

EST

SUD

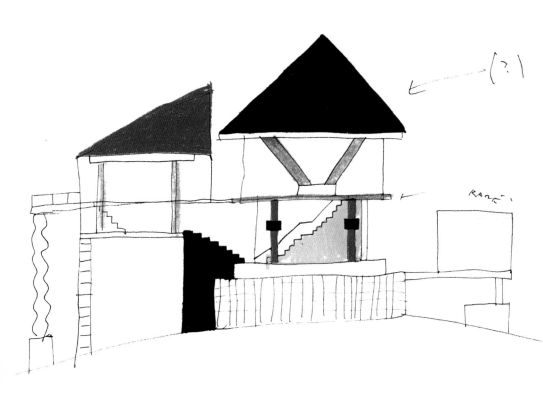

KANT

(?)

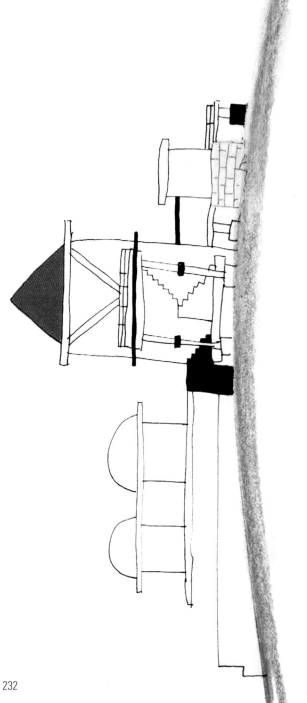

PARIS 1959

36

PER il COLORADO

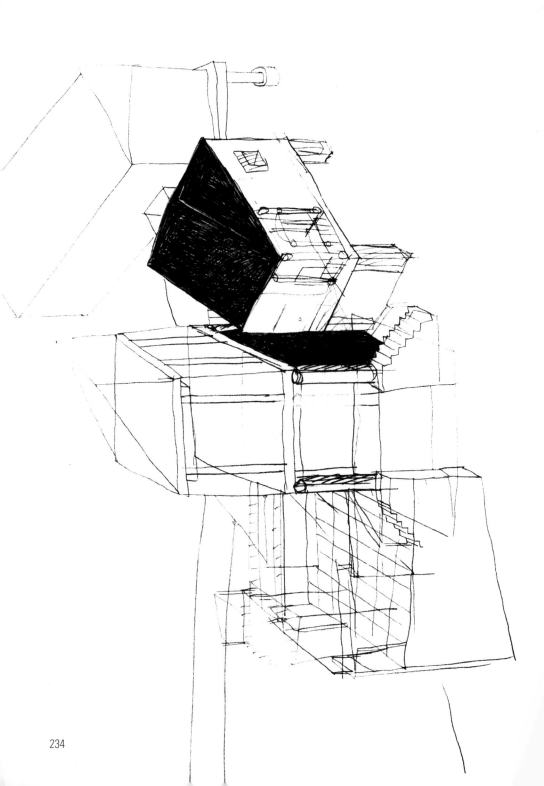

234

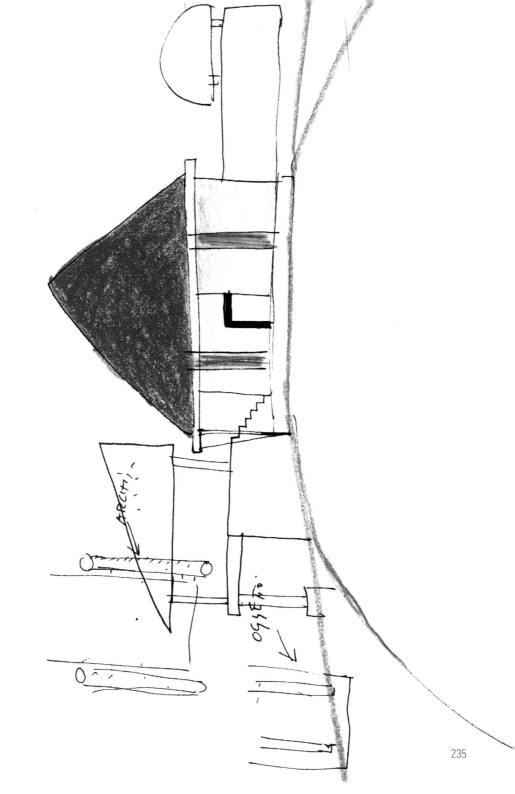

235

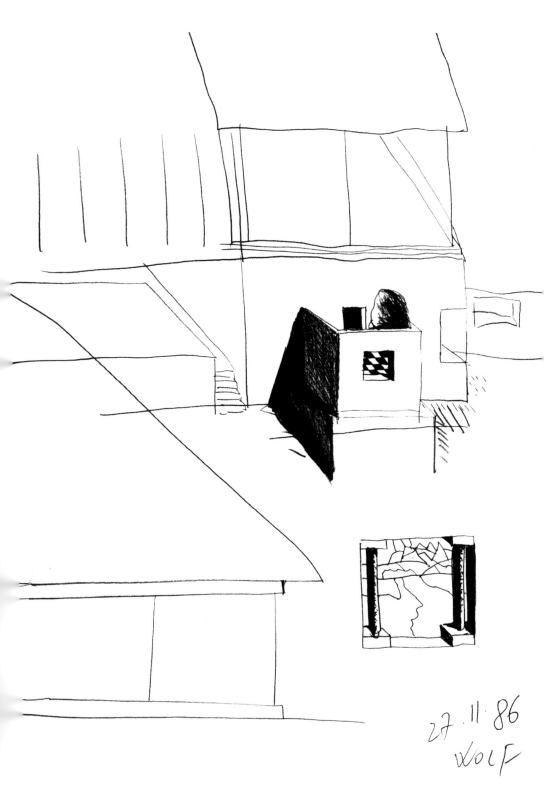

27.11.86
WOLF

27·11·86.
(ʃIʃASI)

CON SPAZIO
SPECIALE

239

3.9.1986
OTERO
MIDALO

240

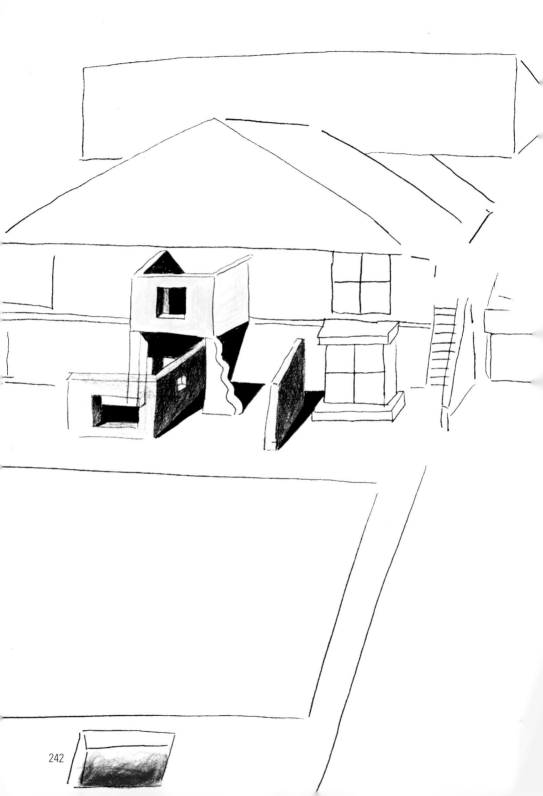

242

243

MILANO
1 MAGGIO
SOTTSASS

244

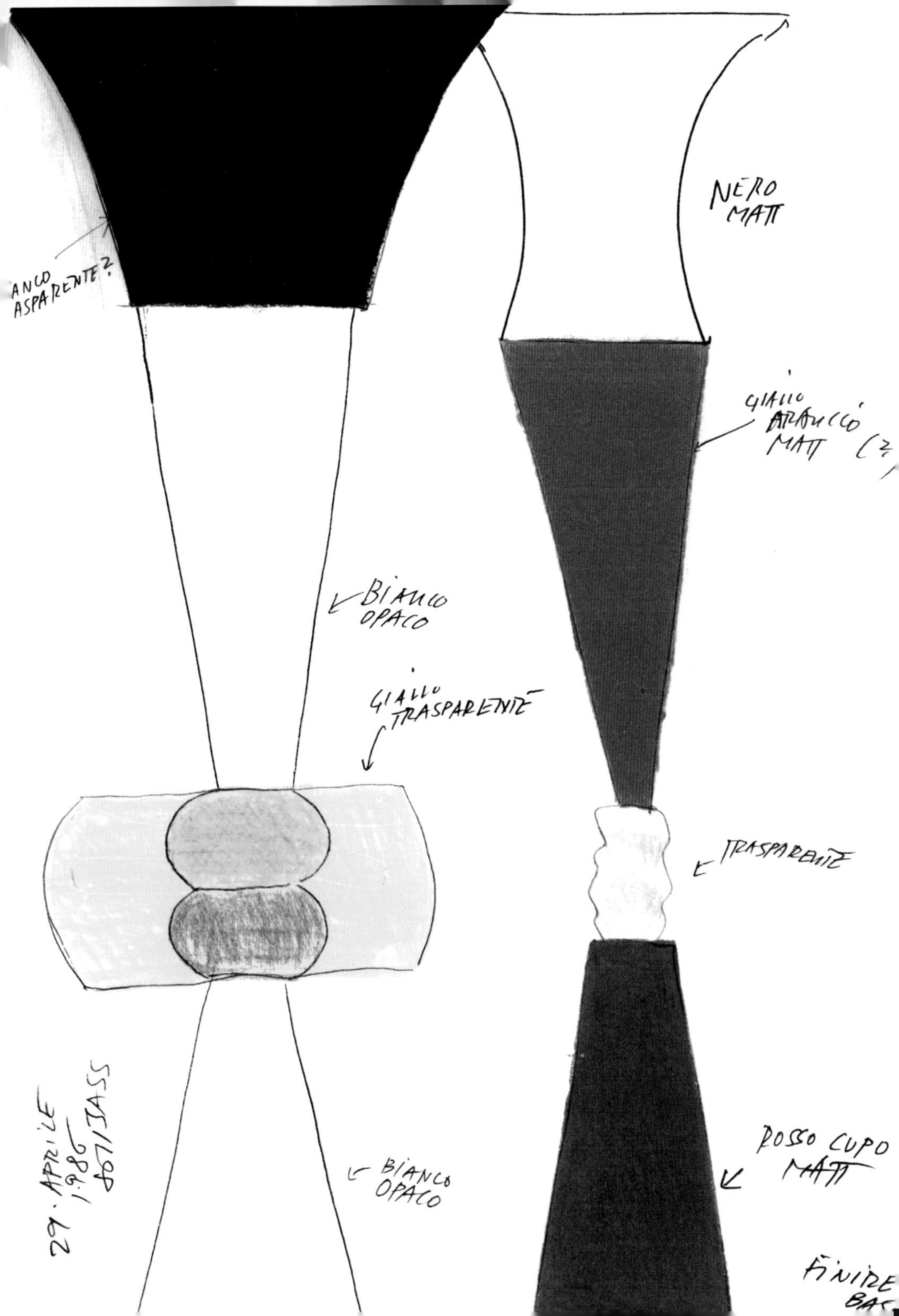

ANCO
ASPARENTE?

NERO
MATT

BIANCO
OPACO

GIALLO
ARANCIÓ
MATT (?)

GIALLO
TRASPARENTE

TRASPARENTE

29·APRILE
1·986
267/IASS

BIANCO
OPACO

ROSSO CUPO
MATT

FINIDE
BAS

7
MAGGIO 1980   MILANO

TRASPA-
RENTE

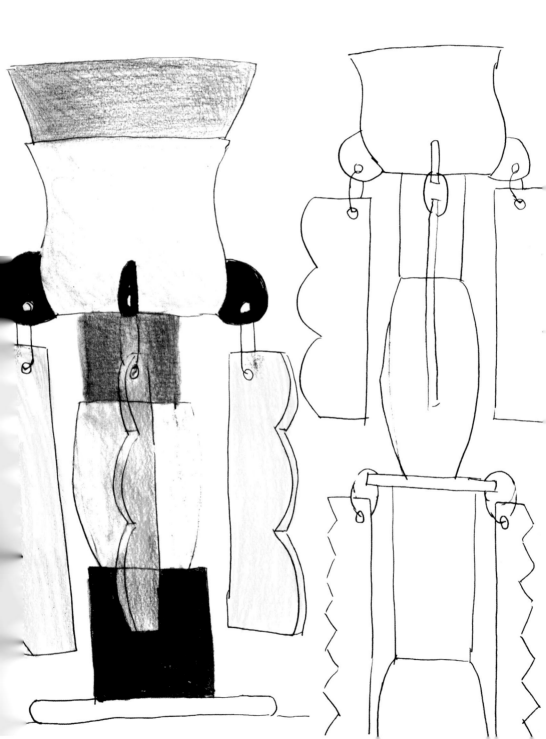

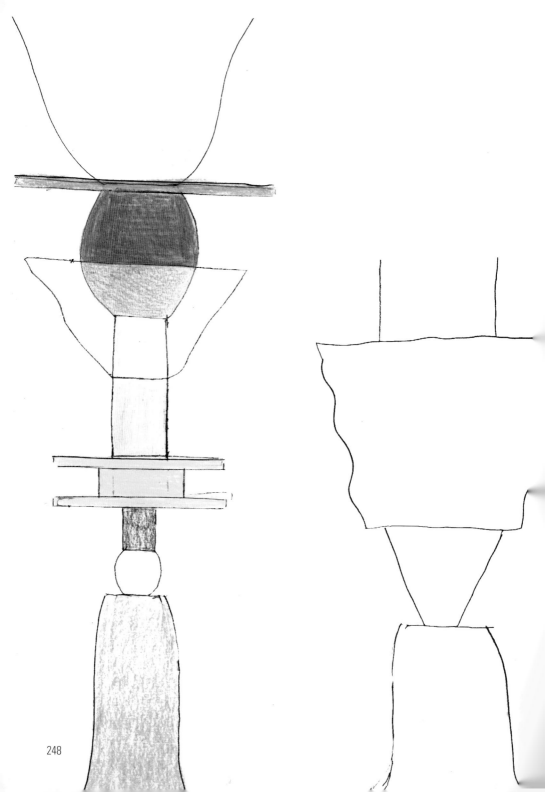

248

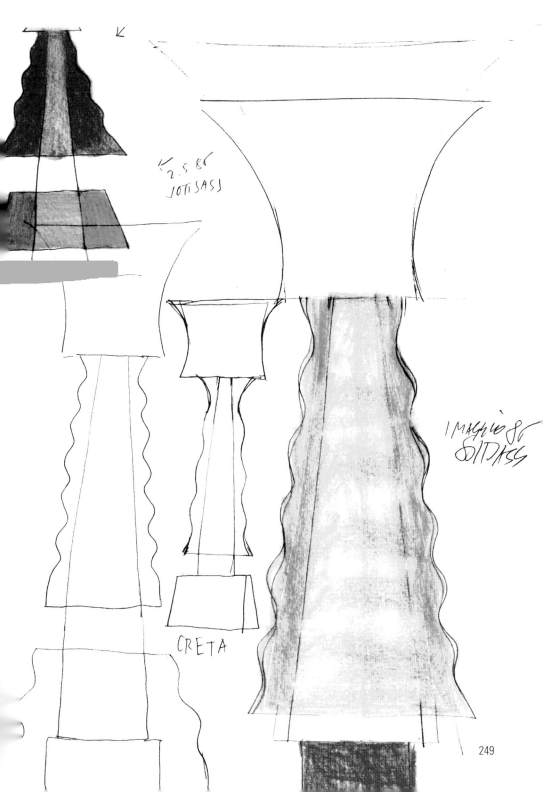

K

2.5 86
JOTISASS

I MAGGIO 86
SOTTSASS

CRETA

249

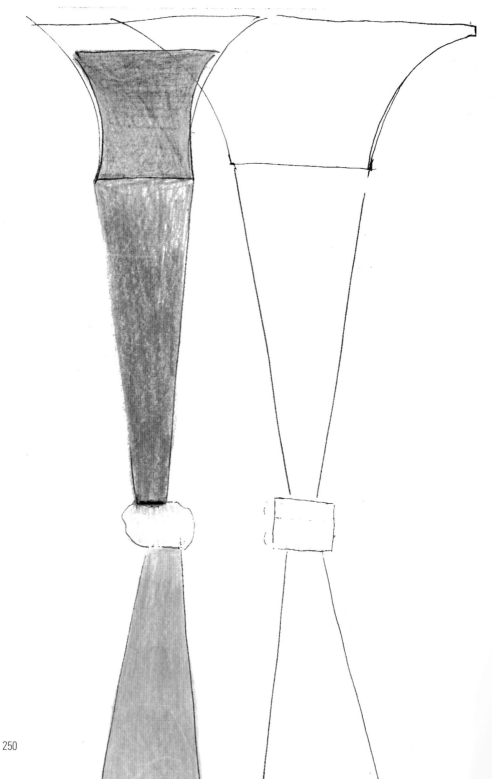

250

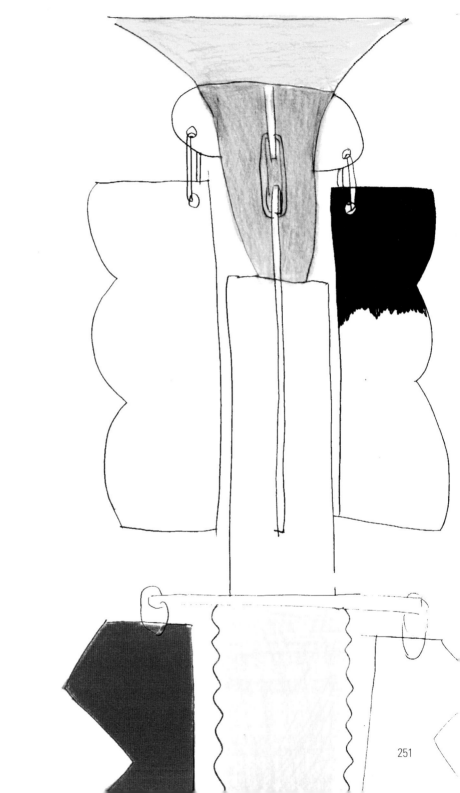

251

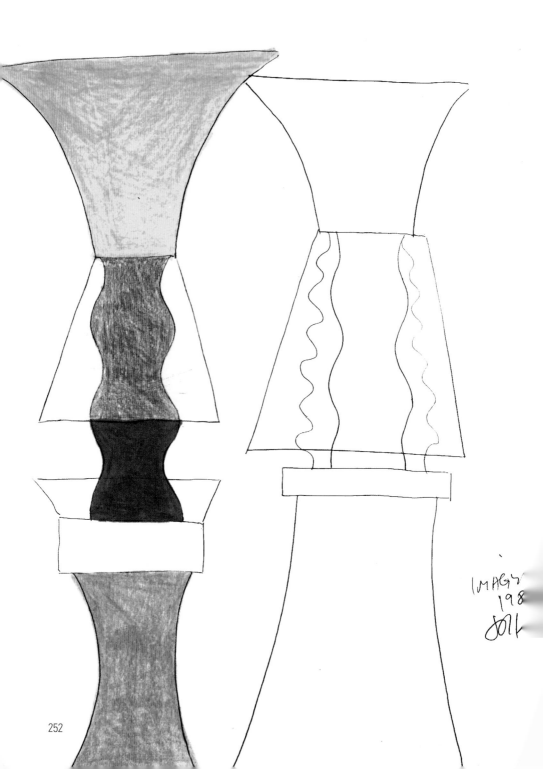

252

IMAGY
198
JO??

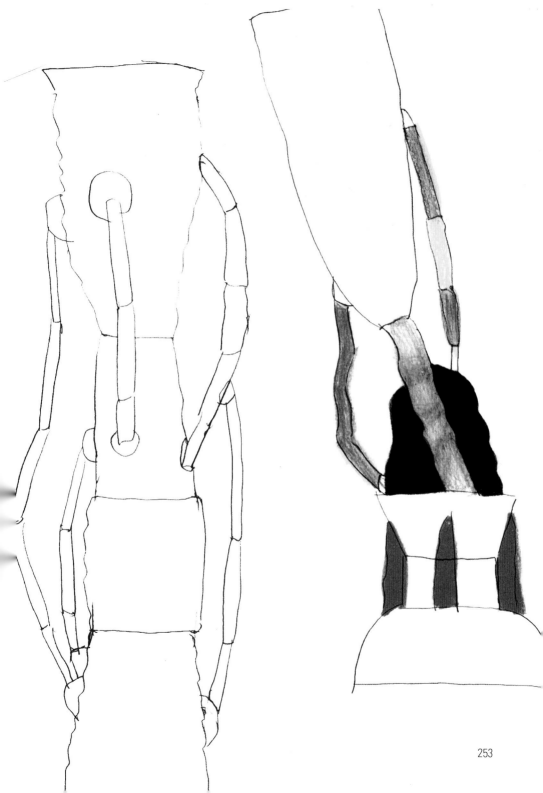

253

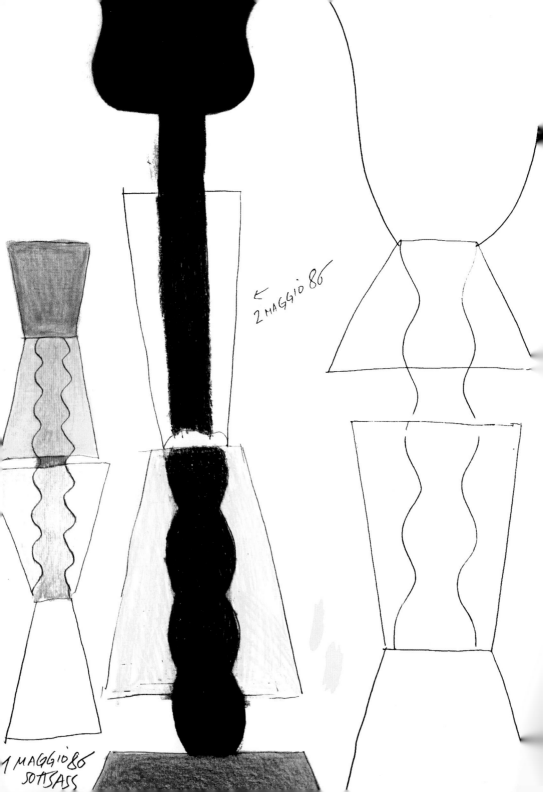

2 MAGGIO 86

1 MAGGIO 86
SOTSASS

2 MAGGIO 1980
SOTTSASS

255

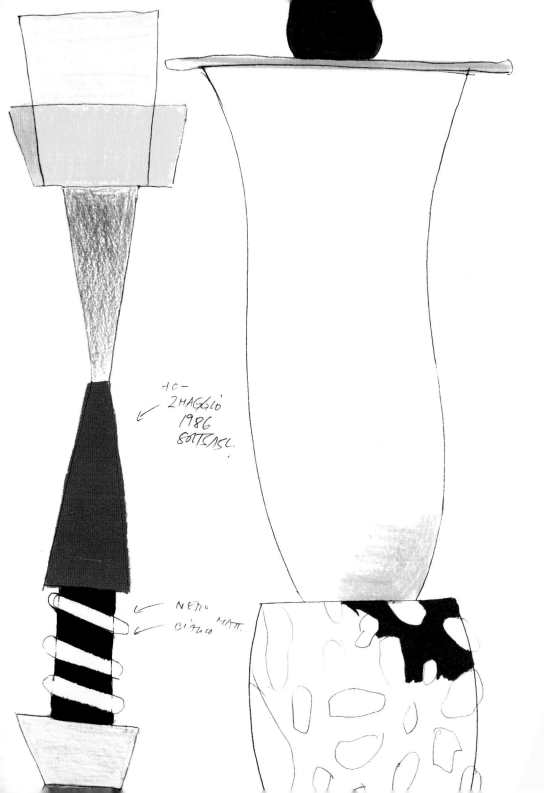

HO—
2 MAGGIO
1986
SOTTSASS.

NERO
BIANCO MATT.

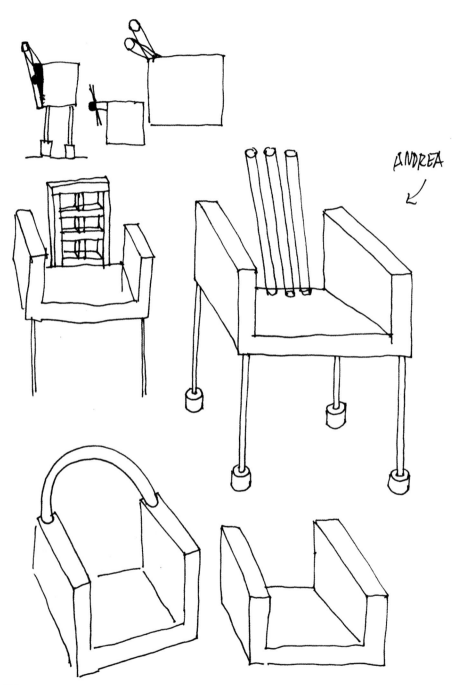

ANDREA

258

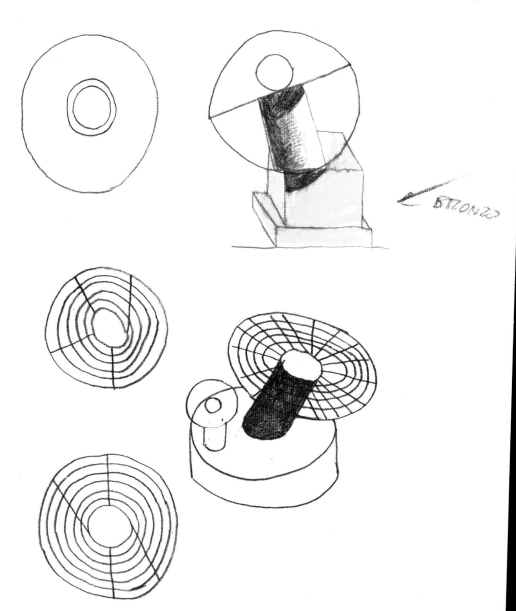

BRONZO

260

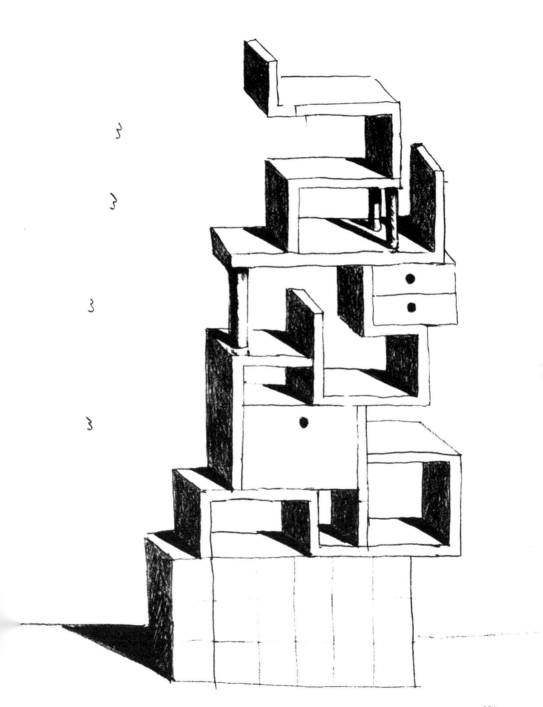

261

VECCHIO
SISTEMA / MA

TENSIONI
DIVERSE

↓ QUESTO
NON È
MALE

5. 3. 87

262

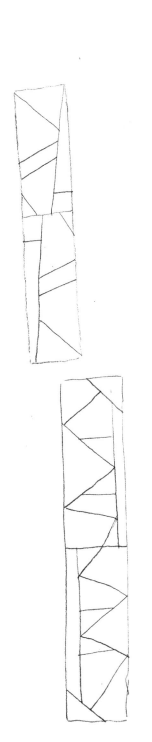

7.3.82
(11345)

?

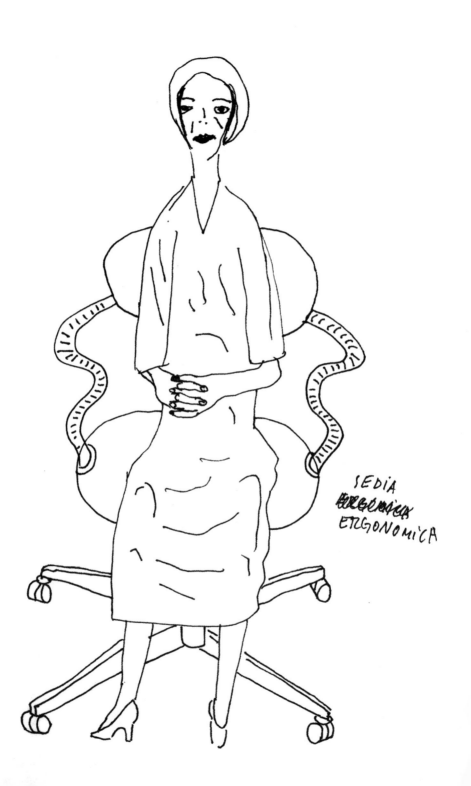

SEDIA
~~ERGONOMICA~~
ERGONOMICA

RADAR
PER COCCINELLE

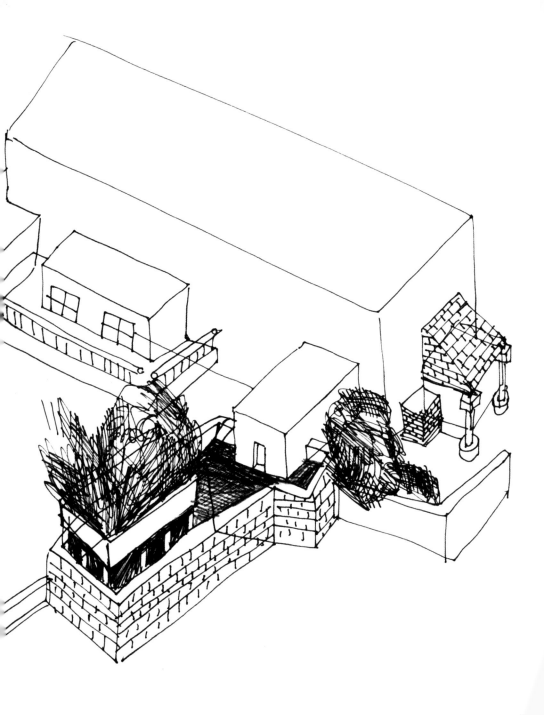

266

Δ CASA PER BRUNO E JOJO IN AUTUNNO

ETTORE 12·12·82

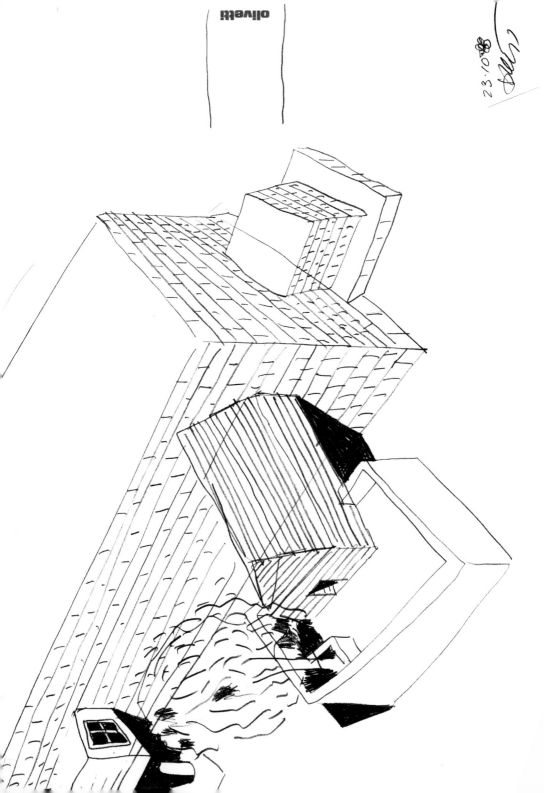

olivetti

23·10

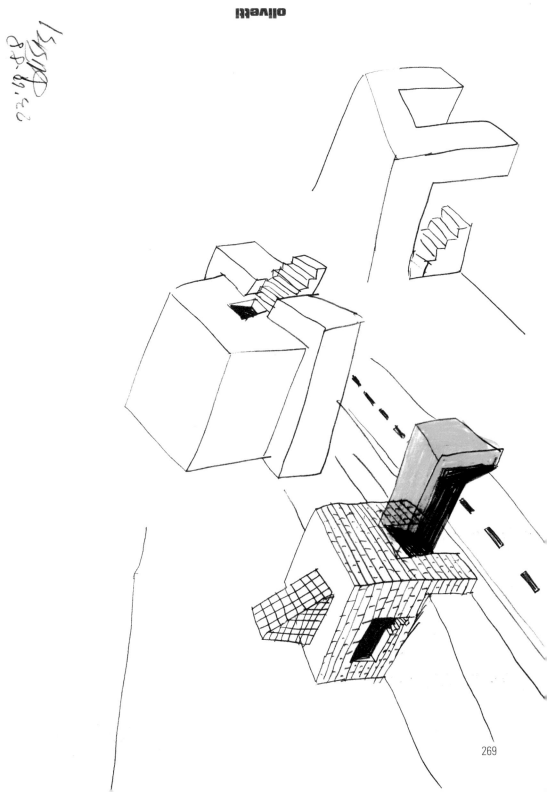

23.08.88
15.51

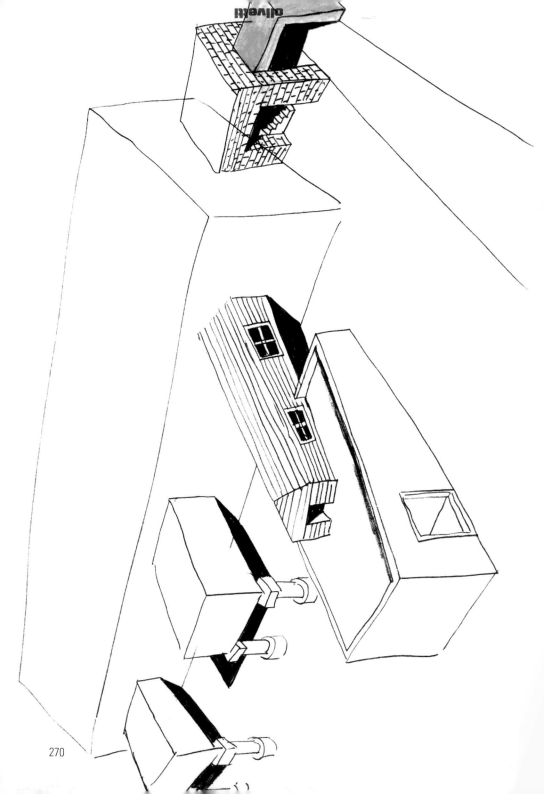

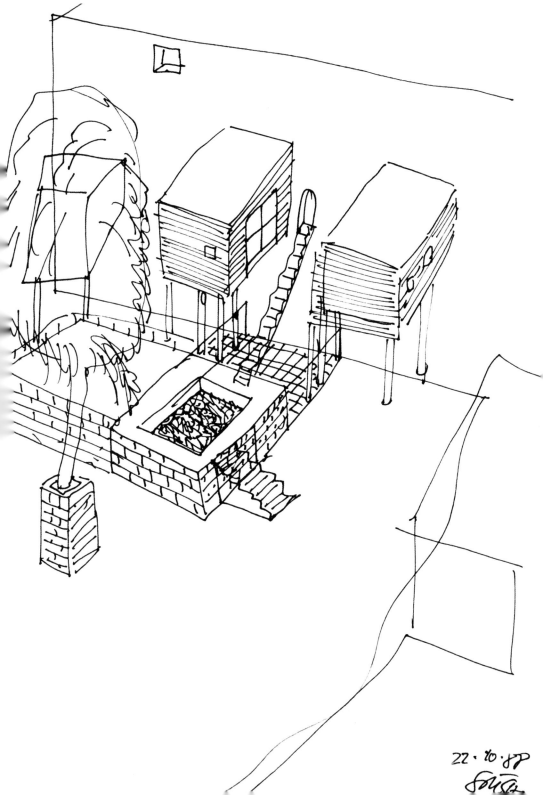

22·10·87

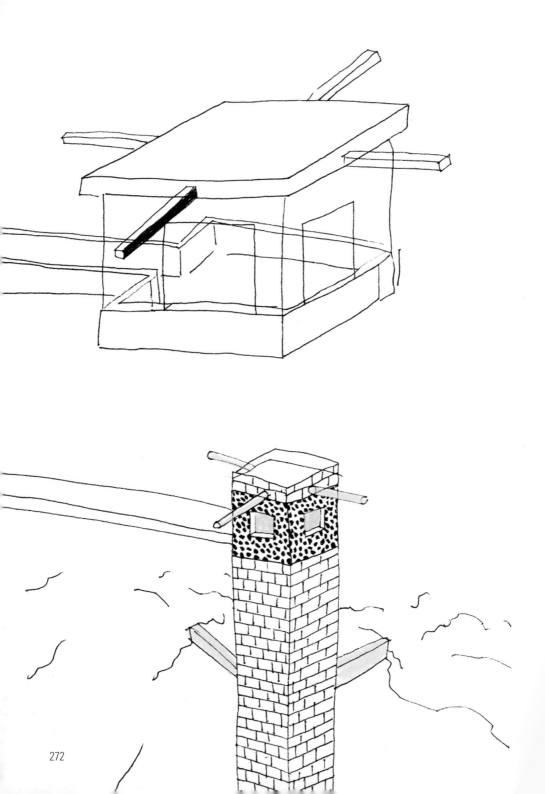

1287
SOTTSASS
MILANO

273

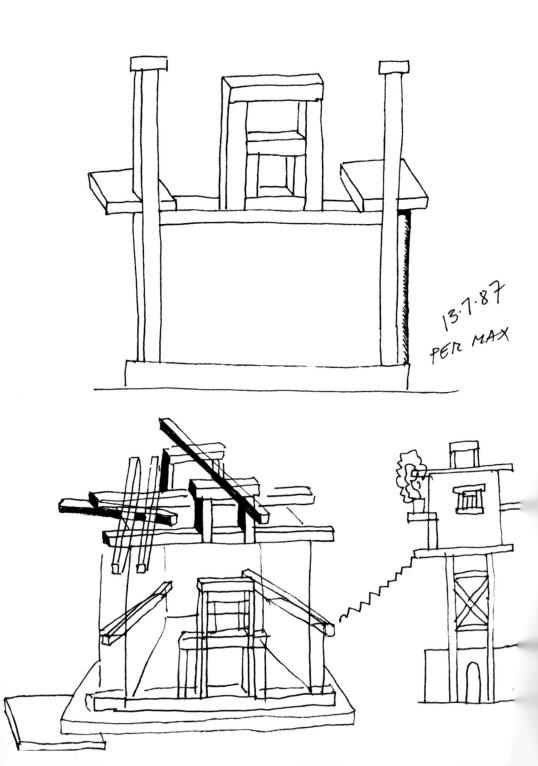

13.7.87
PER MAX

22.1.88

R MAX
11.1.88
SOTTSASS

277

Son Son
11·1·88
For M...

279

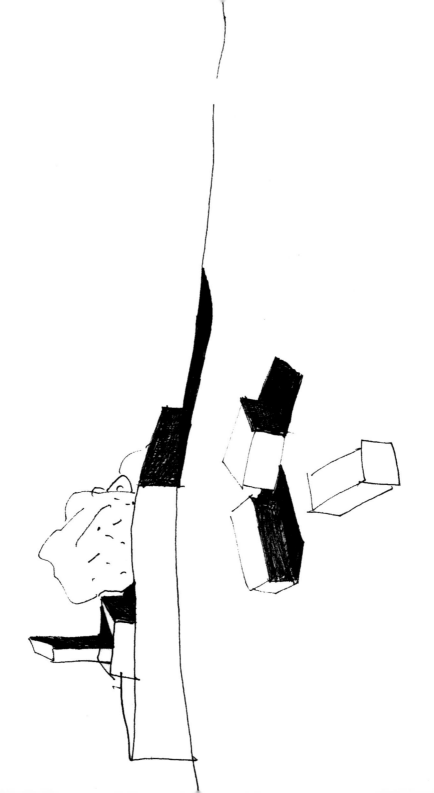

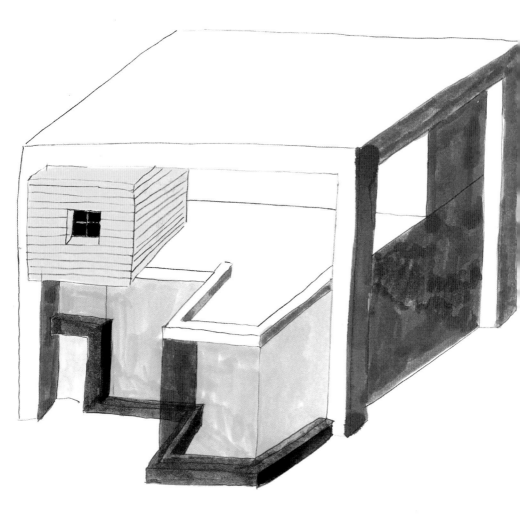

Milano
10.3.89
BN3A9 SI
PER GEORGIE MIULLER

285

288

2.4.88
SOUSA

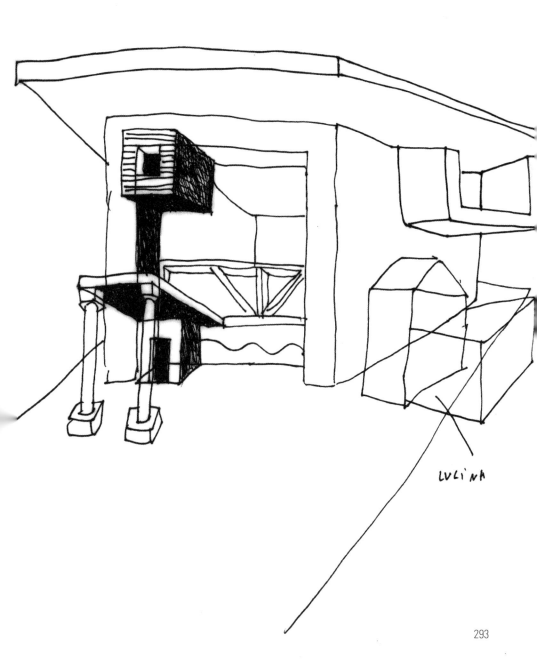

LVLINA

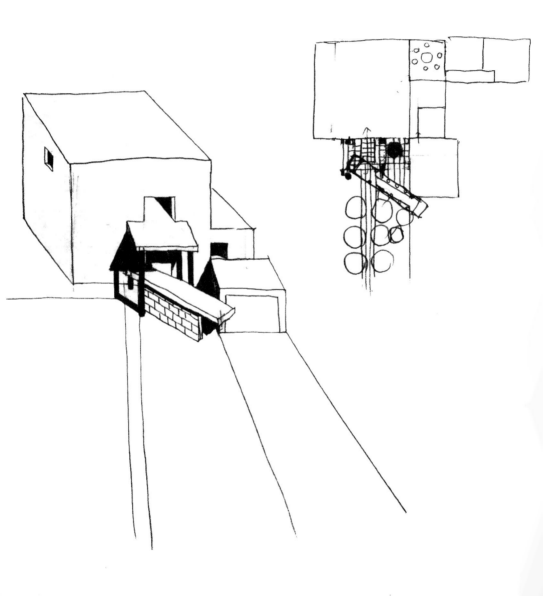

13.8.89

IN A CLOUDY DAY

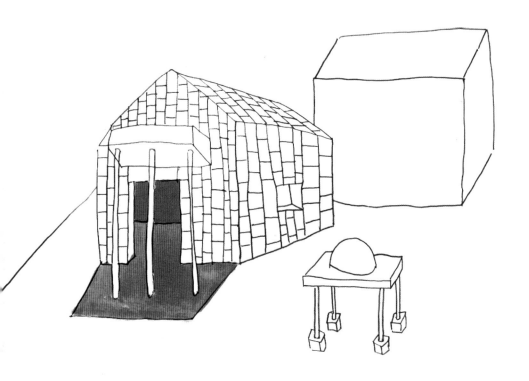

VERGONETTO
13.3.89

305

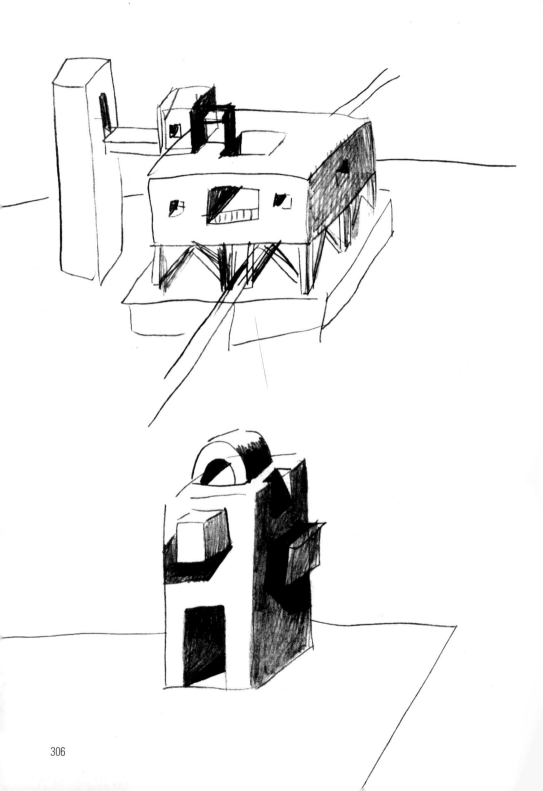

306

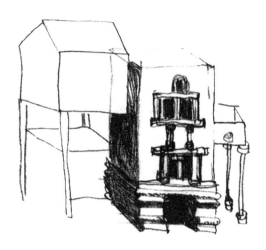

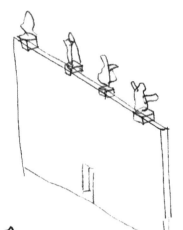

↑ MURO CON I VENTI DEL NORD

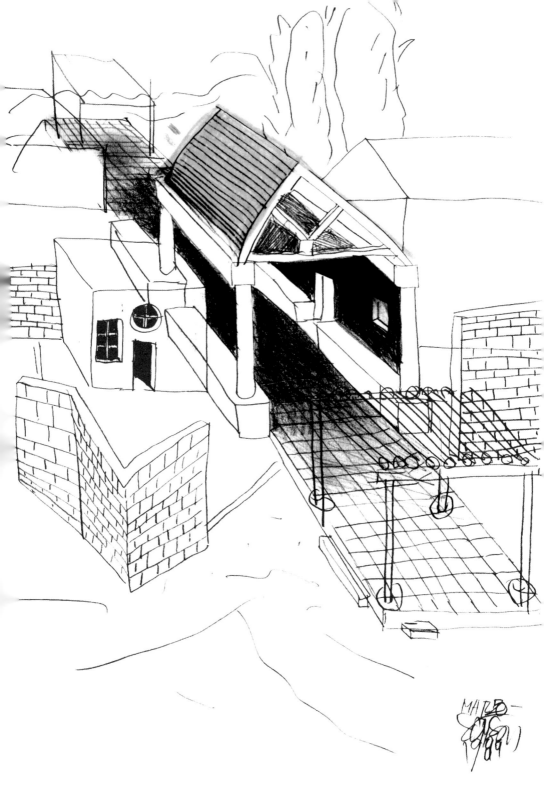

MARZO 89

311

312

THE HOUSE OF THE ASTRONAUT

SOTTSASS '89
MARZO

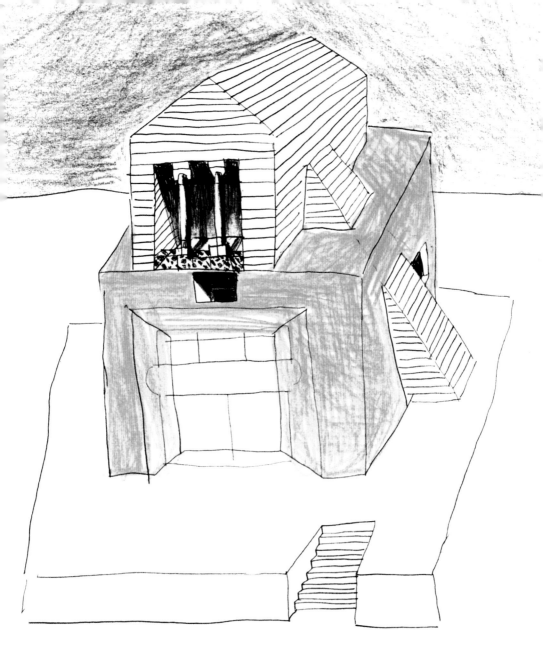

315

IL CASTELLO
DI LE CORBUSIER

Filicuoli
'90

APRILE '90

DAMMI UNO SPAZIO
DOVE POSSO SAPERE CHI SONO...
FORSE.

321

323

19.3.96

326

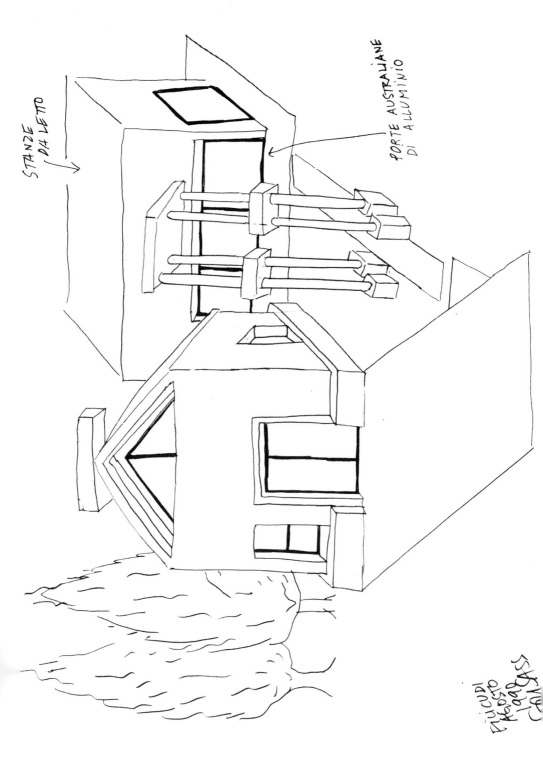

STANZE
DA LETTO

PORTE AUSTRALIANE
DI ALLUMINIO

FILICUDI
AGOSTO
1988
CALABA

CORTILE CON
GRANDE ALBERO

UNA CASA
ABBANDONATA

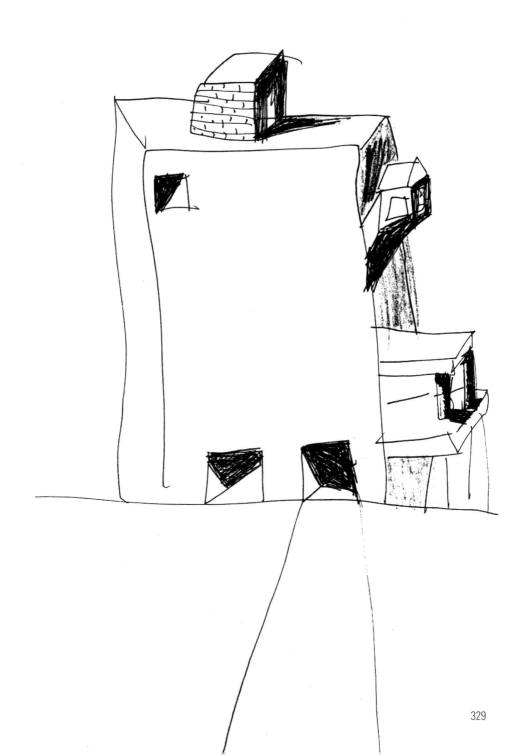

329

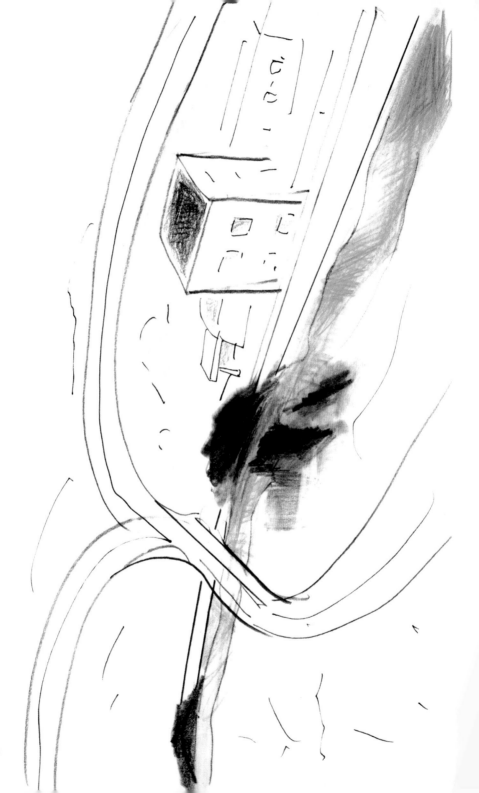

CONFINI NON RETTILINEI

CONFINI (MURETTI) NASCOSTI NEL VERDI

STRADE ALLE VILLE:
QUALCUNA STORTA!
QUALCUNA DIRITTA CON "ALBERI"

SEMPRE + O – VISTA SUL MARE

ALLARGAMENTI AGLI INCROCI

PORTO – CLUB – SHOPPING CENTER – MAIN STREET –

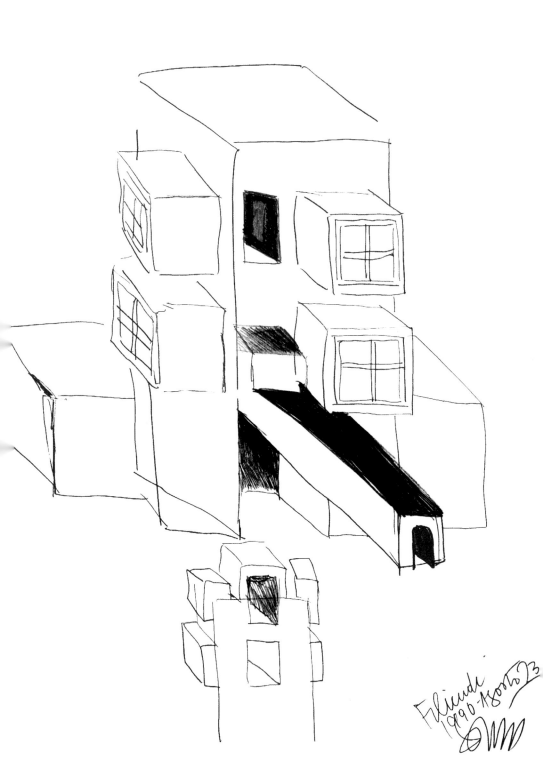

Filiandi
1990-Agosto 93

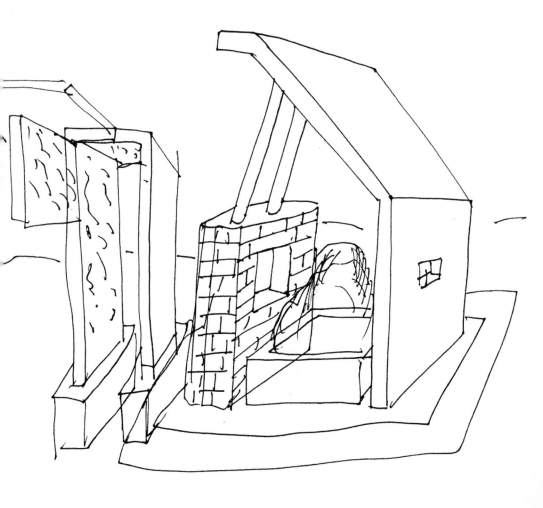

28.1.80
UNA SEDS COMPAÑÍA
DISEÑO

SUPER CASTELLO *

GIOVEDÌ SERA 23.8
FILICUDI
SOTTSASS

339

AGOSTO 90
ALICUDI

345

CASTELLO,
FILICUDI
1990

CASTELLO
AGOSO
LIGUDI
1990

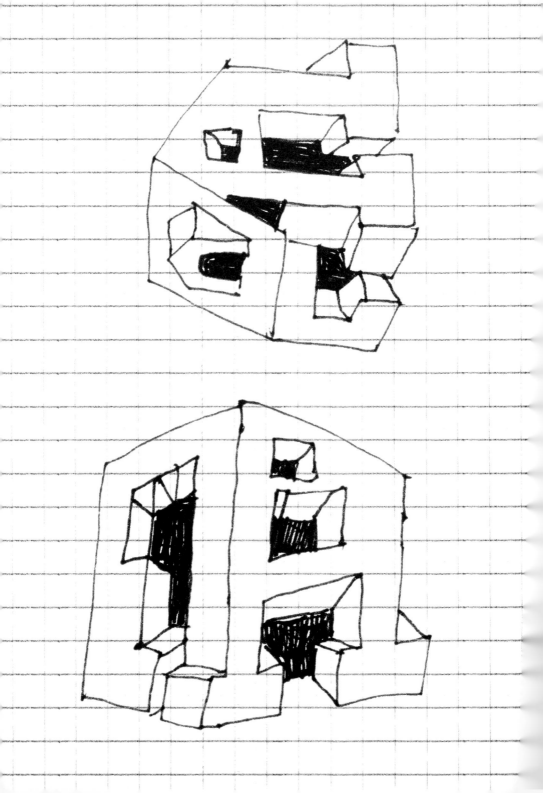

LEGN

CERAMICA

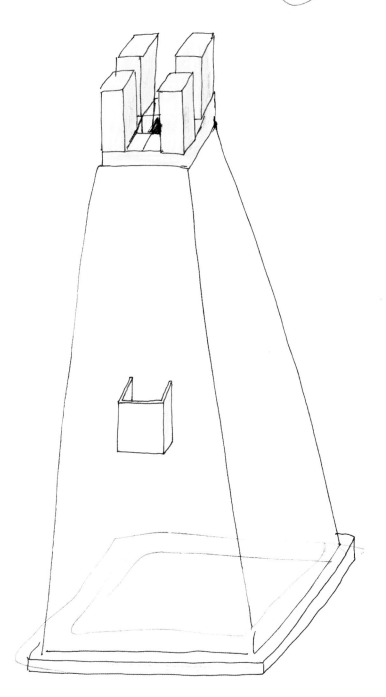

PER SEVRES

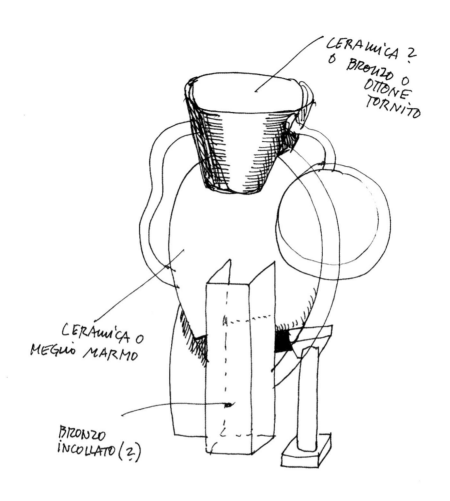

CERAMICA ?
O BRONZO O
OTTONE
TORNITO

CERAMICA O
MEGLIO MARMO

BRONZO
INCOLLATO (?)

GRANDE VASO

(VEDI DISEGNO)

PER ...

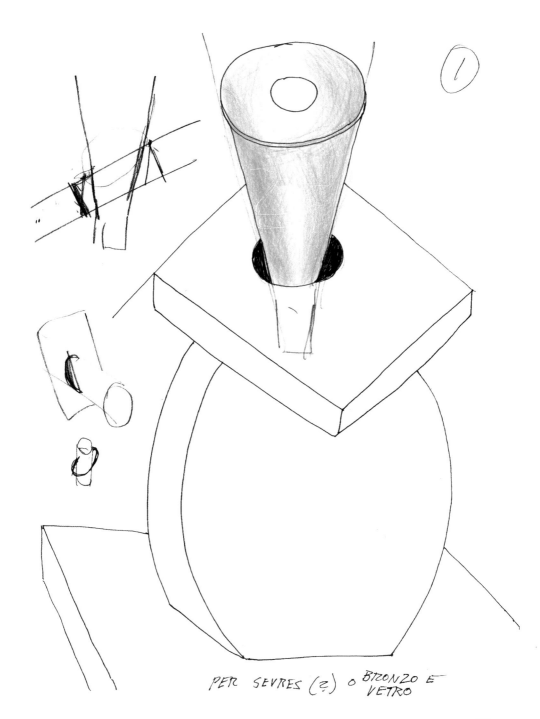

PER SEVRES (?) O BRONZO E VETRO

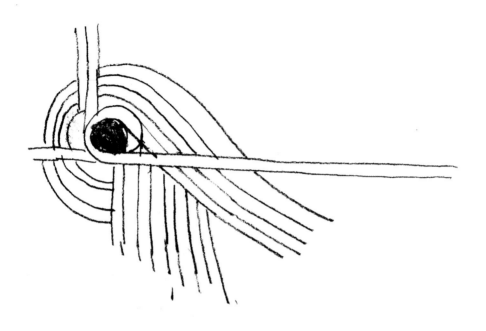

1990

CONTINUARE A LAVORARE ?

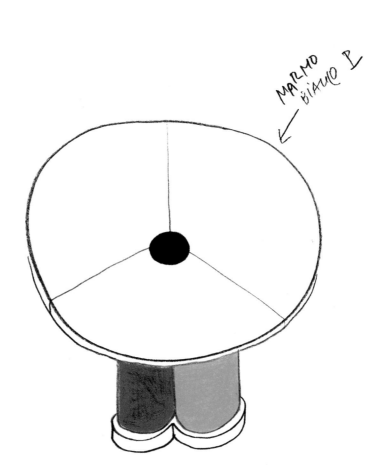

MARMO
BIANCO I

SOTTS
NOV. 90

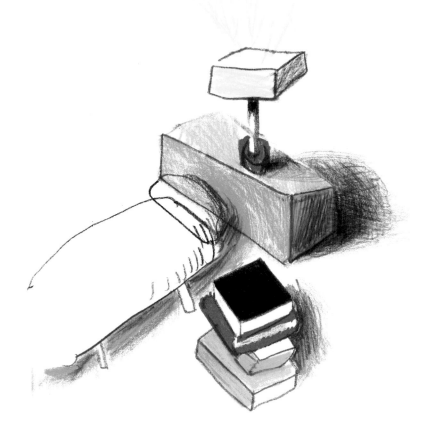

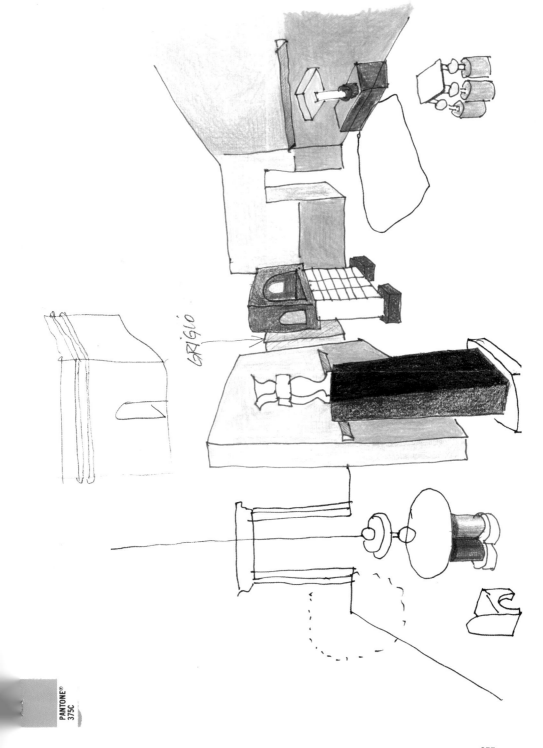

GRIGIO

357

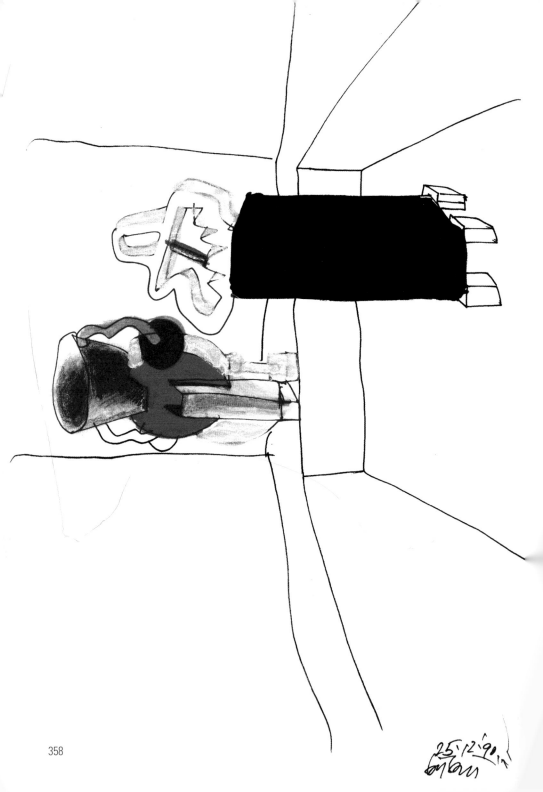

358

25-12-1990

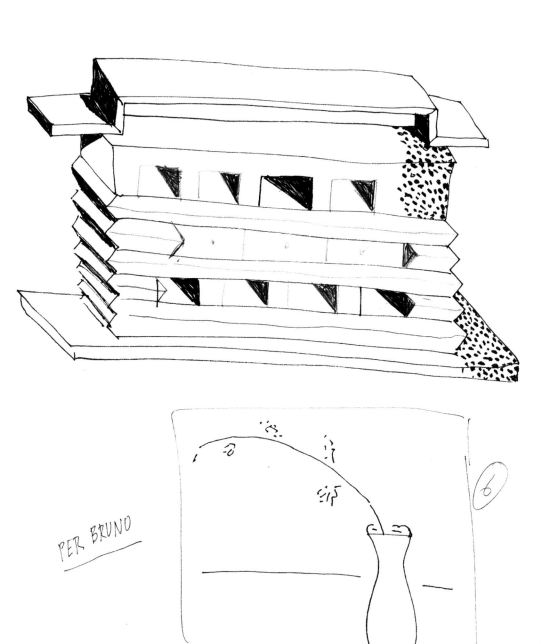

PER BRUNO

olivetti

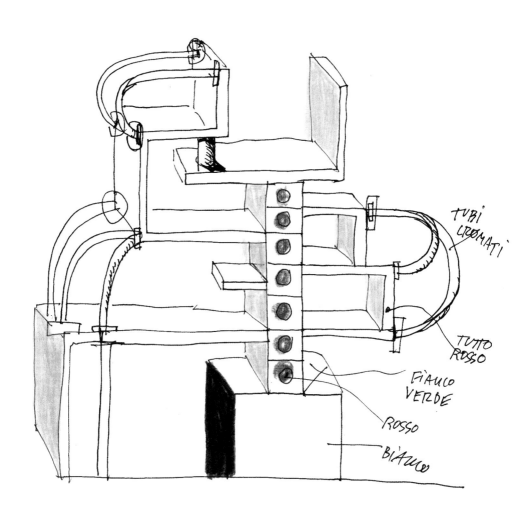

TUBI
CROMATI

TUTTO
ROSSO

FIANCO
VERDE

ROSSO

BIANCO

(VEDI SCHIZZO)

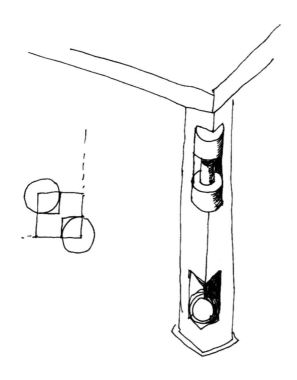

TAVOLO PER BRUNO

NR ③

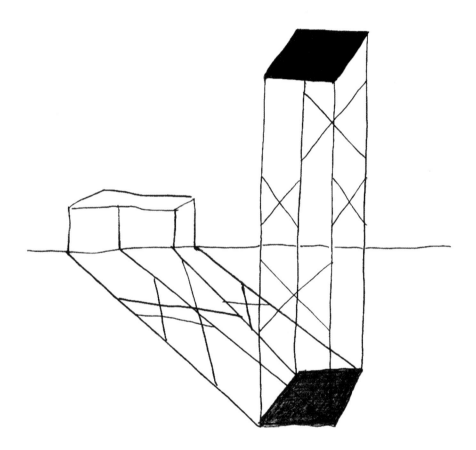

BIANCO
FORO APERTO

365

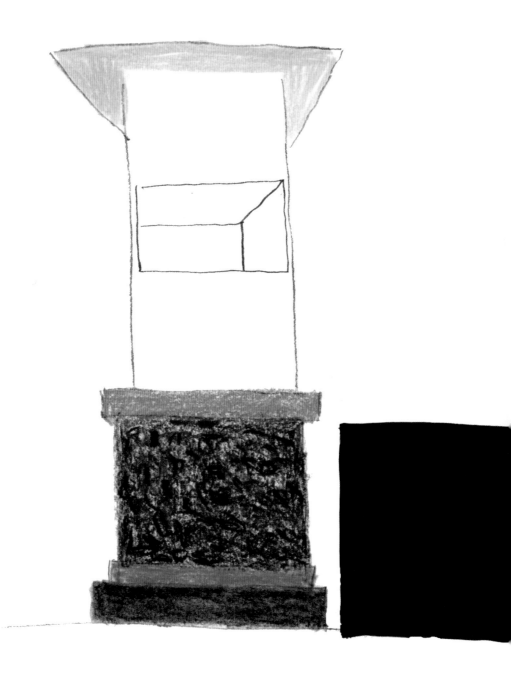

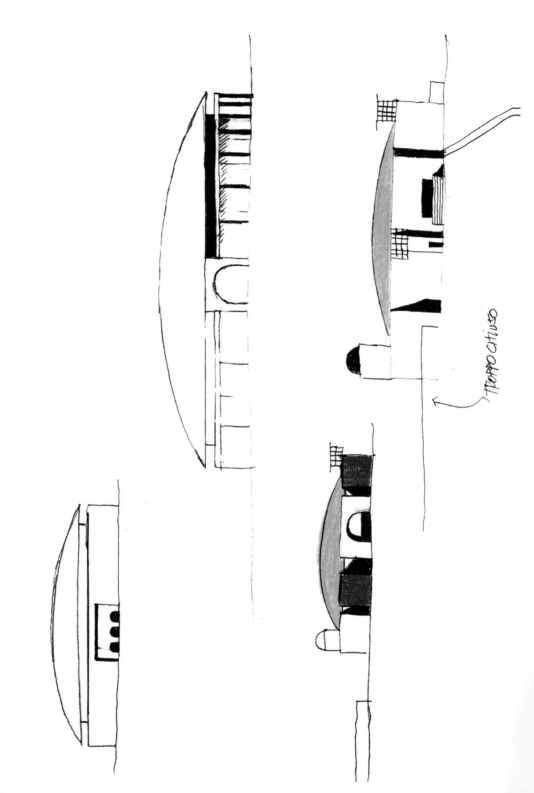

TROPPO CHIUSO

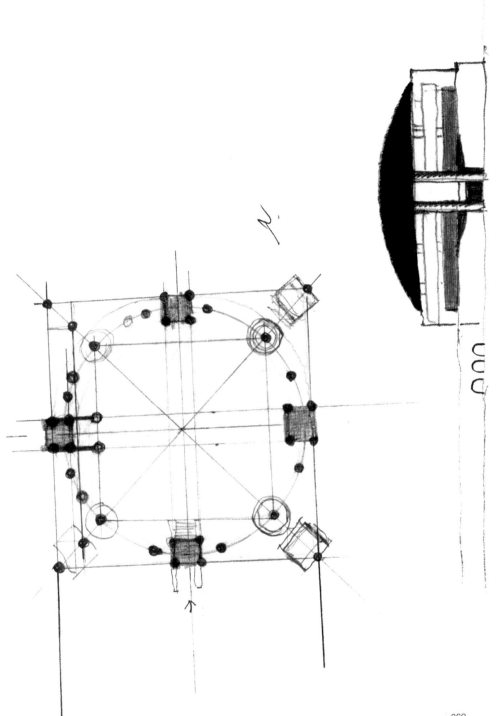

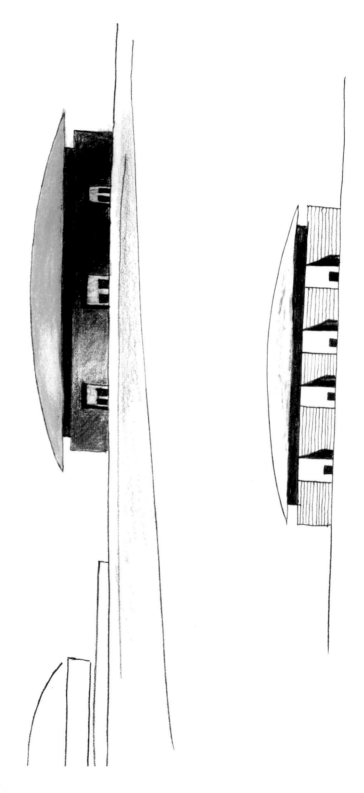

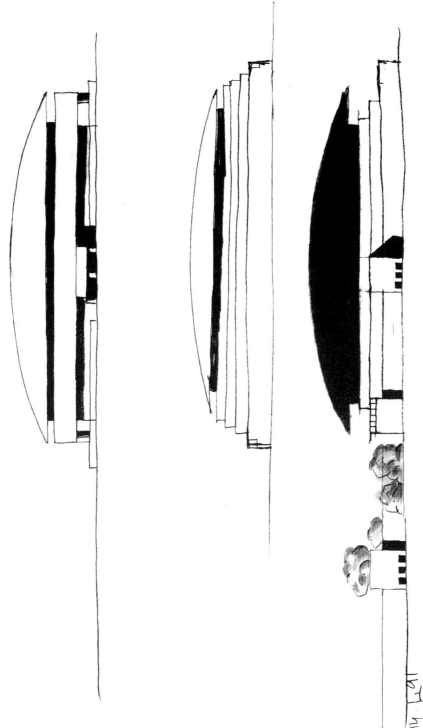

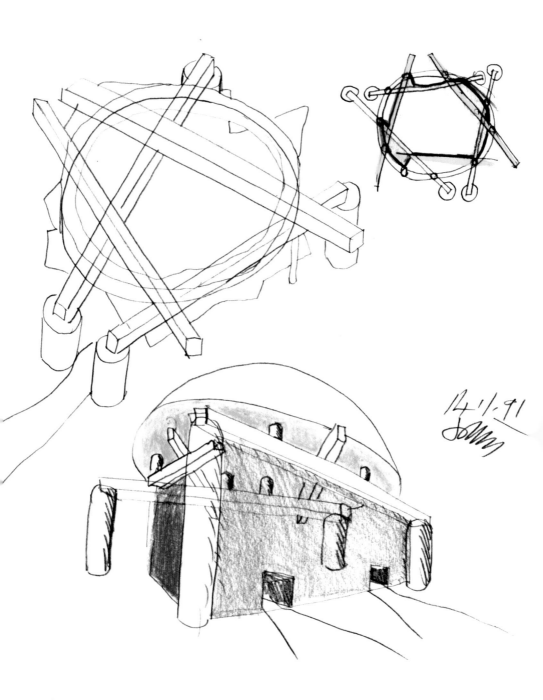

14·11·91

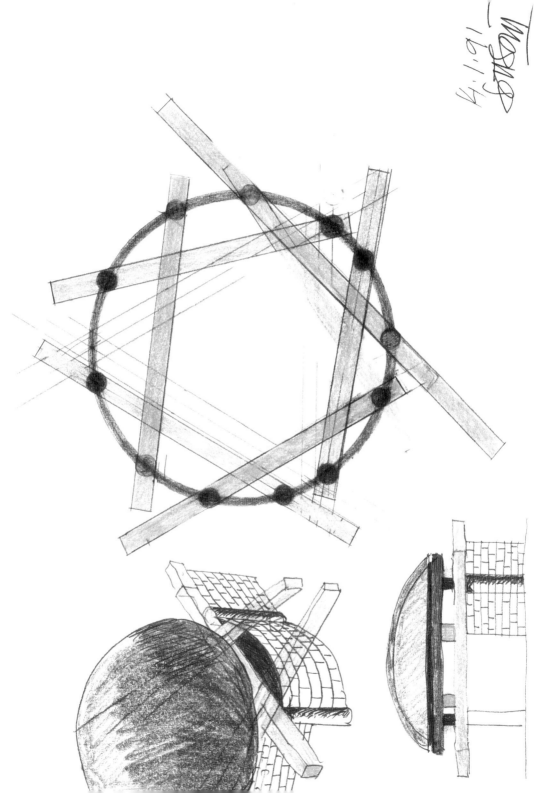

DESASTROUS
HIGH TECHNOLOGY

TEA CUP

Sottsass
91

376

ESPRESSO CUP 1

91

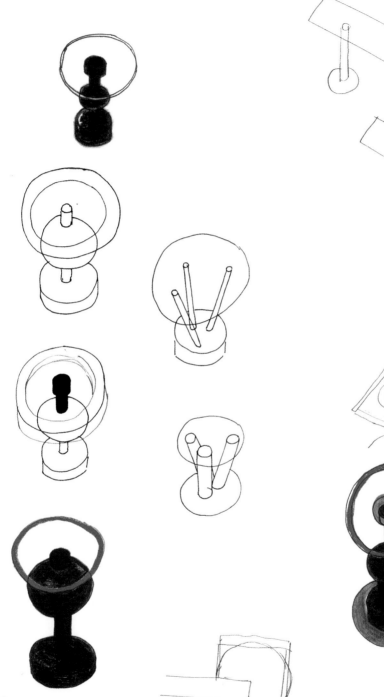
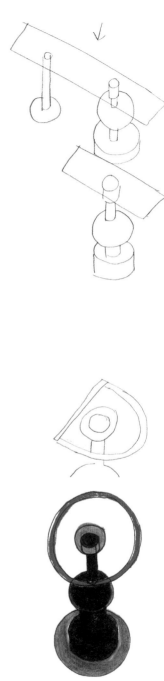

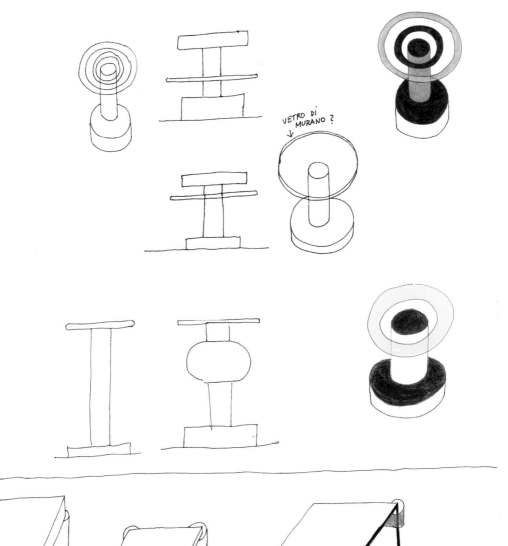

CRISTALLO BIANCO

VETRO DI MURANO ?

379

TRAFILATI

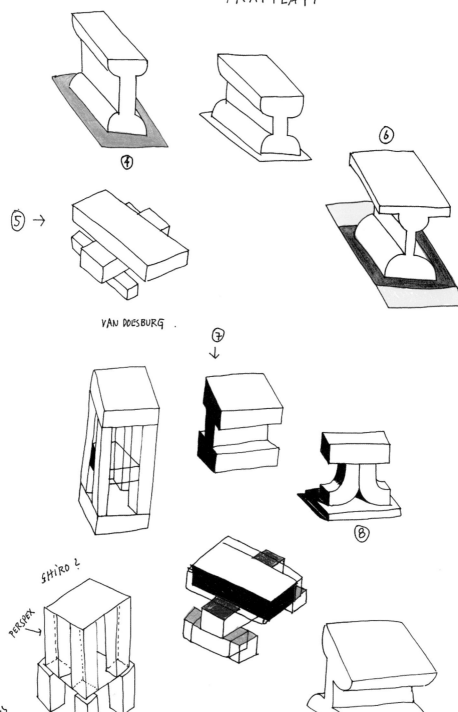

④

⑤ →

⑥

VAN DOESBURG .

⑦
↓

⑧

SHIRO ?

PERSPEX →

1991
SOTTSASS

CRISTALLO BIANCO

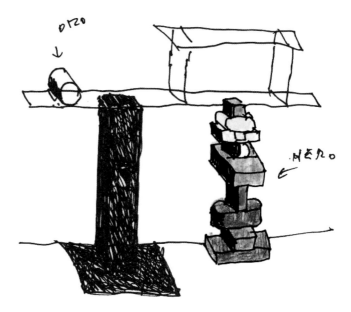

ORZO

NERO

IN AEREO
MT. SINGAPORE
8·8·91

ANCHÉ
SPOSTATI
E
DI DIVERSI
COLORI

TRA TORONTO E MILANO
6.12.92

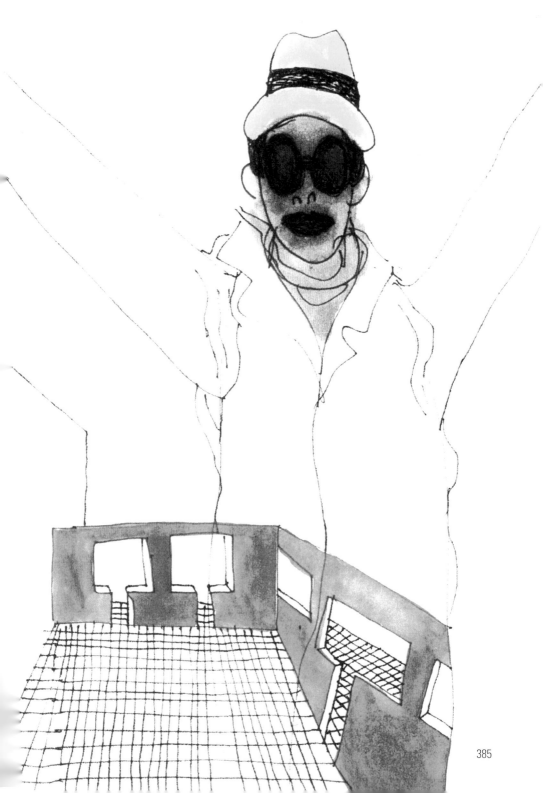

385

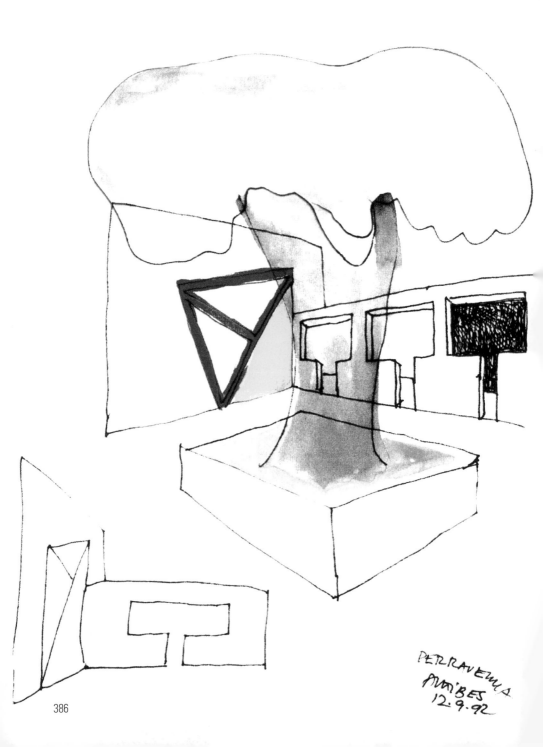

PERRAVELLA
ANTIBES
12.9.92

386

SOTTSASS
SETT '92

VERDE?

NR③

388

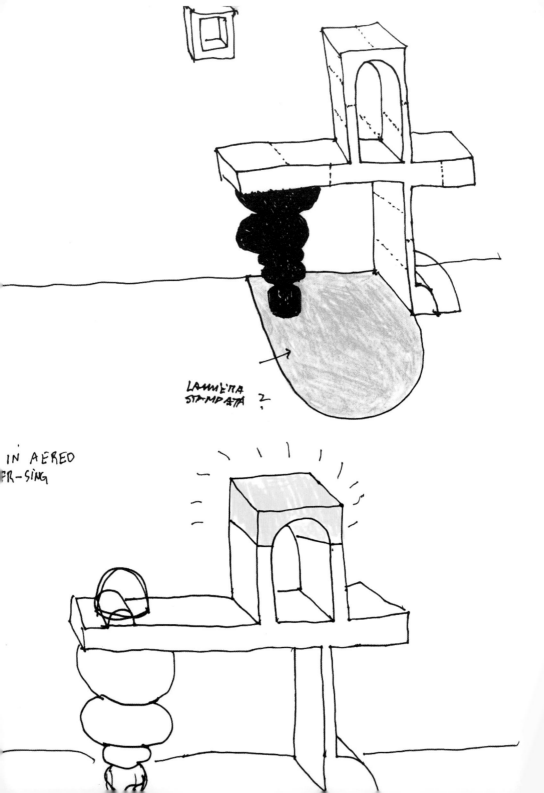

LAMIÉRA
STAMPATA ?

IN AEREO
PR-SING

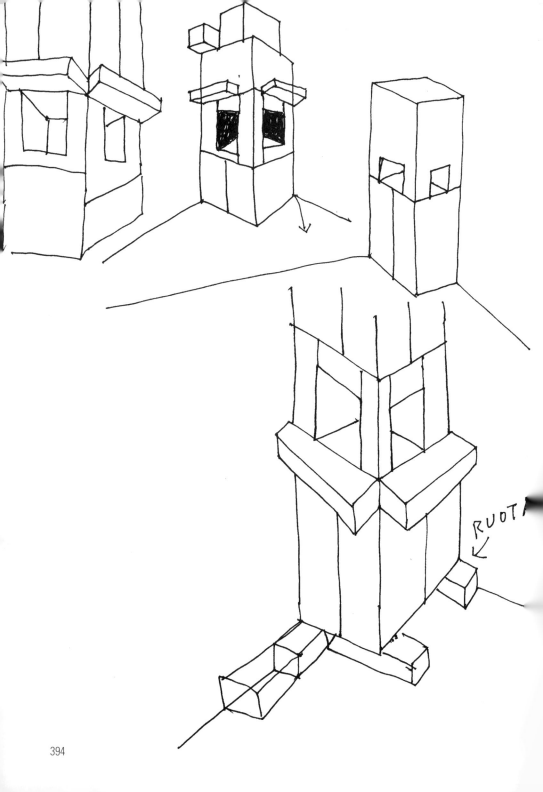

RUOTA

394

SEPARATEZZA

GRIGLIA   METODOLOGICA

TECNICA → POLITICA   (CAPITALE)

ANTROPOLOGICO - SOCIALI

IL BISOGNO CRESCE

SOCIALIZZAZIONE DEL PROGETTO

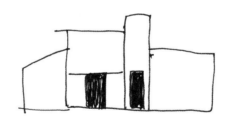

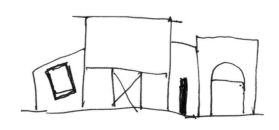

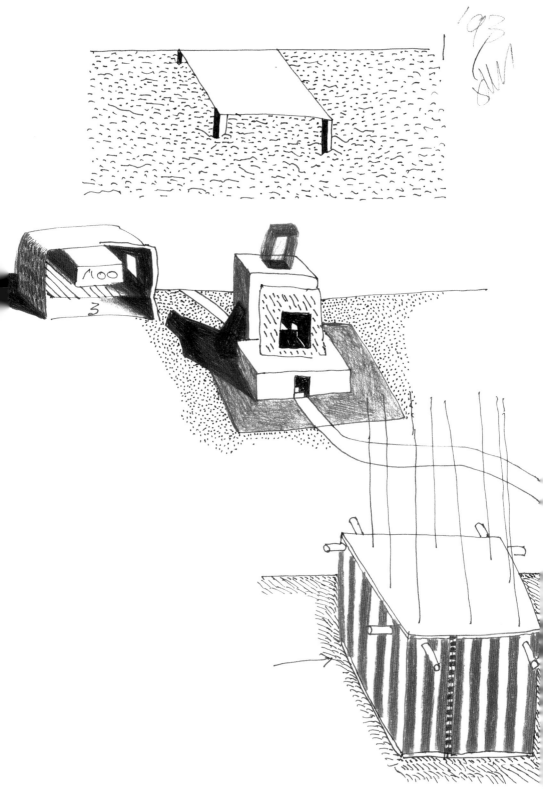

398

400

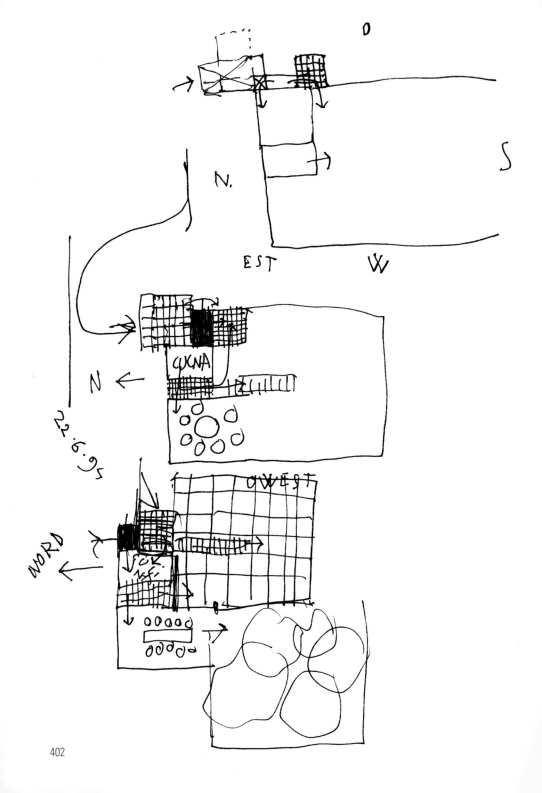

O

S

N.

EST

W

N

CUCINA

22.6.94

OVEST

NORD

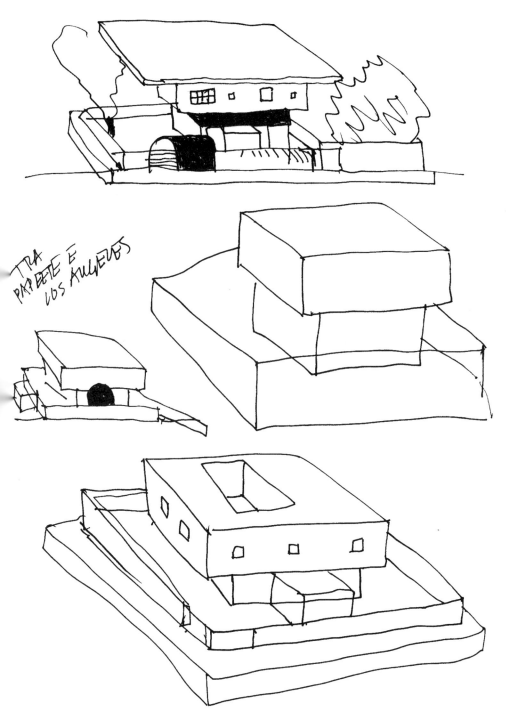

TRA
PAPEETE E
LOS ANGELES

405

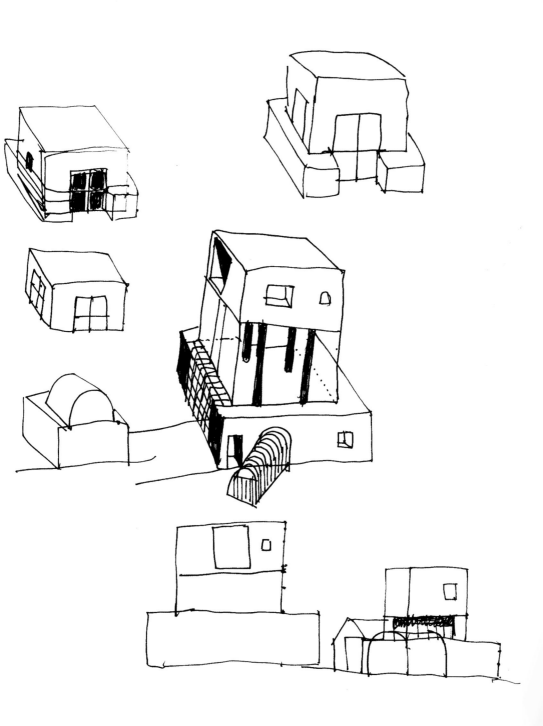

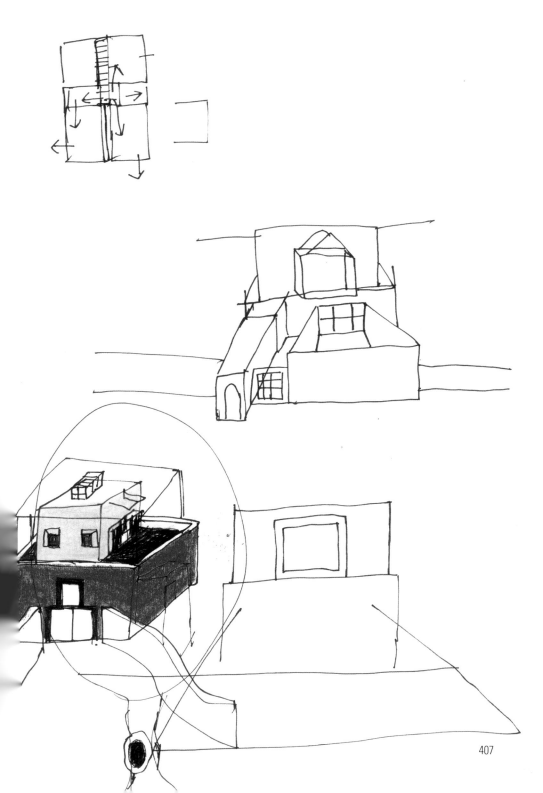

409

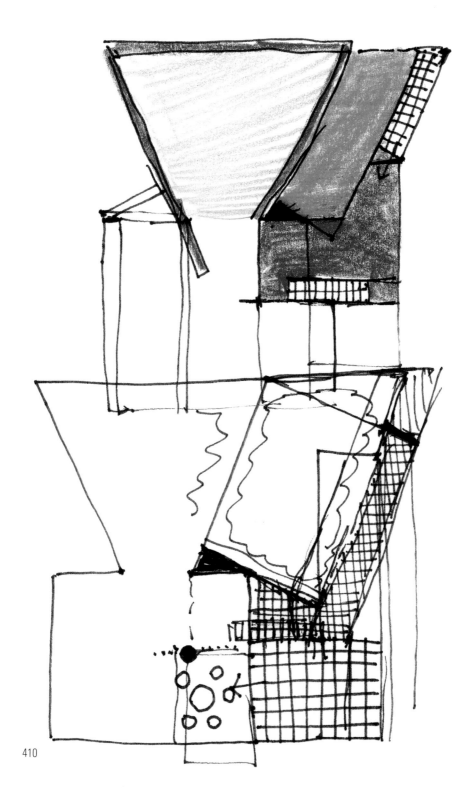

410

IL PIÙ POSSIBILE
MATERIE OPACHE

BIANCO
LATTE

LAMINATO
CON PELI?

CERTE
INFORMAZIONI

ZOCCOLO
SPORGENTE

PAVIMENTO
NERO !!!

NERO?

PILASTRI 2 BEIGE?
MARRONE?
VERDE CUPO?

ARANCIO/ROSA .
GRIGI CALDI
BLU GRIGI CHIARI

411

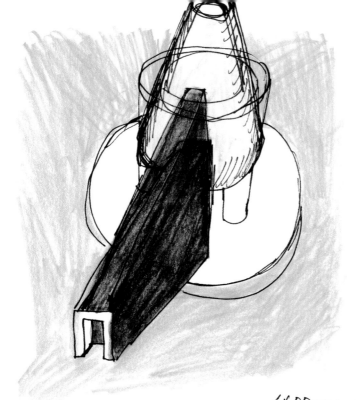

CAPPELLA JEAU CHATOLES
CASTEL BAJAC
1·7·94

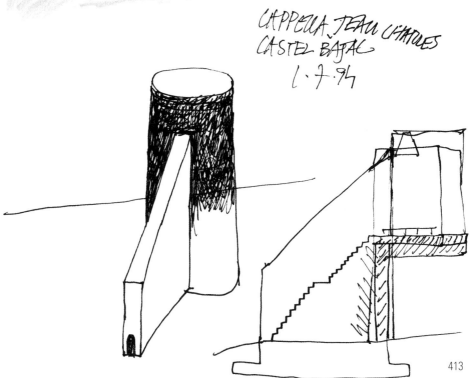

413

CINA 94

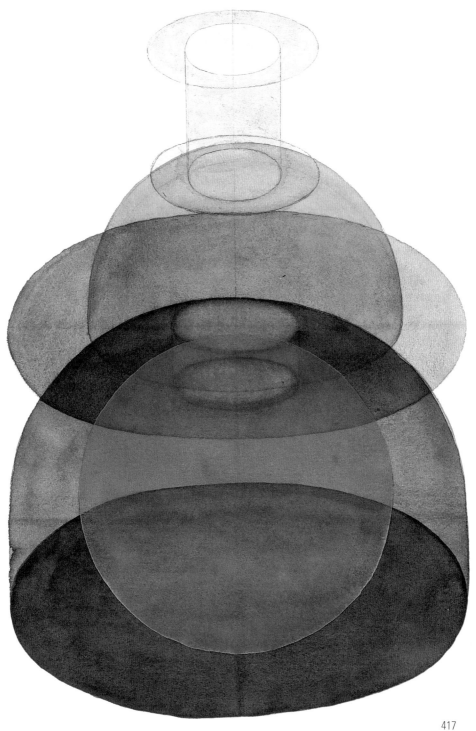

417

418

419

420

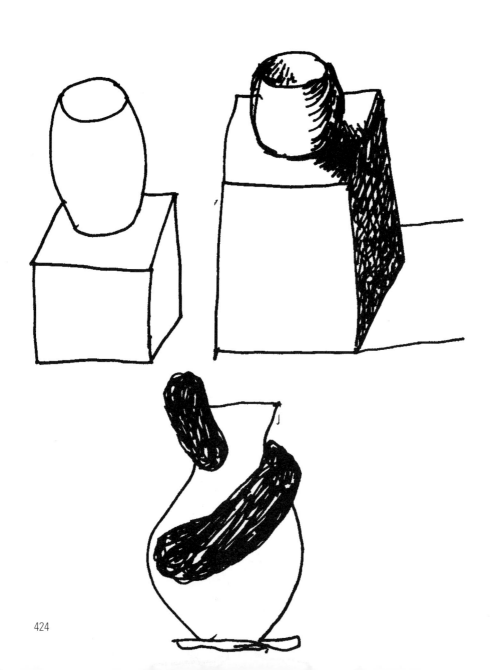

424

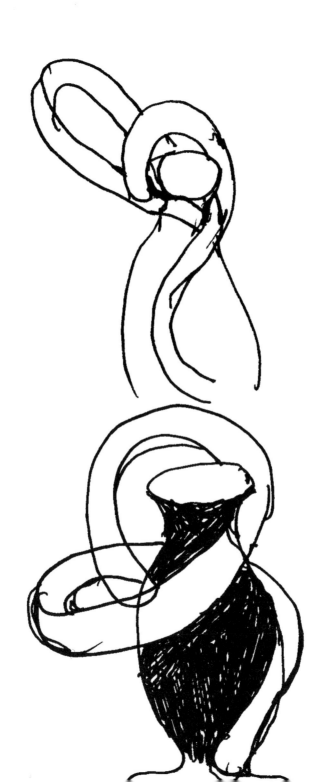

425

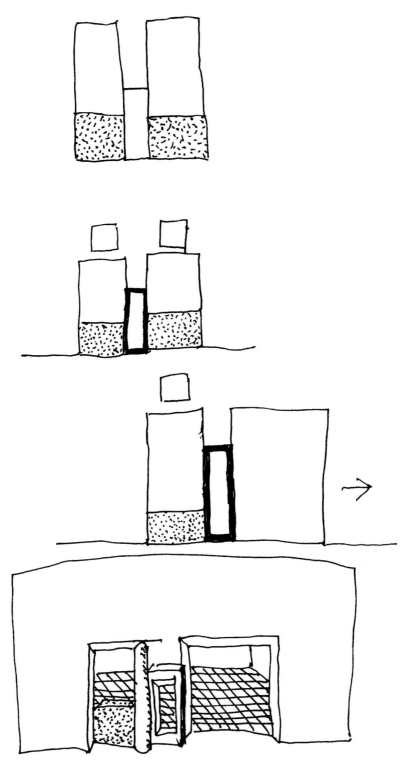

LOSANGELES
↓
ATLANTA.
25·3·95

427

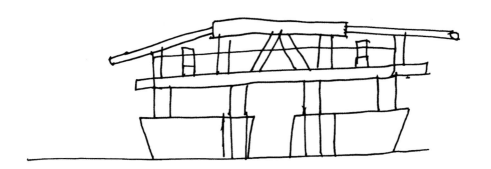

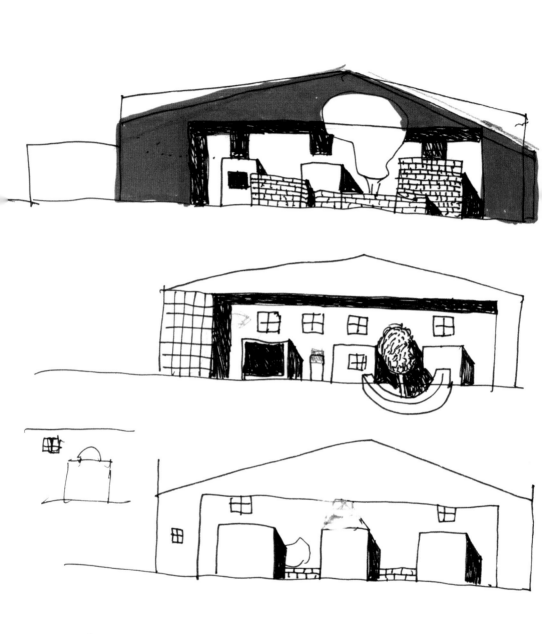

PARIGI
APRILE
1995

429

MILANO 3. 1. 95

SINGAPORE

430

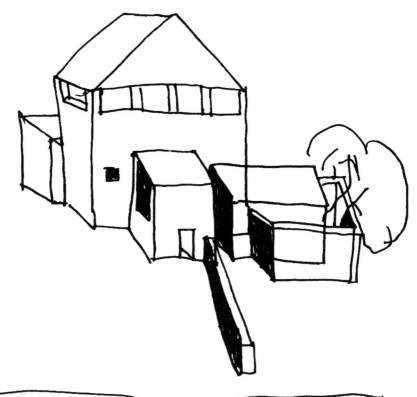

UNA OPERAZIONE INTERATTIVA
(SI METTONO I FIORI), VIRTUALE
(I FIORI SONO ARTIFICIALI) HO
USATO L'INTERNET (PER SAPERE
A QUANTO È QUOTATA IN BORSA
LA RADICA DI PIOPPO) (NON HO
AVUTO RISPOSTA) i FARÒ UN ~~VIDEO
TAPE~~) · SI C.D. ROM ·

APO4
2.1.95
ETTORE

EINRICH ZIMMER

MITI E SIMBOLI ELL'INDIA AG 41

"SEMPLICIOTTI INDISTINGUIBILI L'UNO DALL'ALTRO SI UNISCONO A FORMARE UNA SORTA DI IMPASTO SGRADEVOLE E APPICCICOSO."

(MATSYA PURANA .....)

– KALI YUGA – | 4° PERIODO, LA FINE

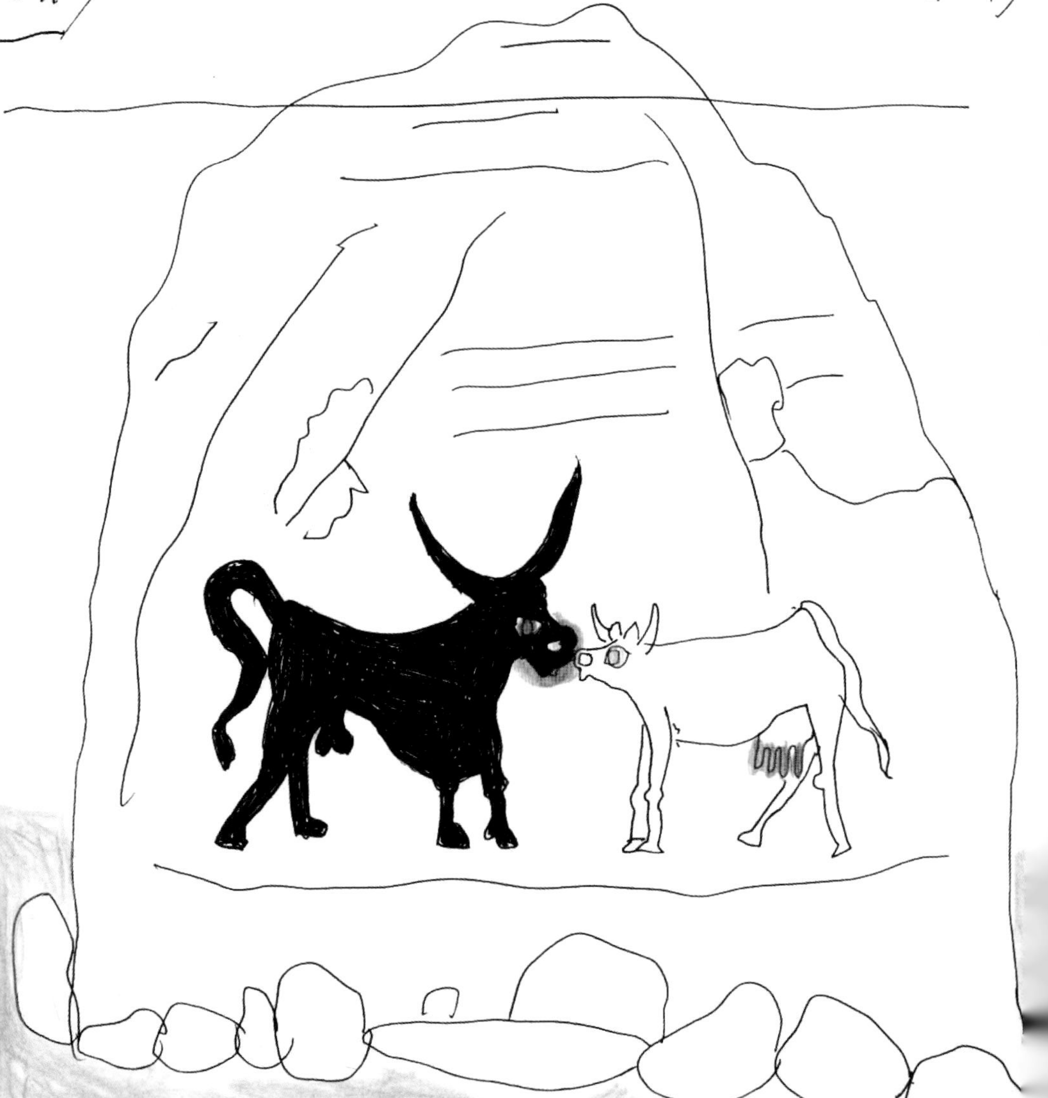

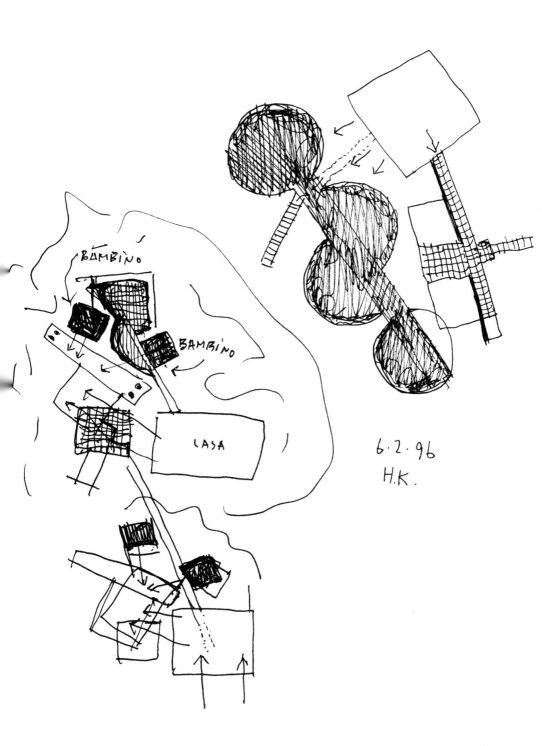

BAMBINO

BAMBINO

CASA

6·2·96
H.K.

435

21.1.98
PETS ETWEST.

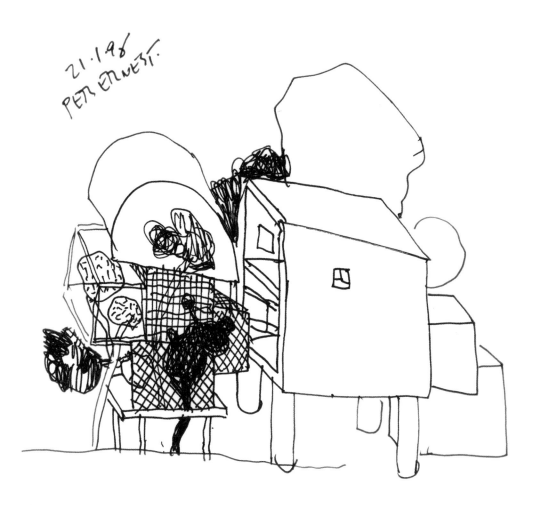

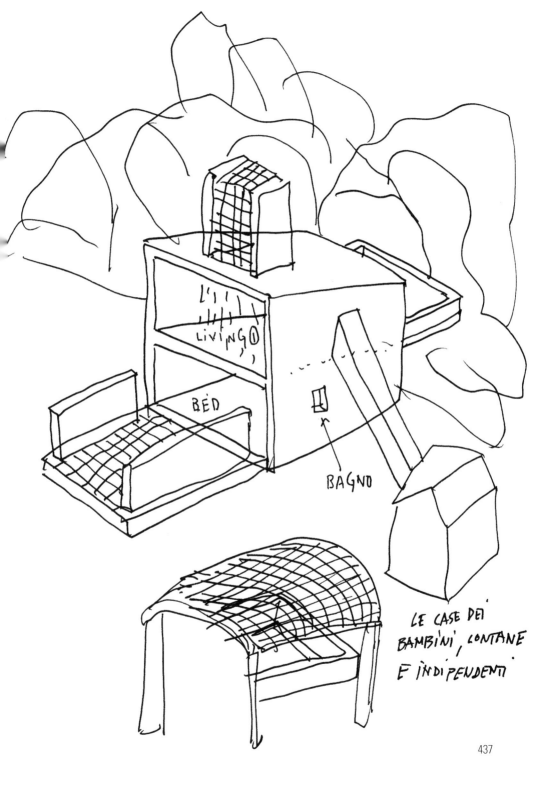

L'... LIVINGO

BED

BAGNO

LE CASE DEI BAMBINI, LONTANE E INDIPENDENTI

438

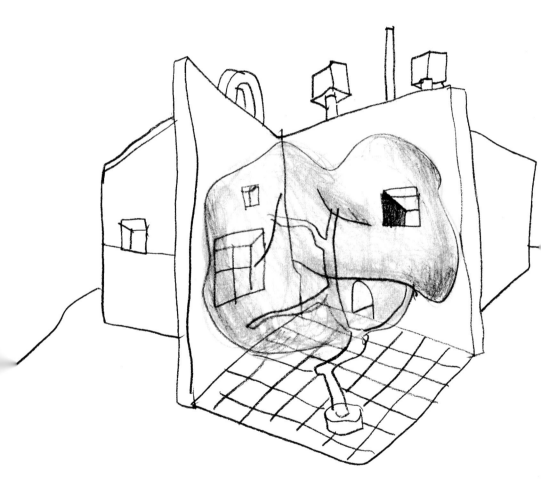

439

442

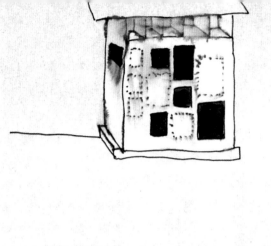

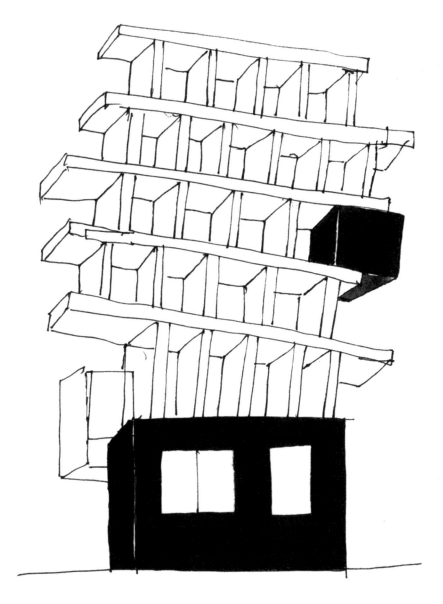

MUSEUM/QUALITY

447

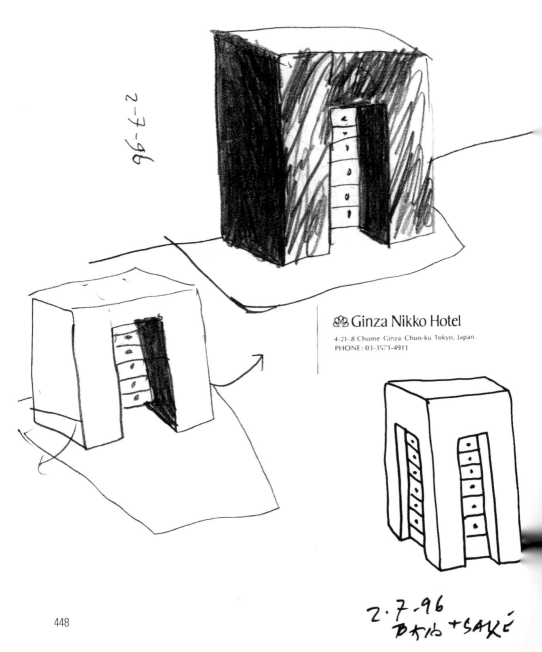

2-7-96

&8 Ginza Nikko Hotel

4-21-.8 Chome Ginza Chuo-ku Tokyo, Japan.
PHONE : 03-3571-4911

2.7.96
TOKYO +SAKÉ

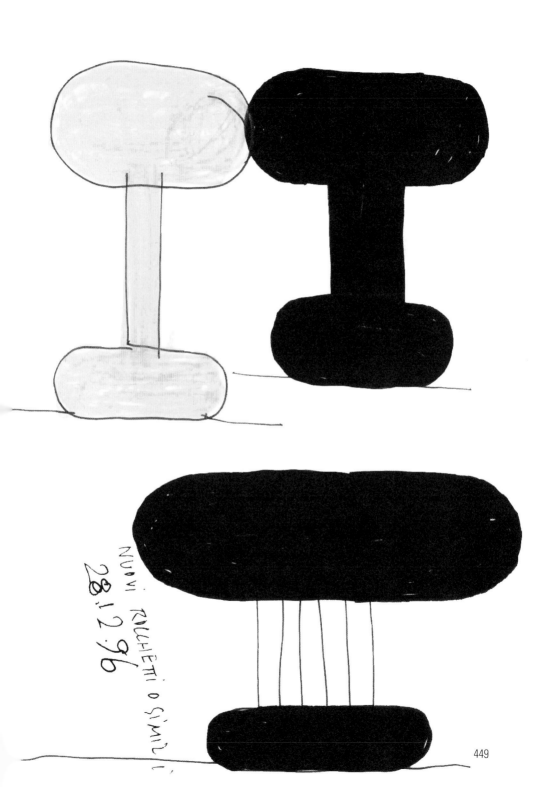

NUOVI ROCHETTI O SIMILI
28.12.96

449

450

FATTO

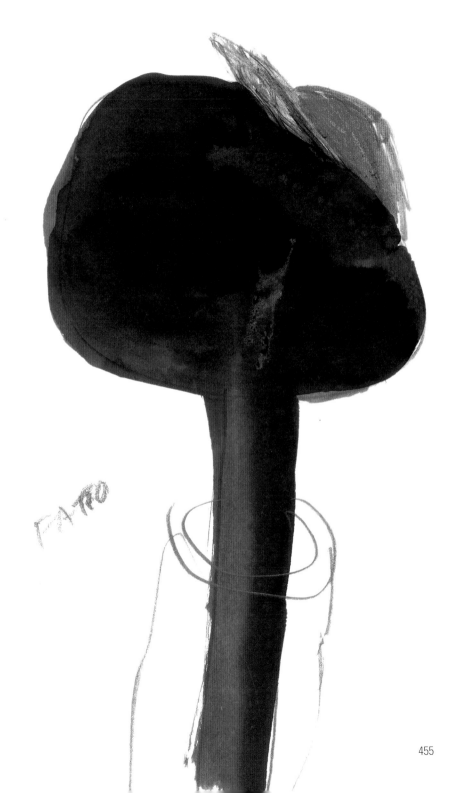

455

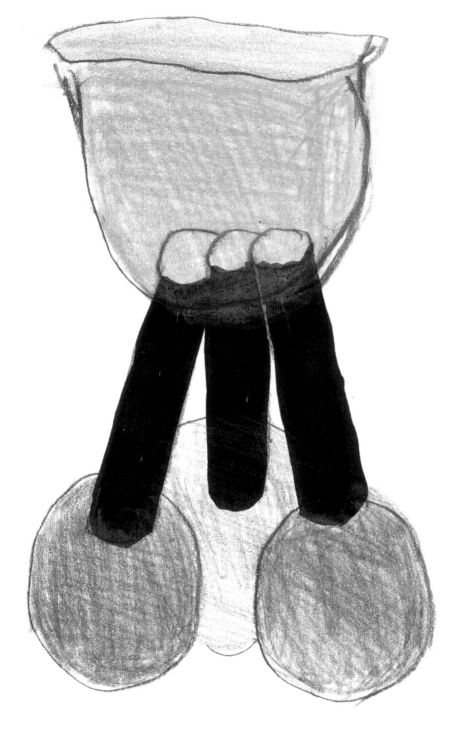

457

459

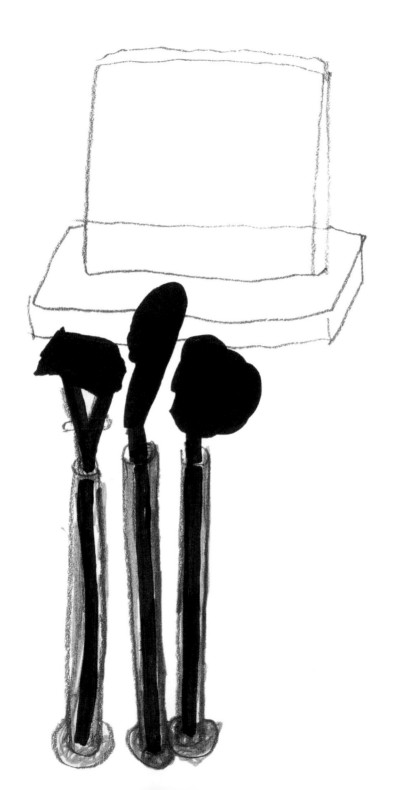

460

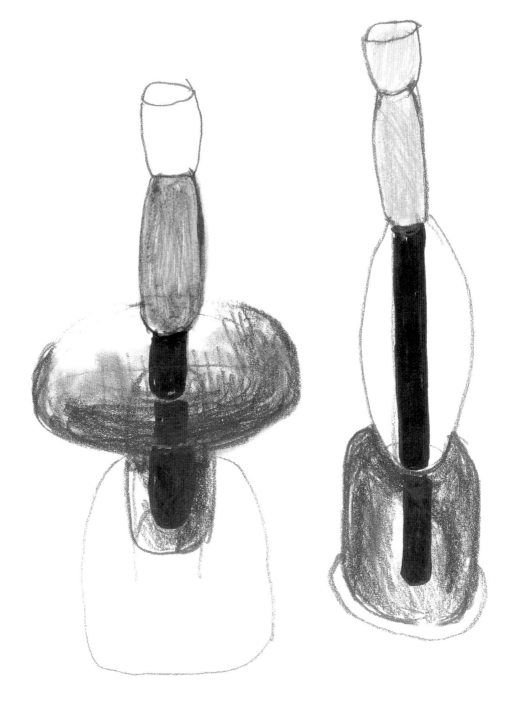

461

VIVALDI 1678 – 1741	SCHUBERT 1797 – 1828
ALBINONI 1671 – 1750	SCARLATTI 1685 – 1757
B. GALUPPI 1706 – 1785	CHOPIN 1810 · 1849
BACH 1685 – 1750	MOZART 1756 – 1791
HAYDIN 1732 – 1809	JOSEPH PLEYEL 1757 – 1831
PERGOLESI 1710 – 1736	BEETHOVEN 1770 – 1827
BOCCHERINI 1734 – 1805	CHERUBINI 1760 – 1842
MERCADANTE 1795 – 1870	PAGANINI 1782 – 1840
STALDER 1725 – 1765	CARL MARIA VON WEBER 1786 – 1826

GRIEG
1843 - 1907
MARTUCCI
1856 - 1909
M. GIULIANI
1770 - 1841
RAVEL
1875 - 1937
SAINT-SAËNS
1835 - 1921
FRANK
1822 - 1890
DEBUSSY
1862 - 1918
SCHUMAN
1810 - 1856

F. MENDELSSOHN
1809 - 1847
JOAQUIN TURINA
1882 - 1949

[
KURT WEILL
1900 - 1950
OTHMAR SCHOECK
1886 - 1957

MALIPIERO
1882 - 1973 †
ROTA
1911 - 1979 †
RESPIGHI
1879 - 1979
36

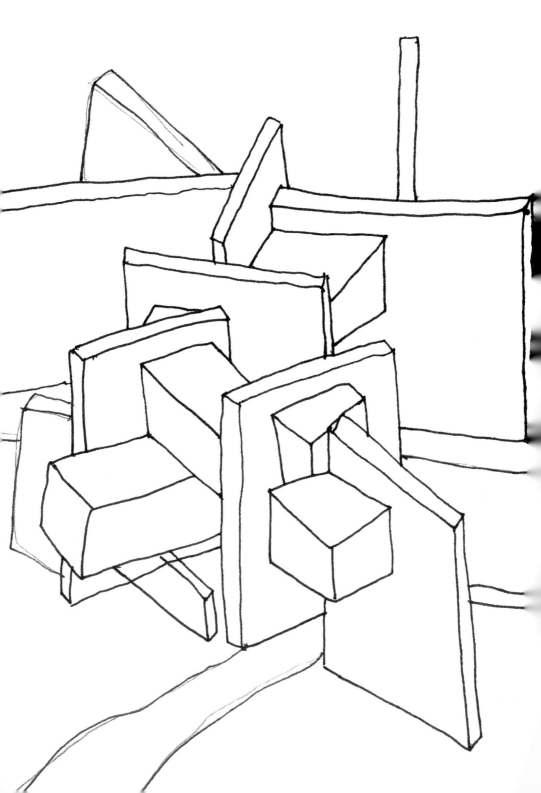

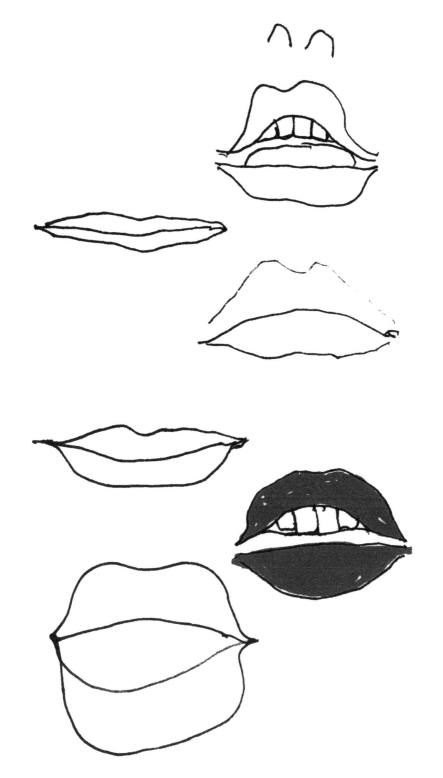

465

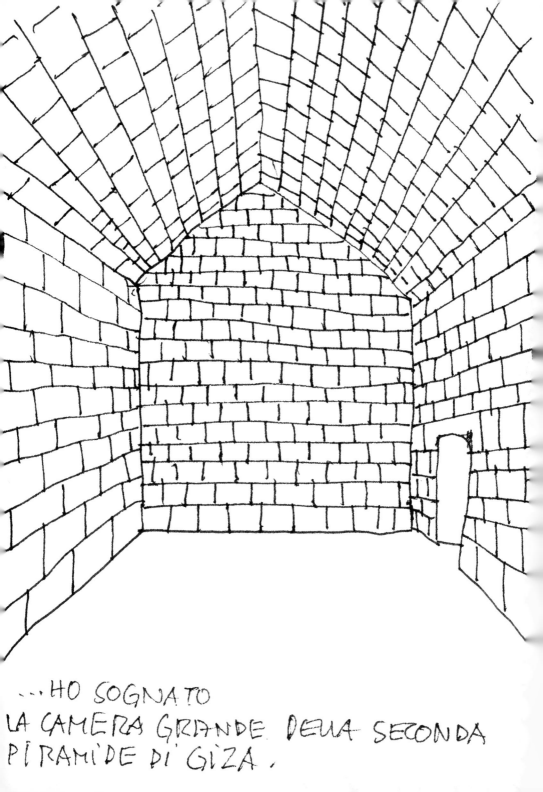

...HO SOGNATO
LA CAMERA GRANDE DELLA SECONDA
PIRAMIDE DI GIZA.

... TROVERAi SULLA SiNiSTRA
DELLA CASA Di ADE, UNA FONTE
E ACCANTO AD ESSA UN CIPRESSO BIANCO
CHE Si DRiZZA...
A QUESTA FONTE NON AVViCINARTI TROPPO.

(FRAMMENTO ORFICO)

467

20.11.'97

468

IL MONUMENTO

469

HONG KONG
20·2·97

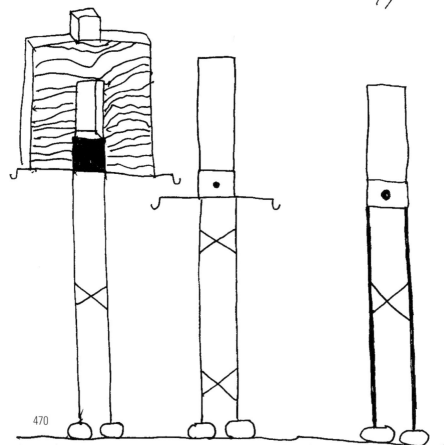

470

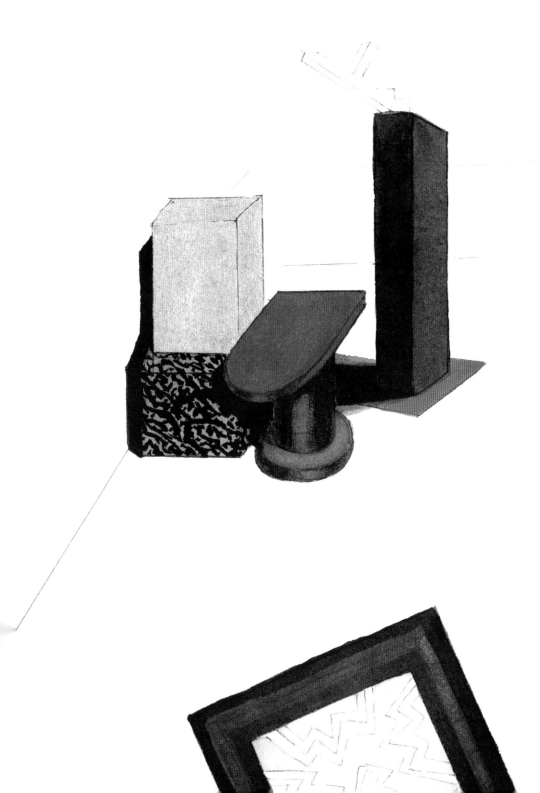

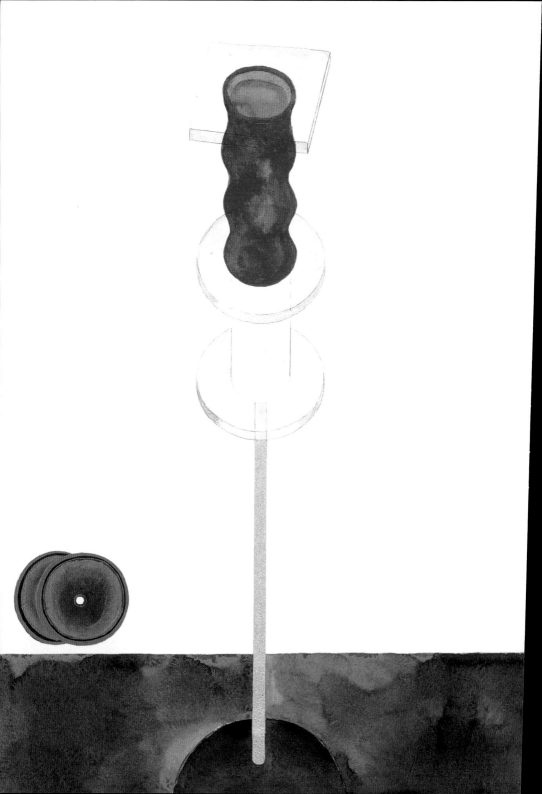

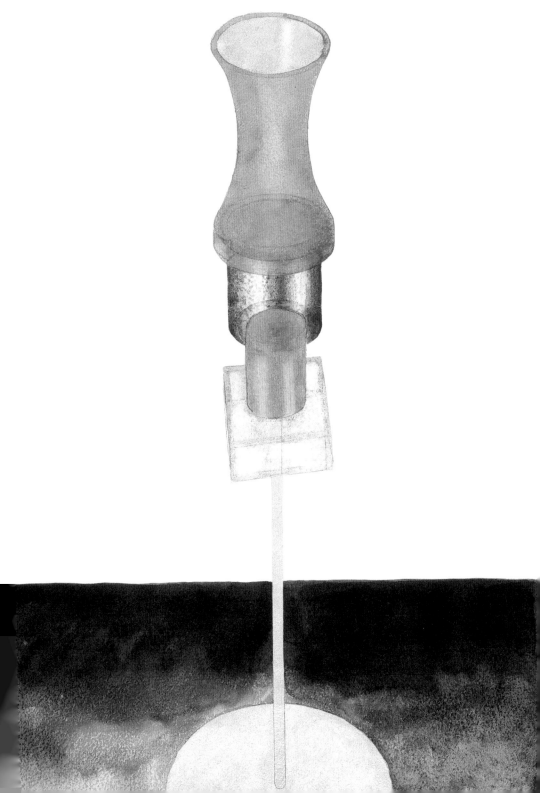

478

479

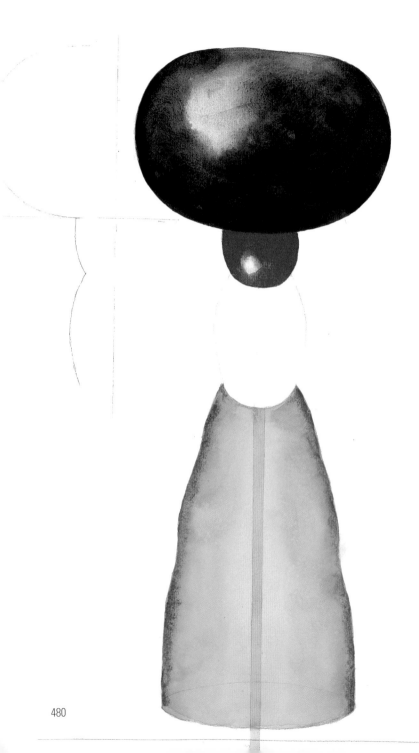

480

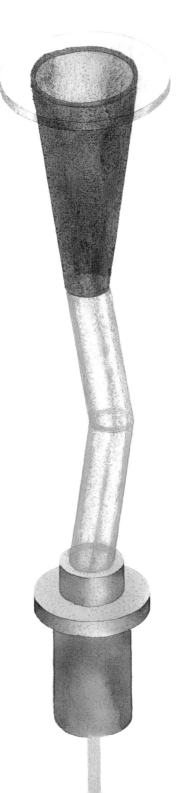

481

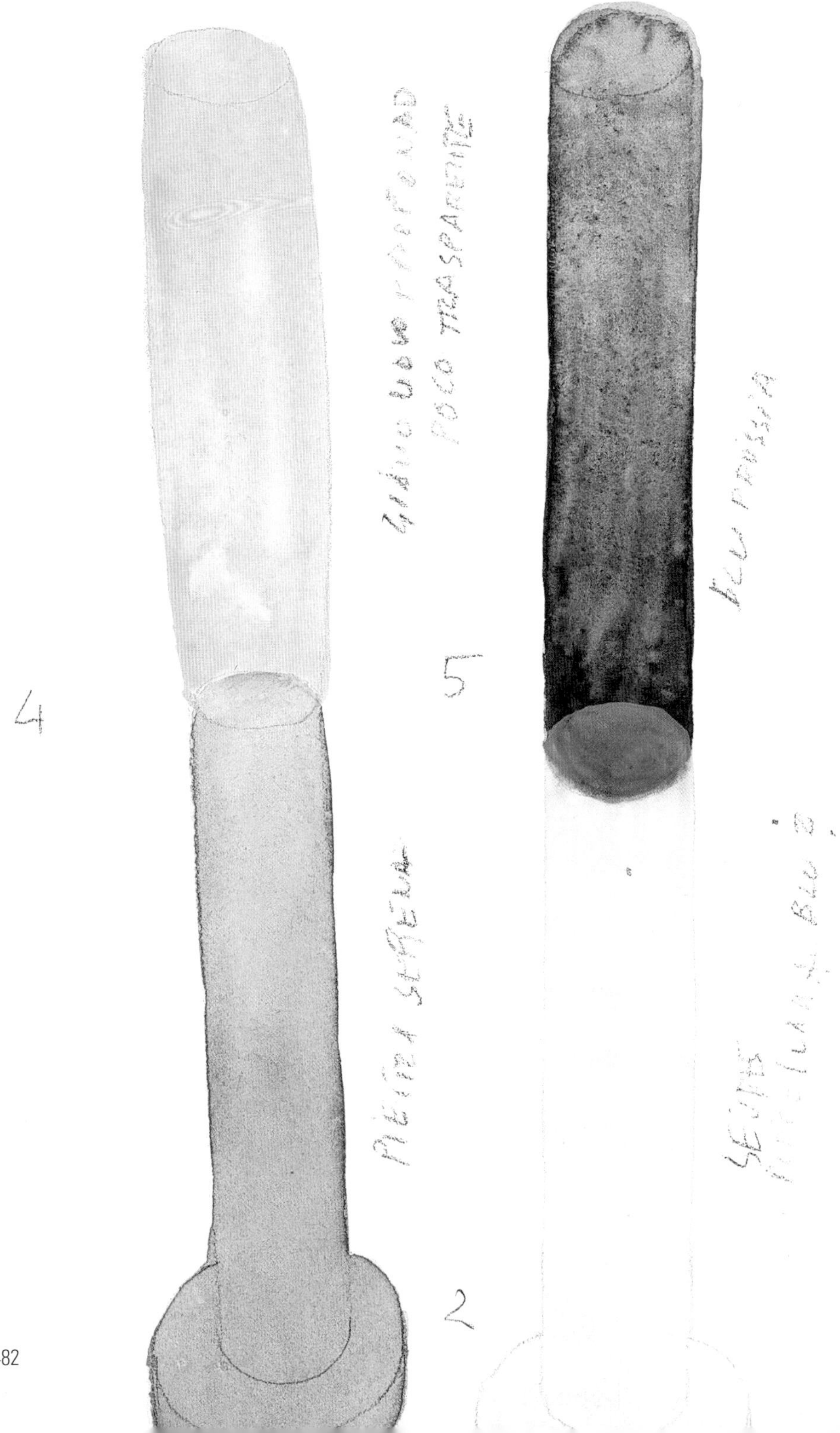

4

5

PROVE DONO VETRE NAD
POCO TRASPARENTE

PIETRA GREZZA

SEGUE
PORCELLANA BLU ?

2

482

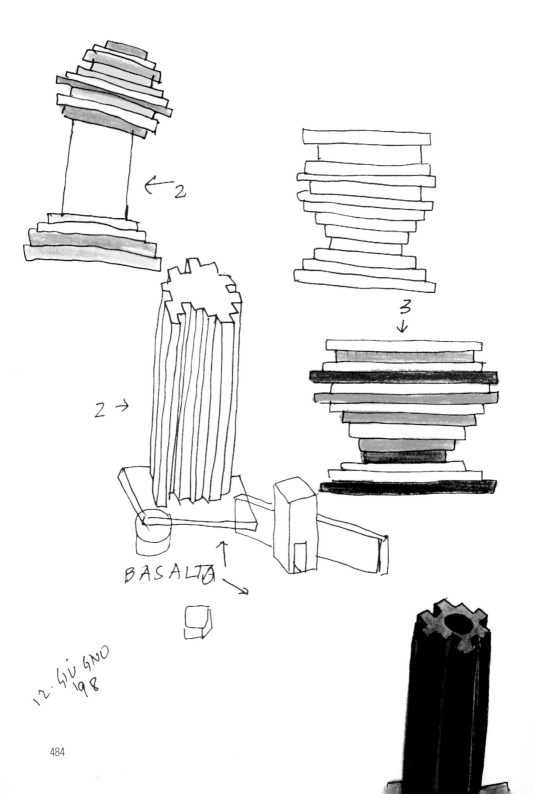

2

3

2 →

BASALTO

12. GIUGNO
'98

484

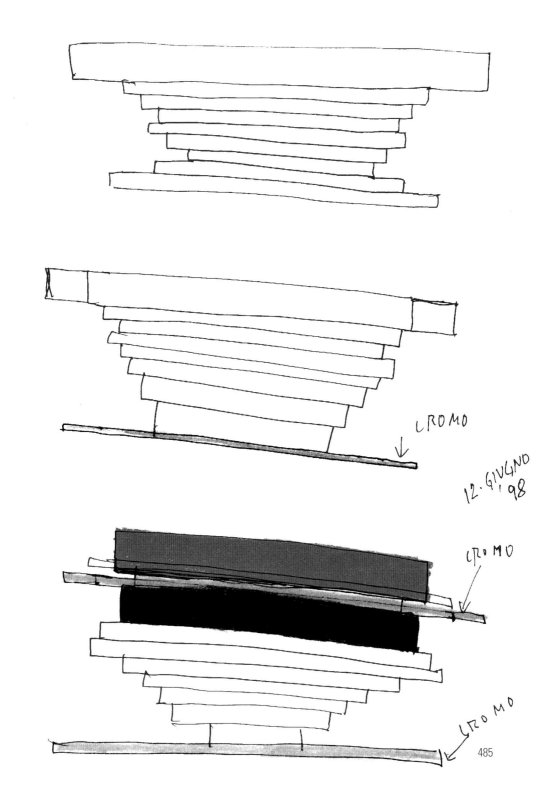

CROMO

12. GIUGNO 98

CROMO

CROMO

485

FILICUDI

DOMENICA 14.6.98

486

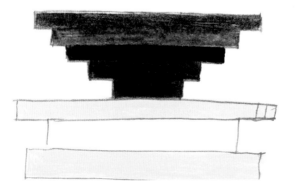

DOMENICA 8.9.98
IQ'71 CUI,

487

490

491

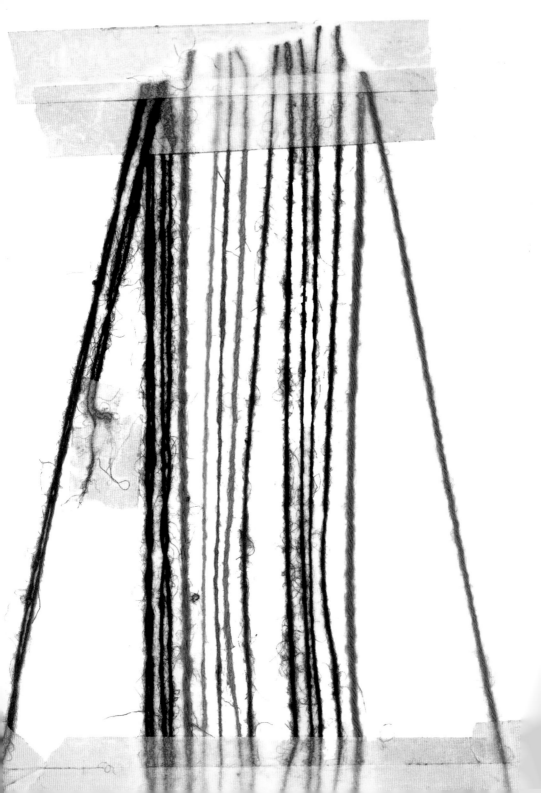

493

494

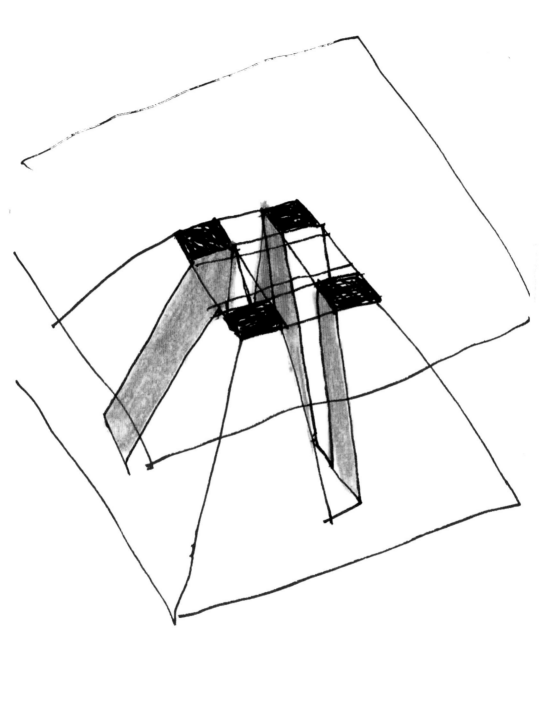

16·11·00

496

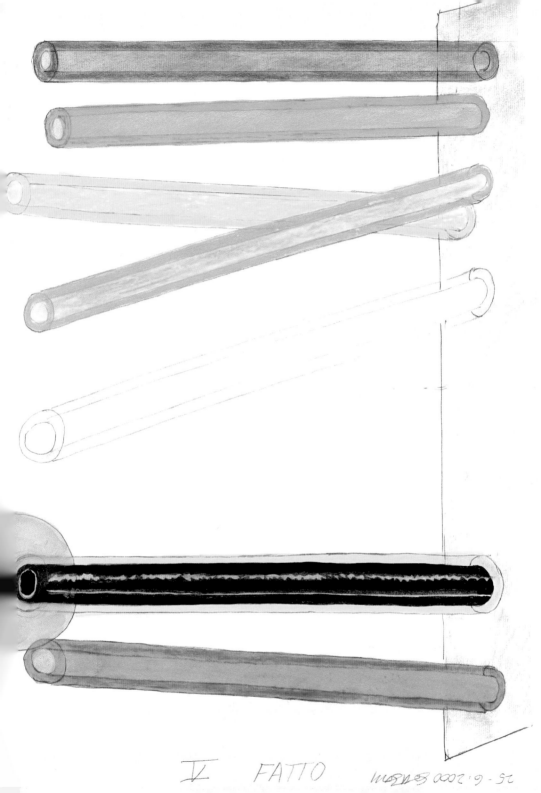

Ⅴ   FATTO

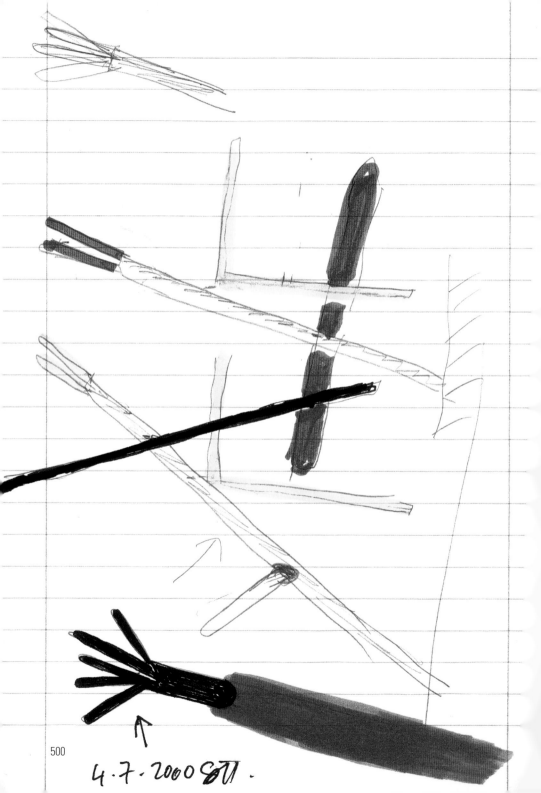

500

4.7. 2000 STI.

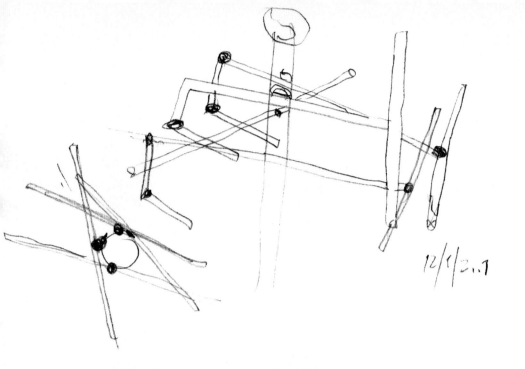

12/1/2.1

① FARE
PENDAGLI
DI VETRO

② ATTACCARE I
PETUDAGLI A UN
BASTONE
DELLA LUNGHEZZA
VOLUTA

③ TROVARE IL
PUNTO PER
OTTENERE
L'INCHIANAZIONE
VOLUTA

④ FARE IL BASTONE
IN VETRO

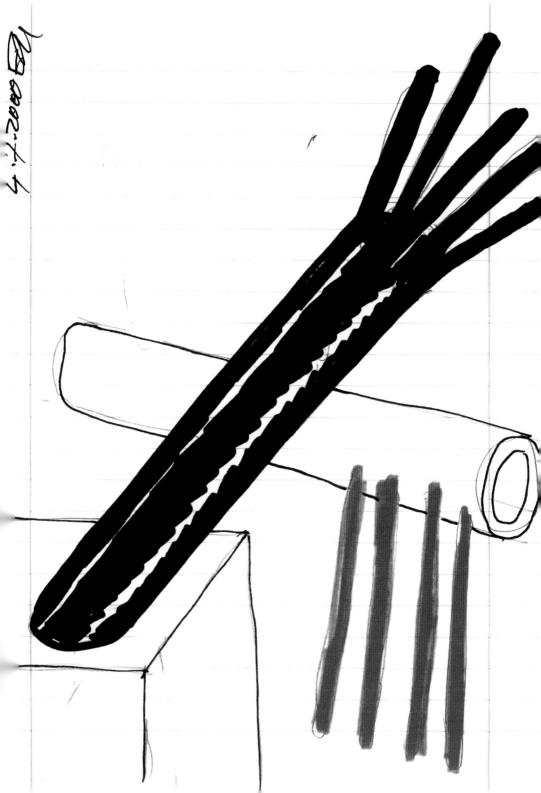

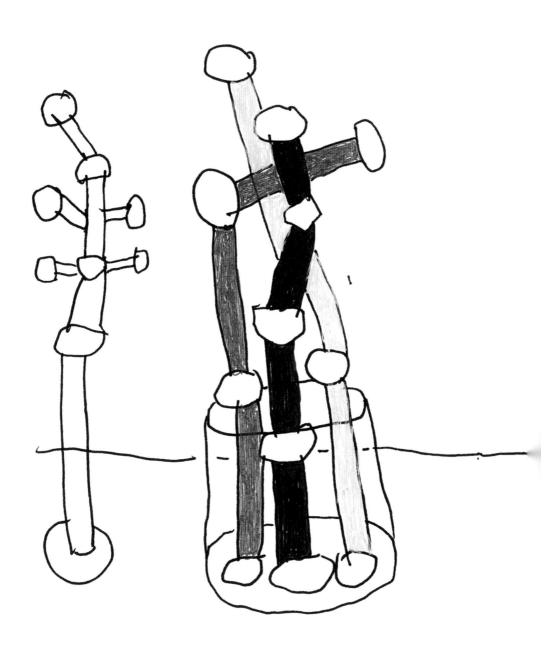

504

17. NOV.

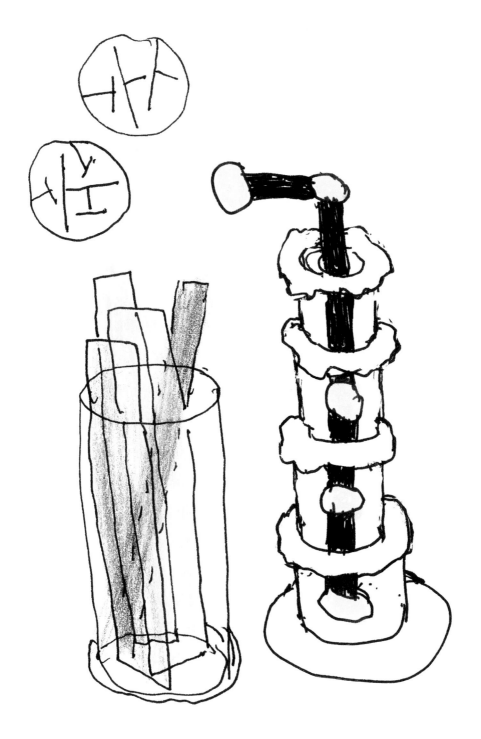

76 NOV. 000
MALIBÙ

506

KĀMA

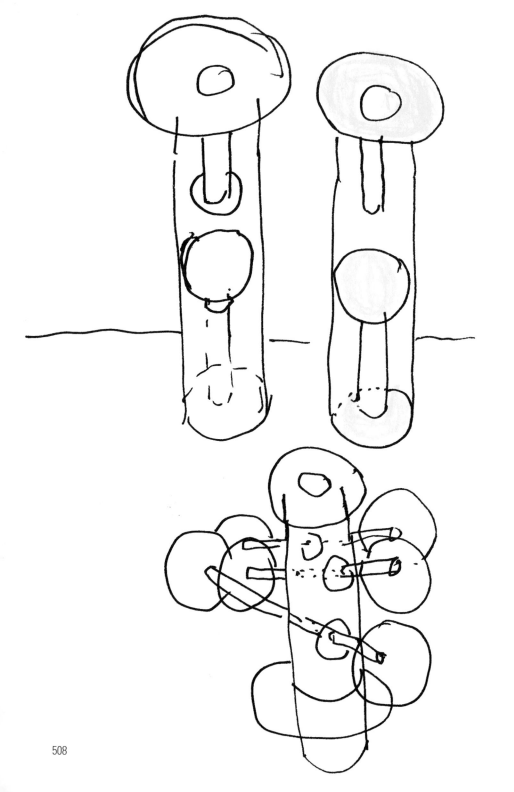

508

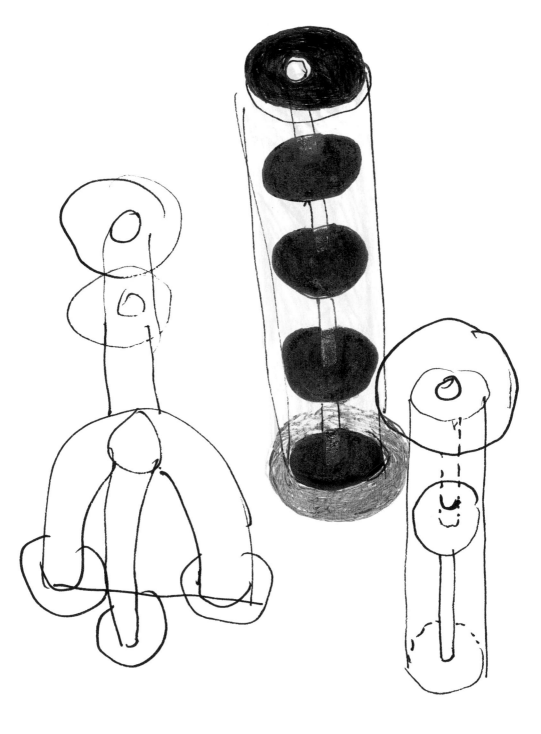

16. Nov. 00

510

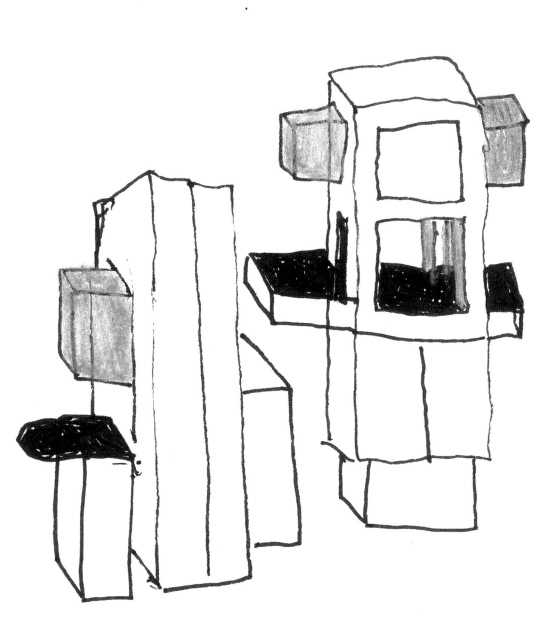

MOSTRA ~~ERNESTO~~: ESERCIZIO FORMALE
NR 6 (?)

MANCANO (2) DISEGNI

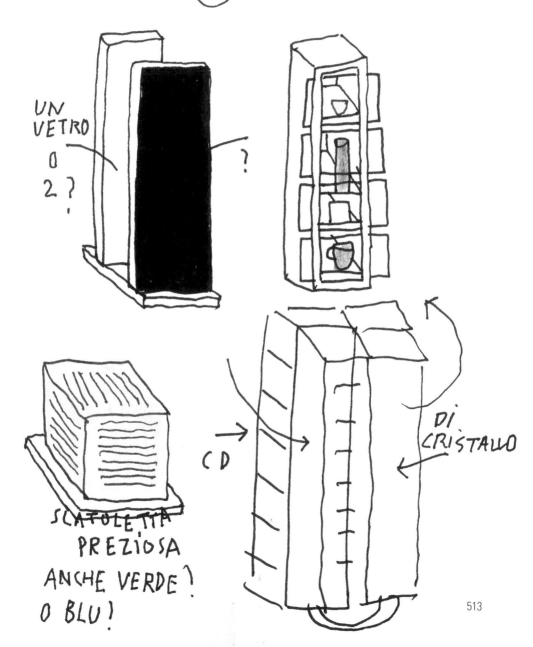

UN
VETRO

0
2 ?

?

DI
CRISTALLO

CD

SCATOLETTA
PREZIOSA
ANCHE VERDE!
O BLU!

513

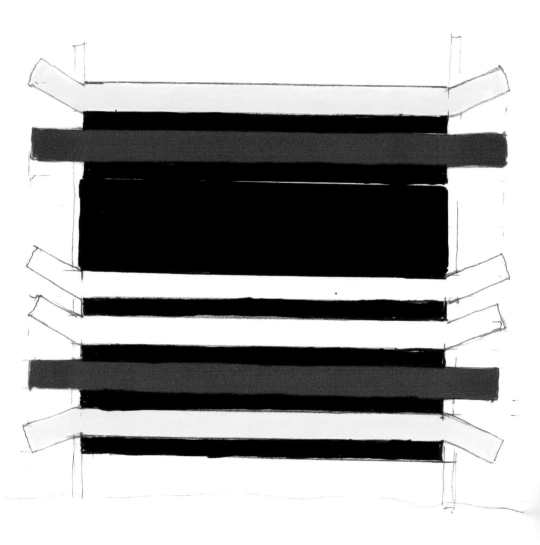

514

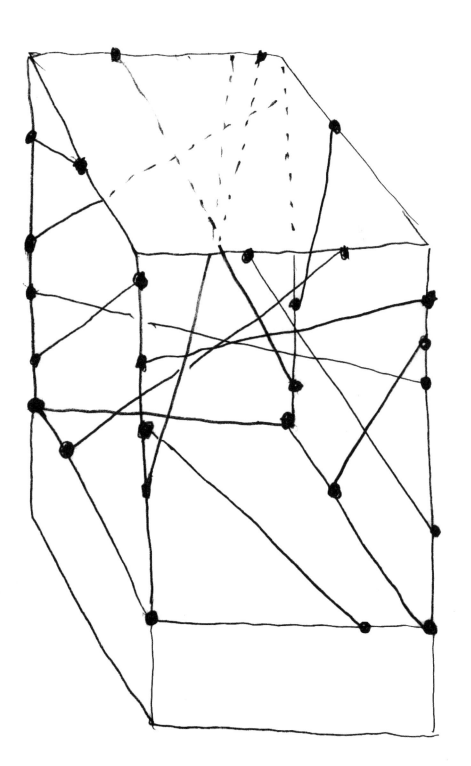

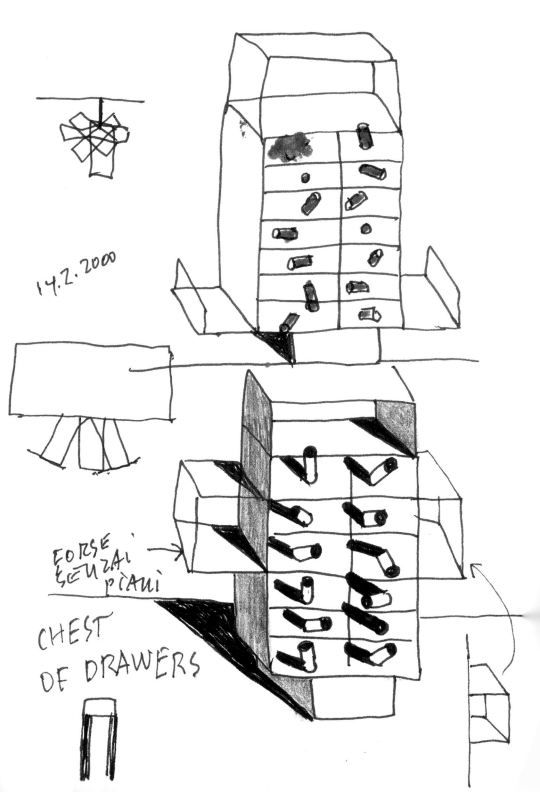

14.2.2000

EORSE
SCUZAI
PTAUI

CHEST
OF DRAWERS

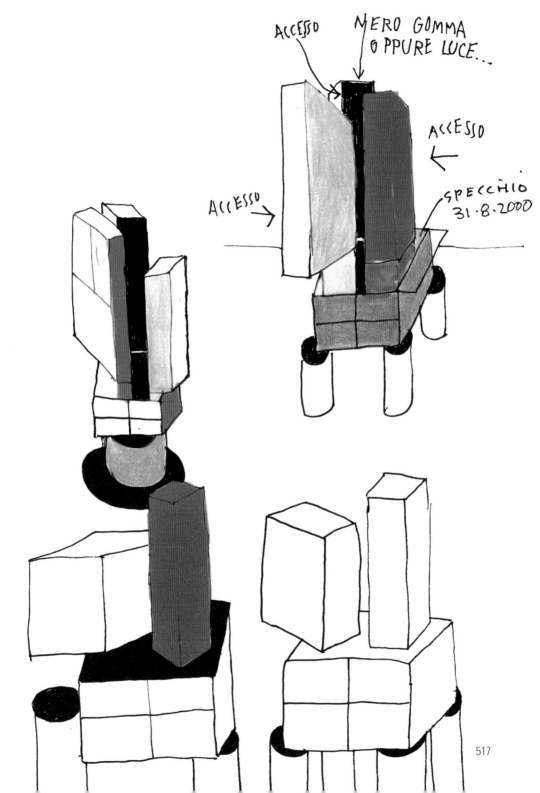

ACCESSO

NERO GOMMA
OPPURE LUCE...

ACCESSO

SPECCHIO
31·8·2000

ACCESSO

517

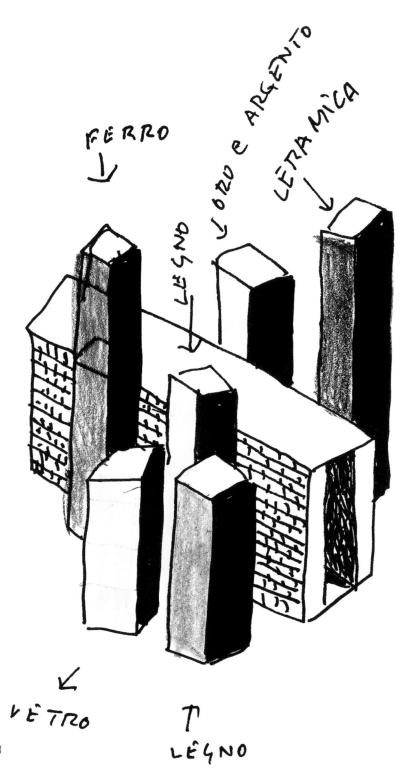

FERRO

ORO e ARGENTO

CERAMICA

LEGNO

VETRO

LEGNO

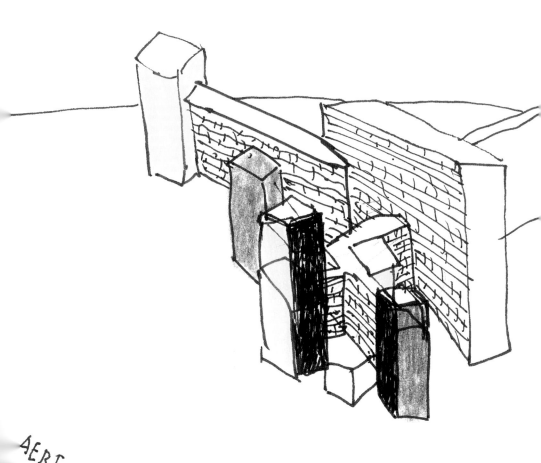

AERED
·11·00

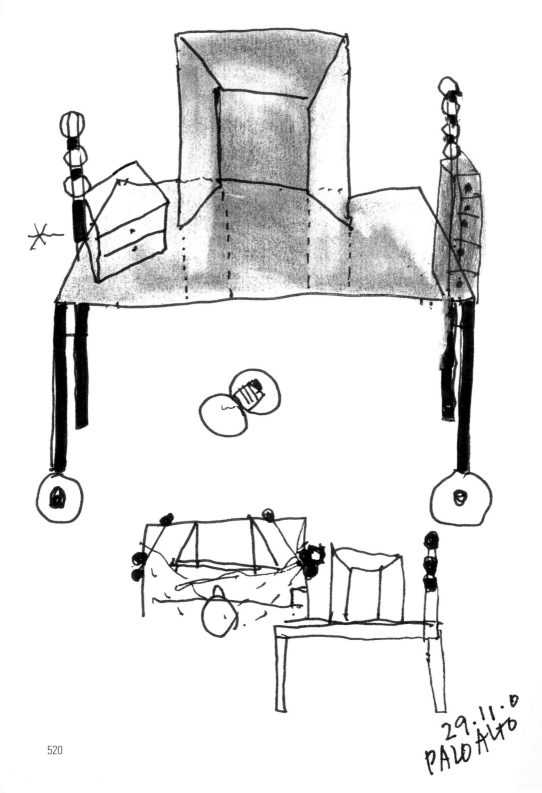

29.11.0
PALO ALTO

521

1·2·2000 - CHENNAI

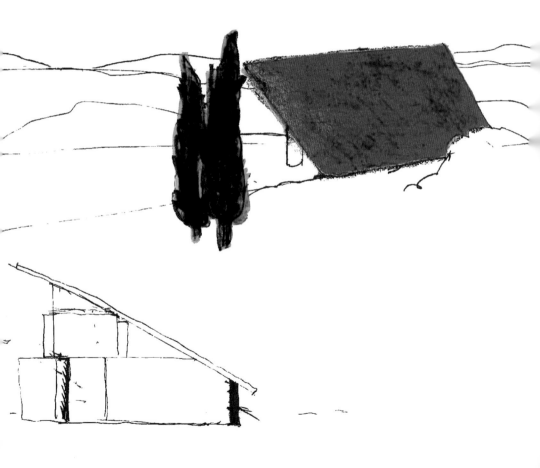

524

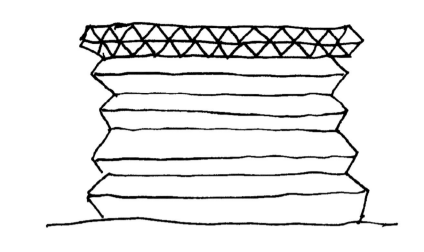

GRIGIO e
GRIGIO VERDINO

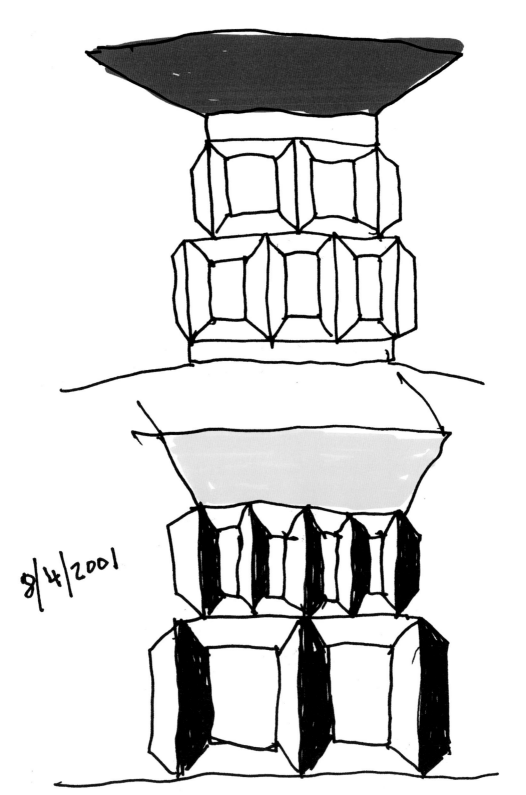

8/4/2001

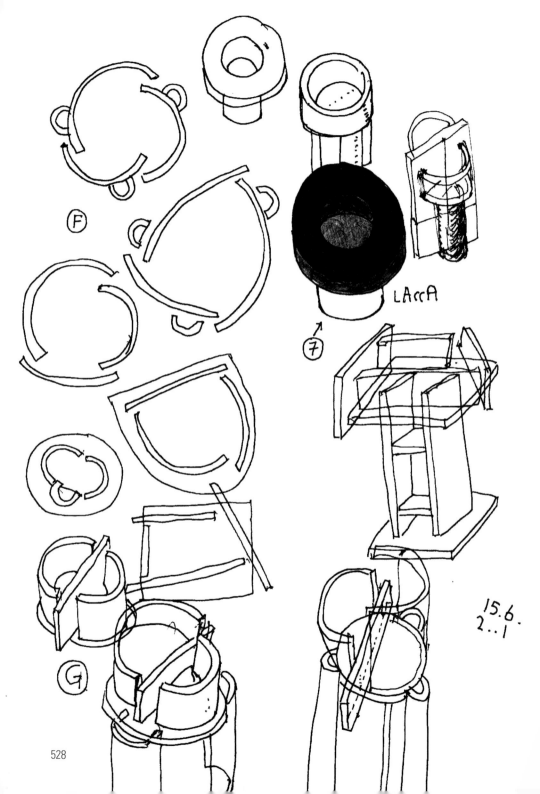

F

LACCA

7

G

15.6.
2..1

528

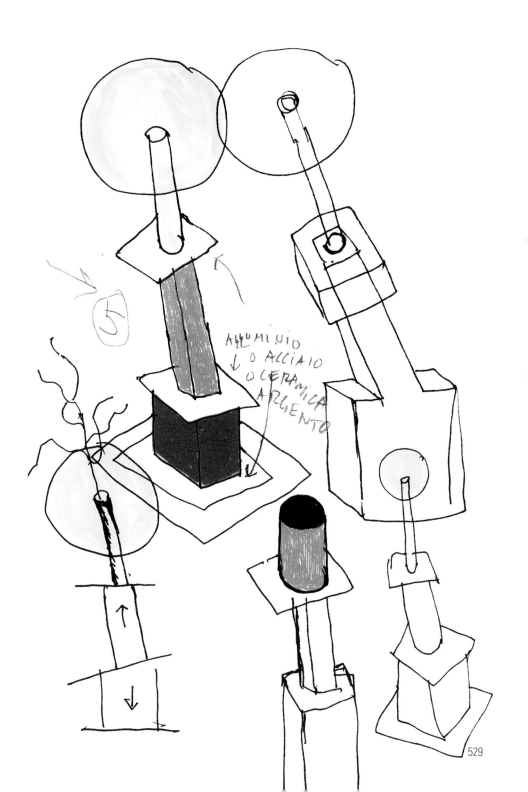

ALLUMINIO
↓ O ACCIAIO
↓ O CERAMICA
ARGENTO

529

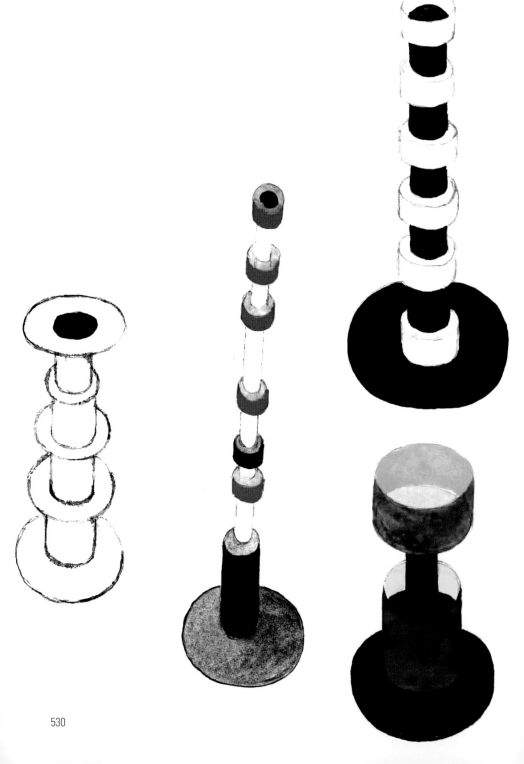

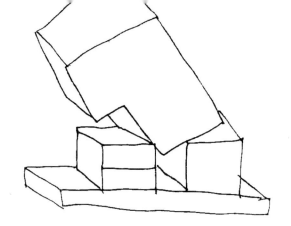

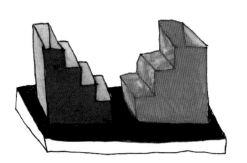

TOLTECHÍ

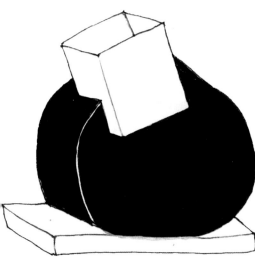

26/6/2..1

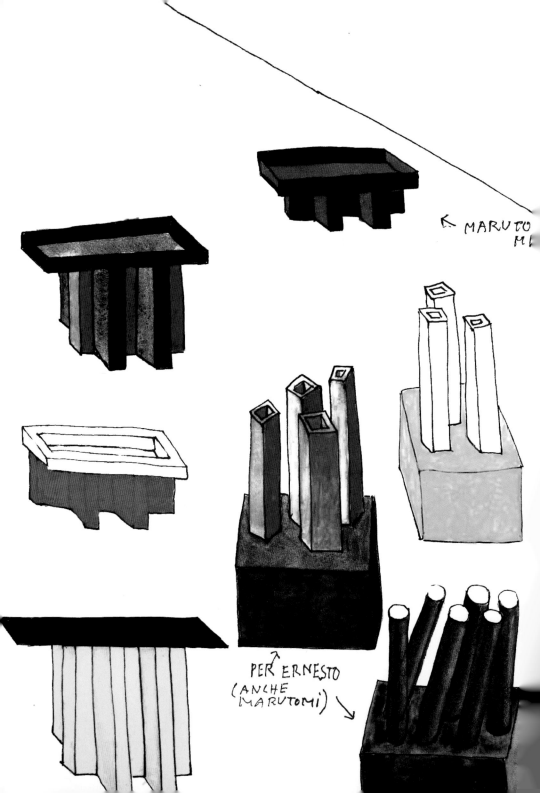

← MARUTO
   MI

PER ERNESTO
(ANCHE
MARUTOMI) ↘

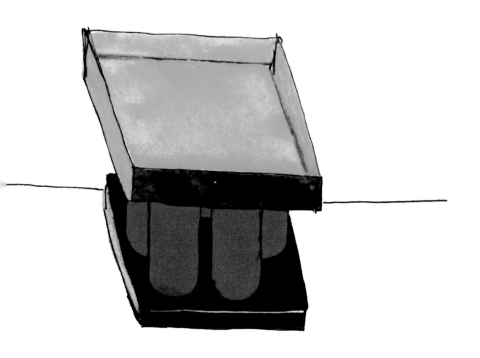

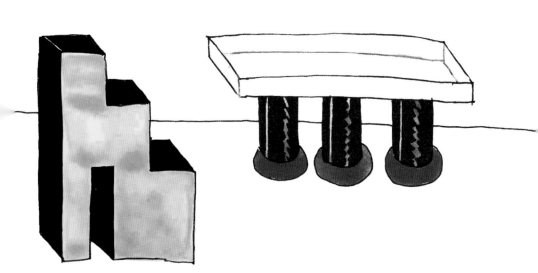

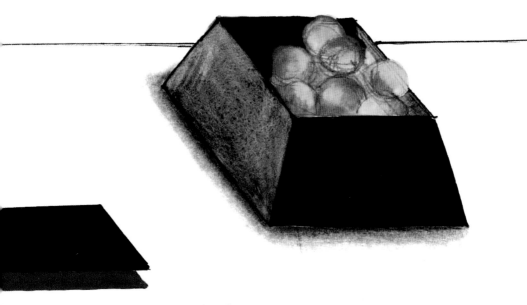

↑
LACCA
GIAPPONESE

COSIDETTO
CENTRO TAVOLA
(FRUTTA)

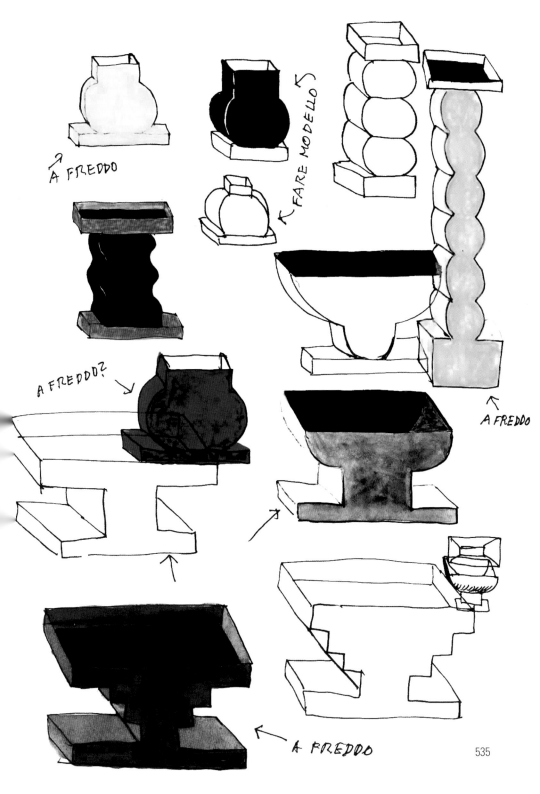

A FREDDO

FARE MODELLO

A FREDDO?

A FREDDO

A FREDDO

535

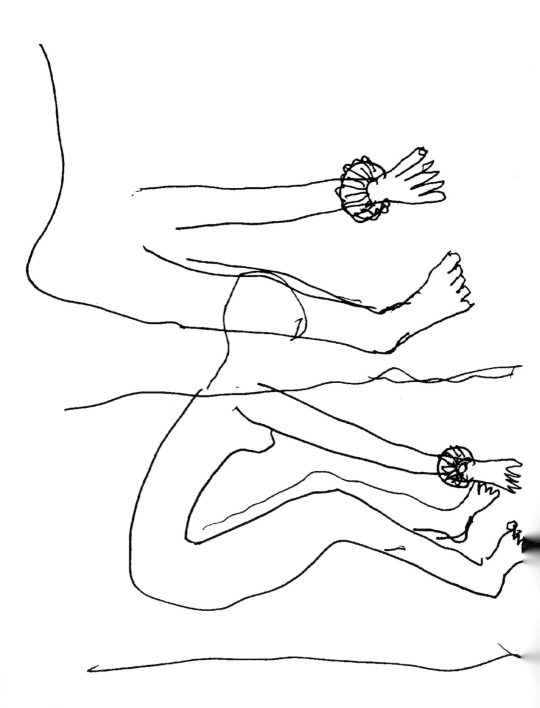

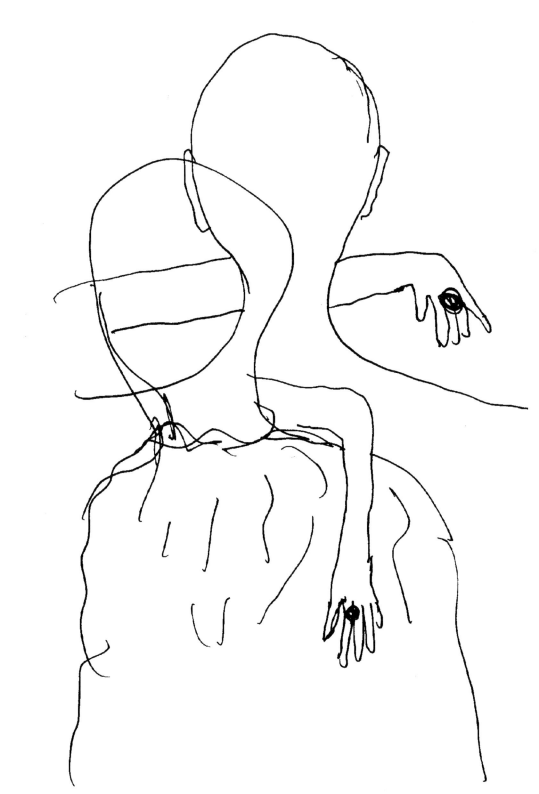

RIVETTI

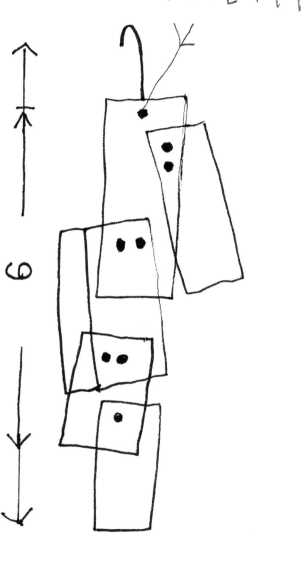

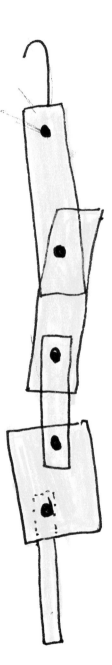

6

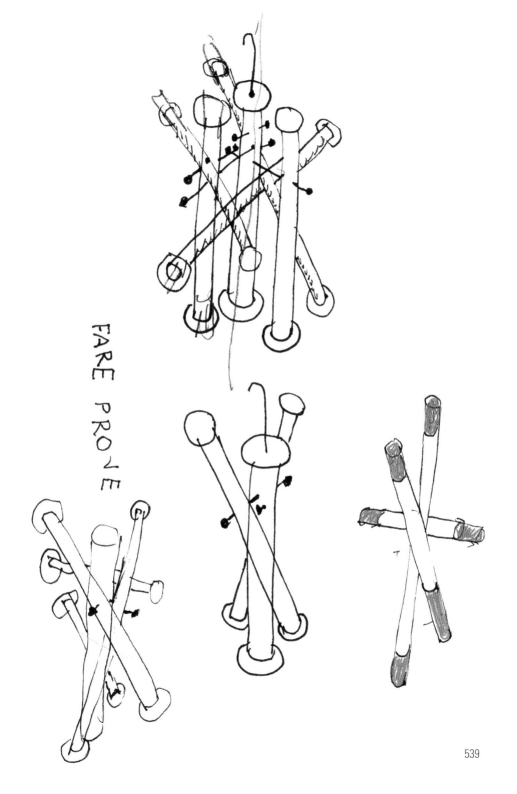

FARE PROVE

539

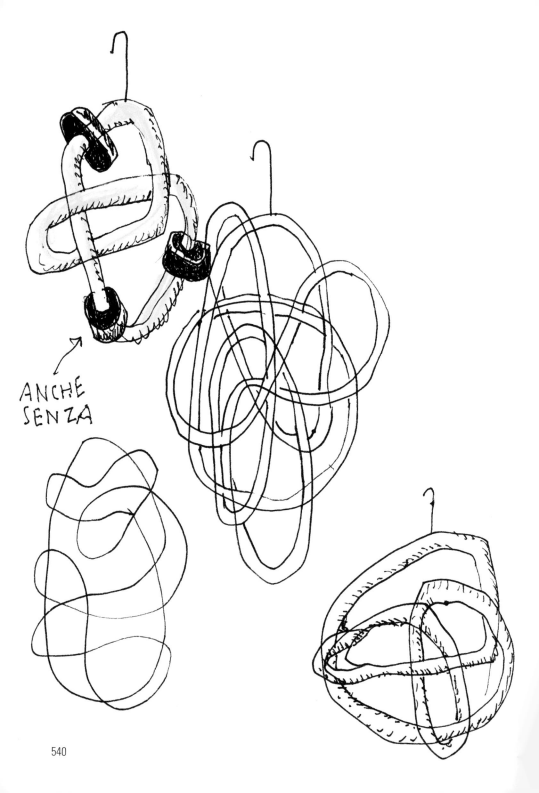

ANCHE
SENZA

540

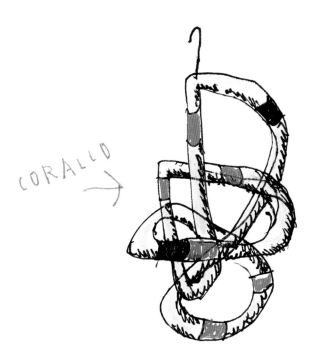

CORALLO →

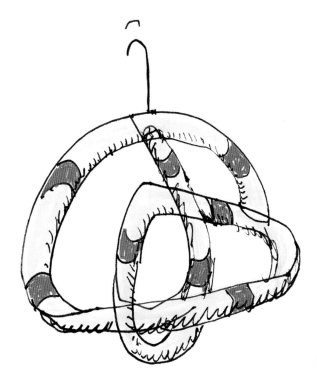

541

4·3·2000

543

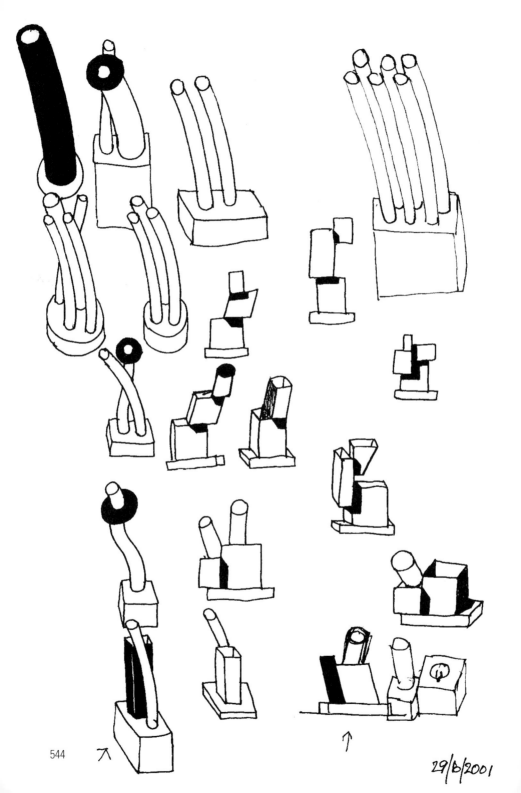

544

AGOSTO
2001

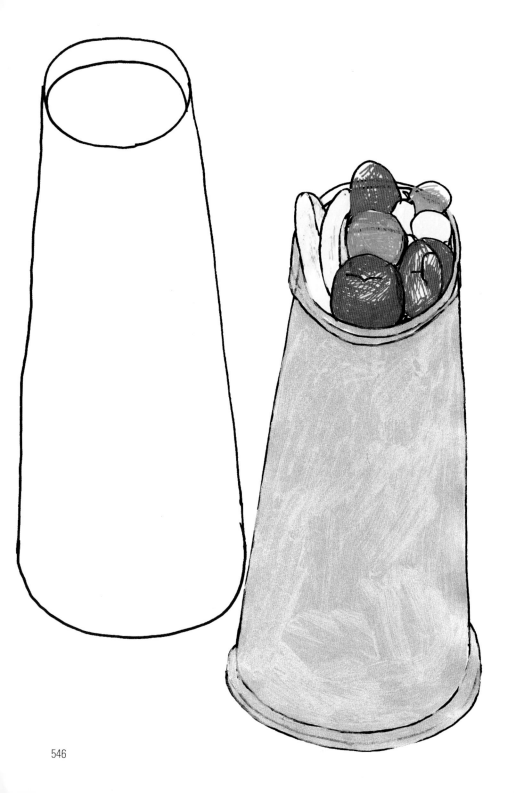

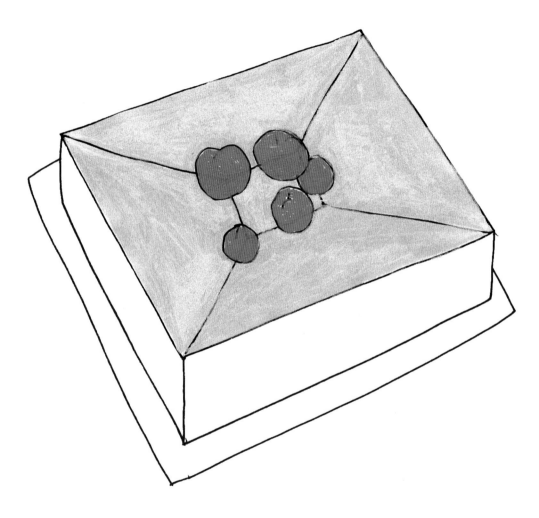

548

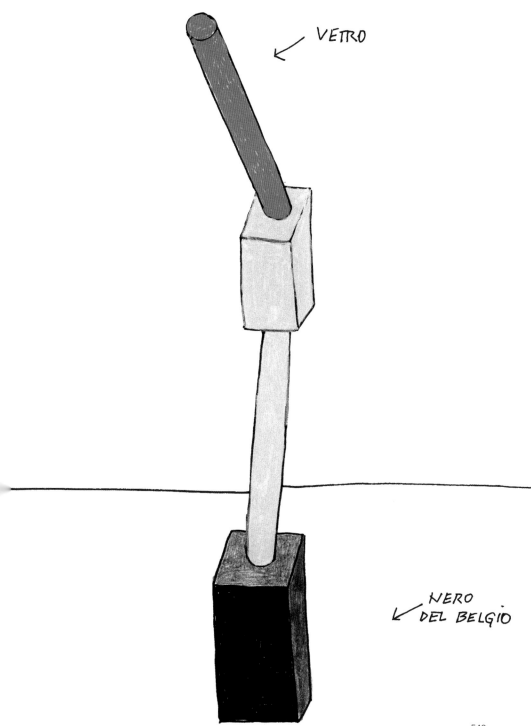

VETRO

NERO
DEL BELGIO

549

TUTÌA LA PAUCA NERA
NELLA STANZA DA LETTO

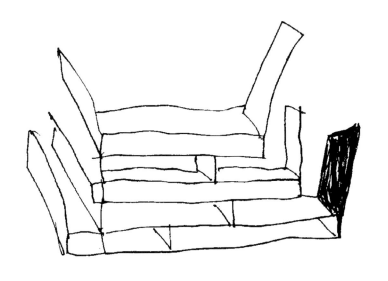

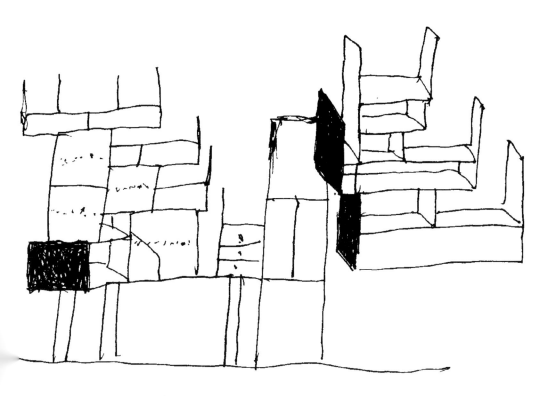

GIUGNO 2001

551

SOPRA LA FAMIGLIA

SOTTO GLI STRA NIERI

ALJEIDE ?

NEGOZIO CON
ABITAZIONE
TERRAZZA, AUTORIMESSA
e GIARDINO

553

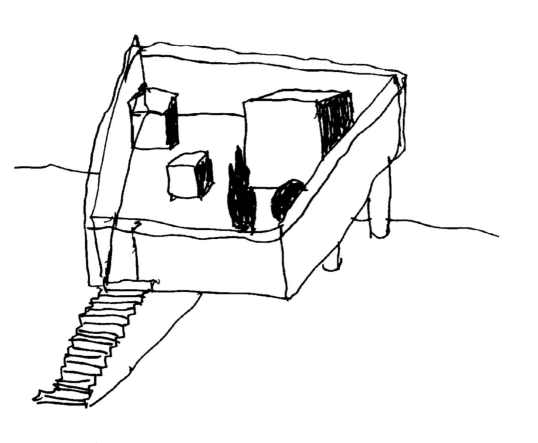

CASTEL PERGINE

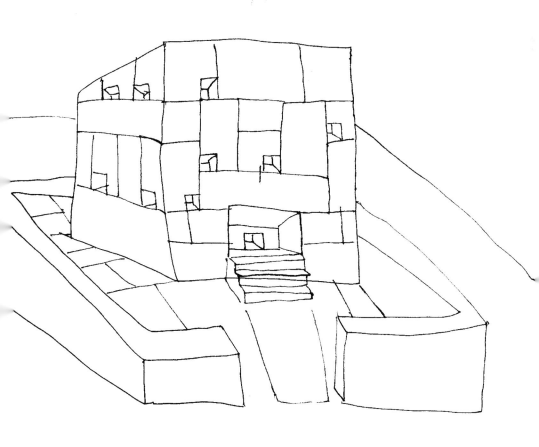

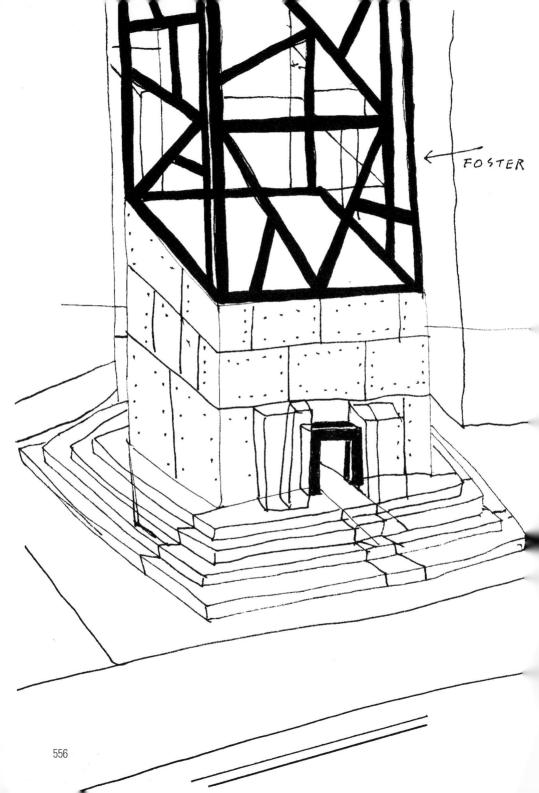

FOSTER

556

NON C'È INCERTEZZA
NON C'È DUBBIO
NON C'È PROFUMO
NON L'È CANTO
NON C'E LUCE
NON
CAPISCO
NON SO
NON MI TROVO

......DEVO ASPETTARE

12-15

558

TAVOLINO

LEGNOCHIARO

TAVOLINO

IL MONTE MERU

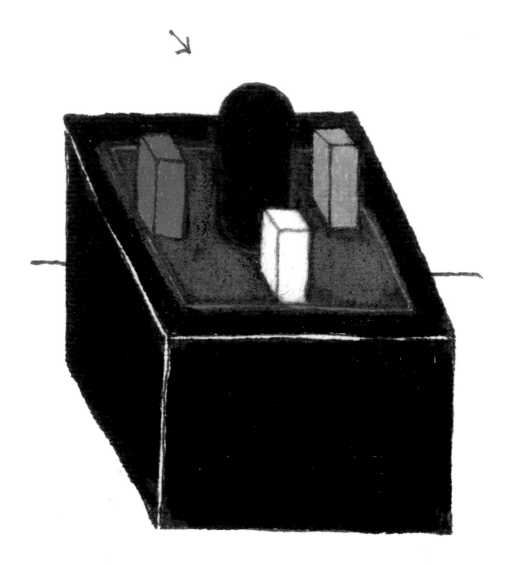

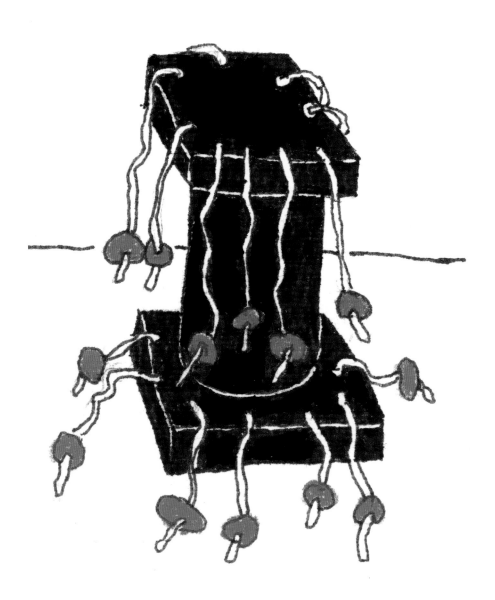

562

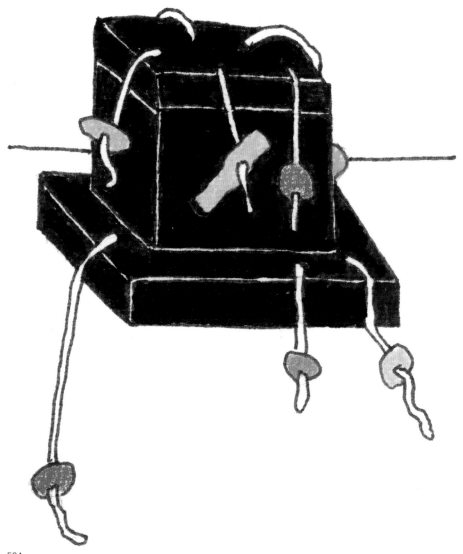

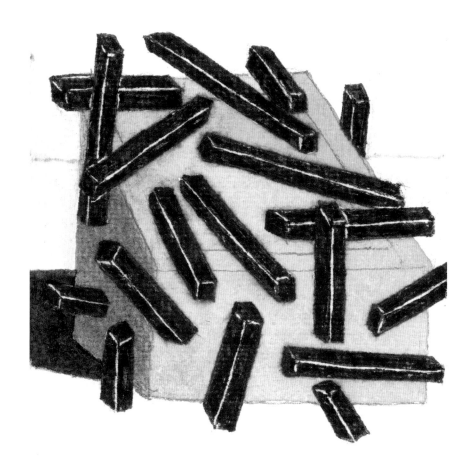

565

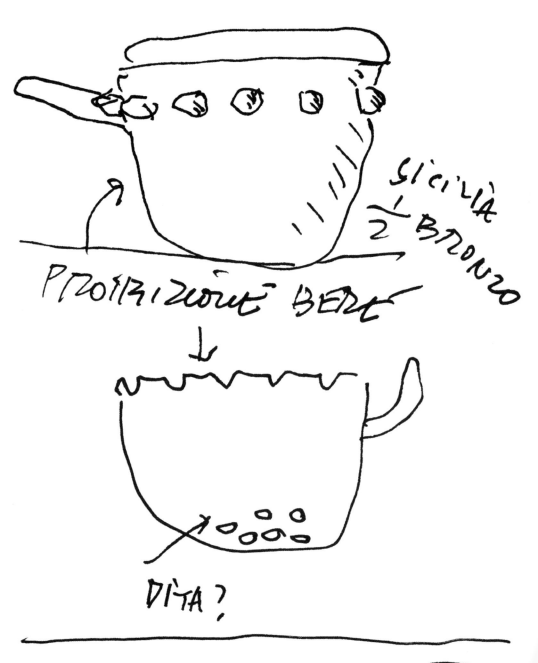

SiciLiA
$\frac{1}{2}$ BRONZO

PROPORZIONI BERE

DITA?

OSSIDIANA MAX

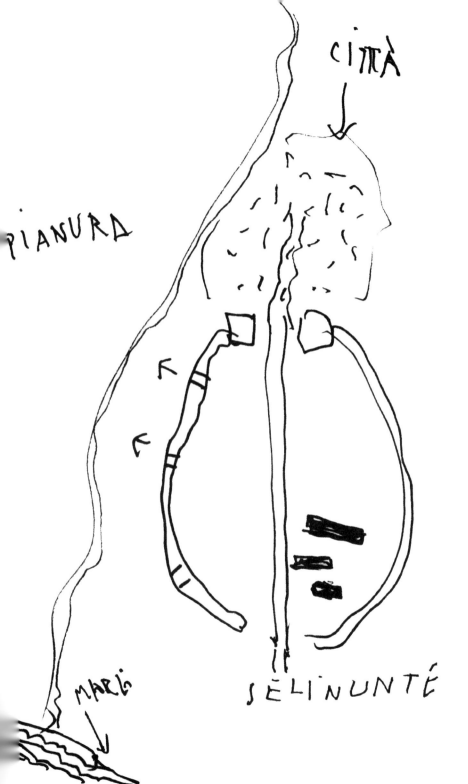

CITTÀ

PIANURA

SELINUNTÉ

MARE

567

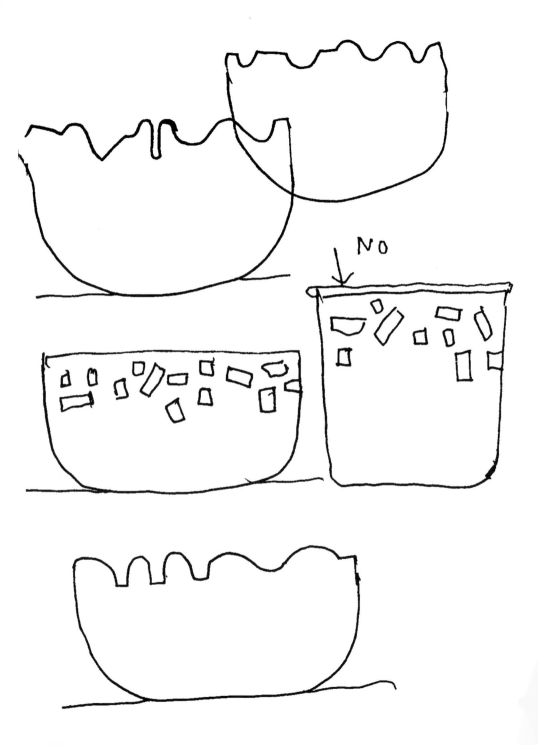

No

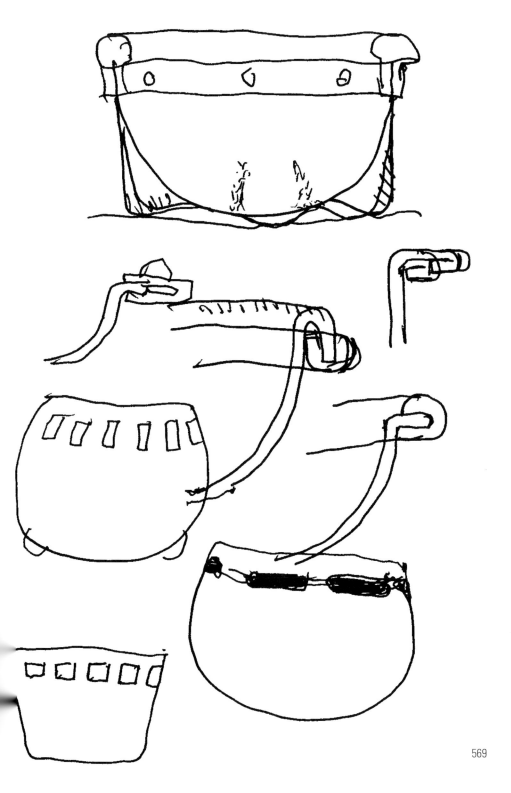

21

22

20

17

571

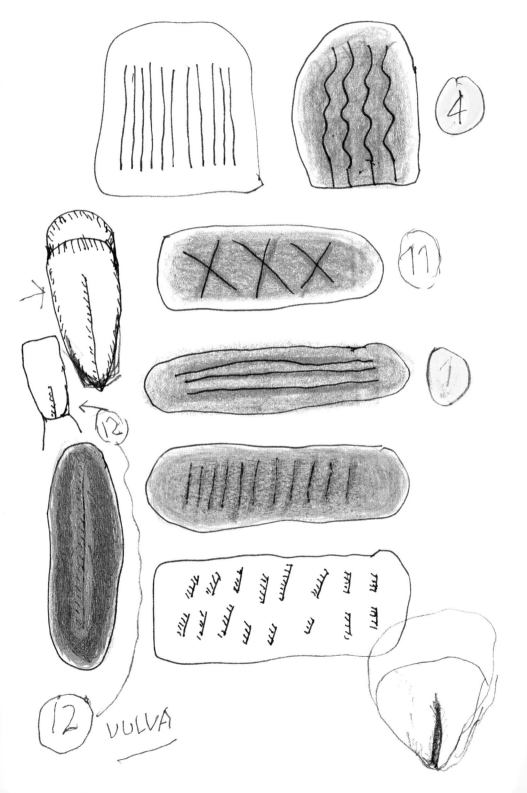

4

11

1

12

12 VULVA

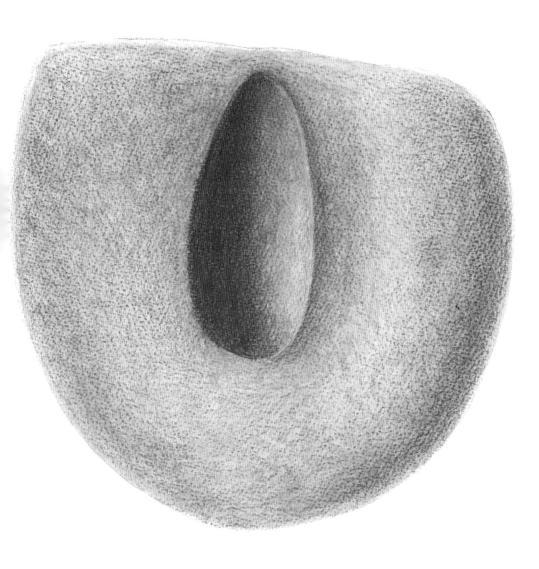

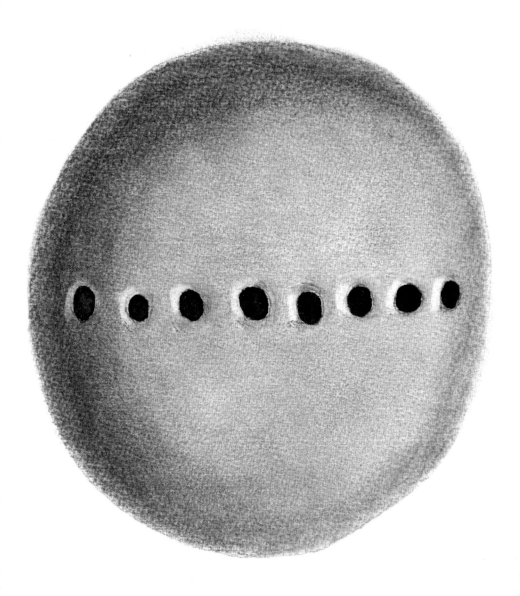

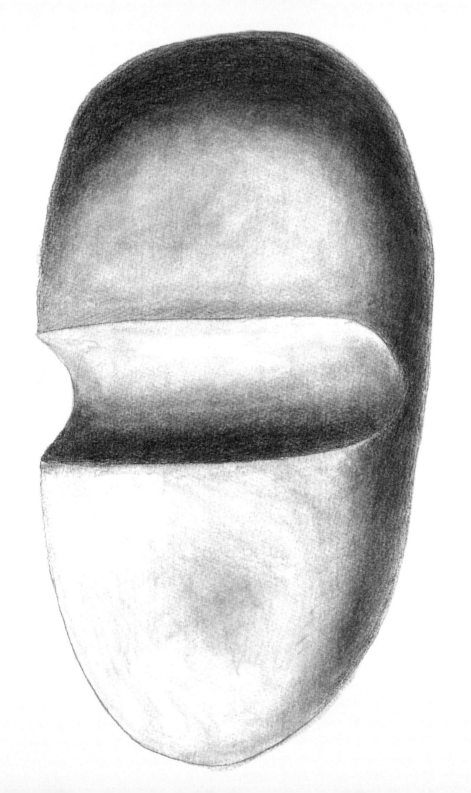

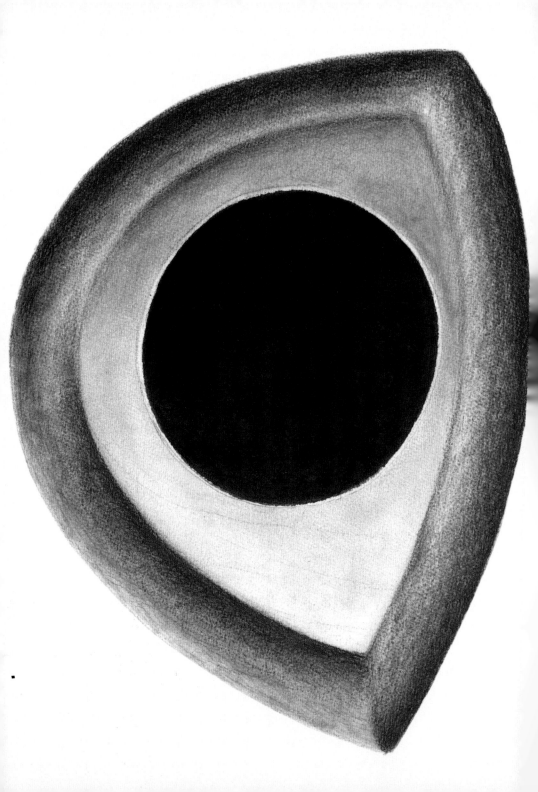

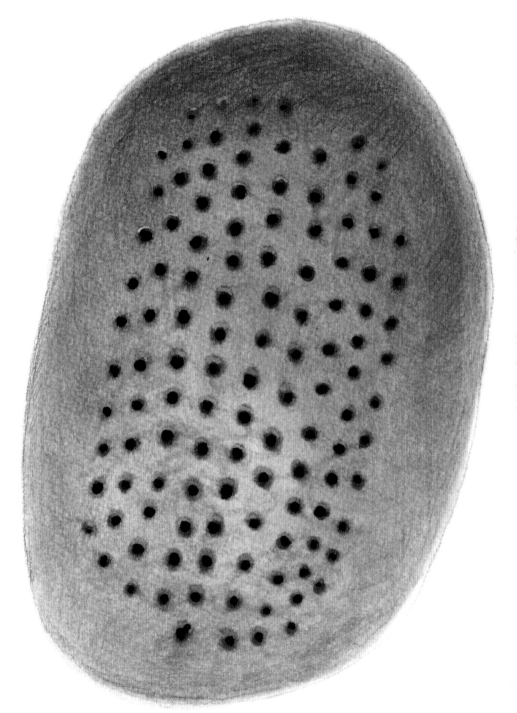

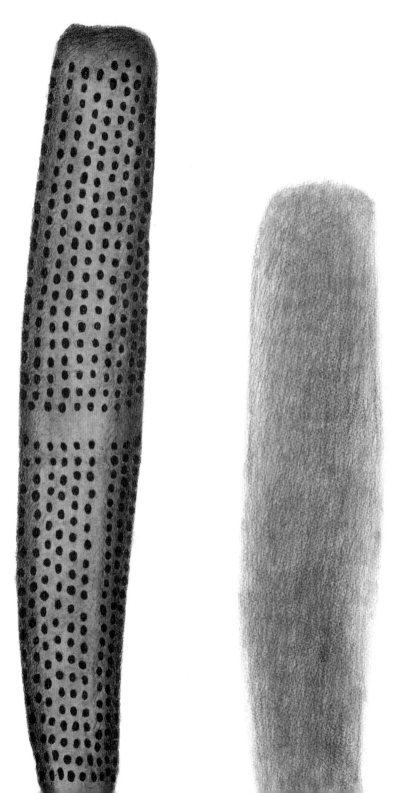

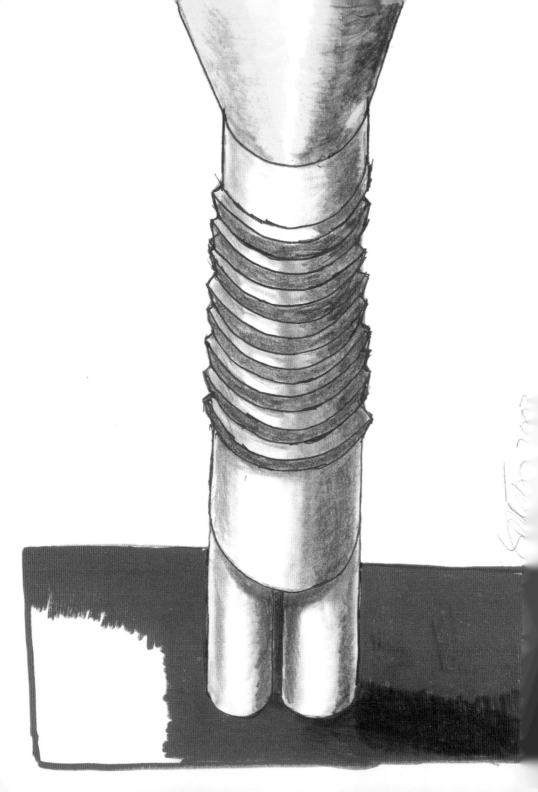

583

584

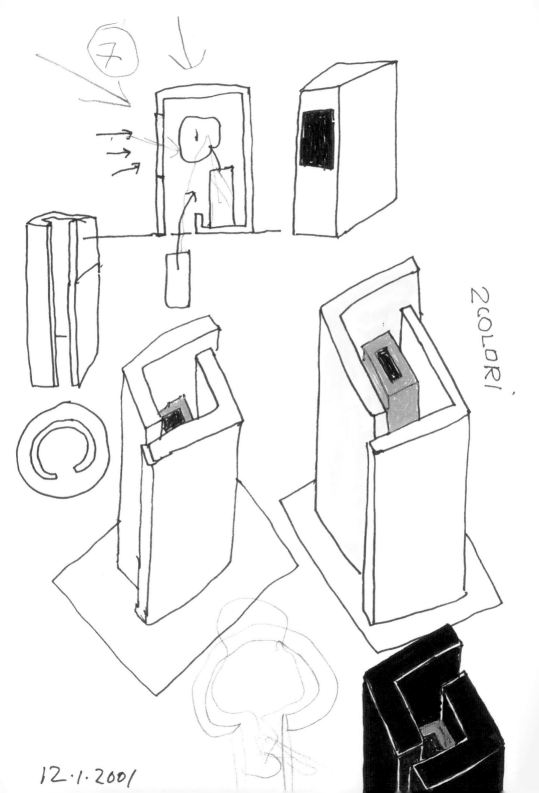

7

2 COLORI

12·1·2001

2·t·2002

LA CIVILTÀ DELLE SCATOLE

25.4.03

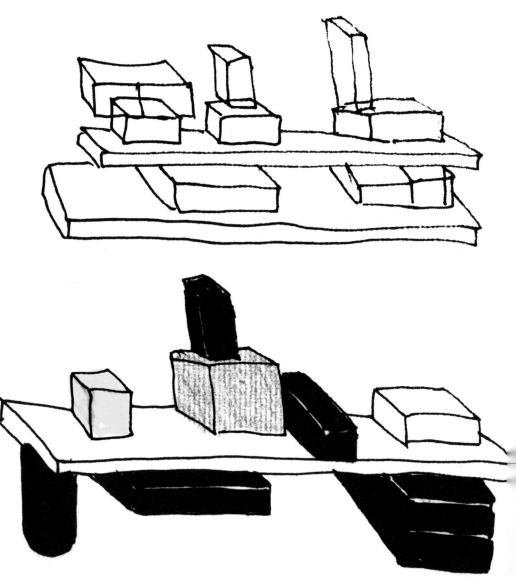

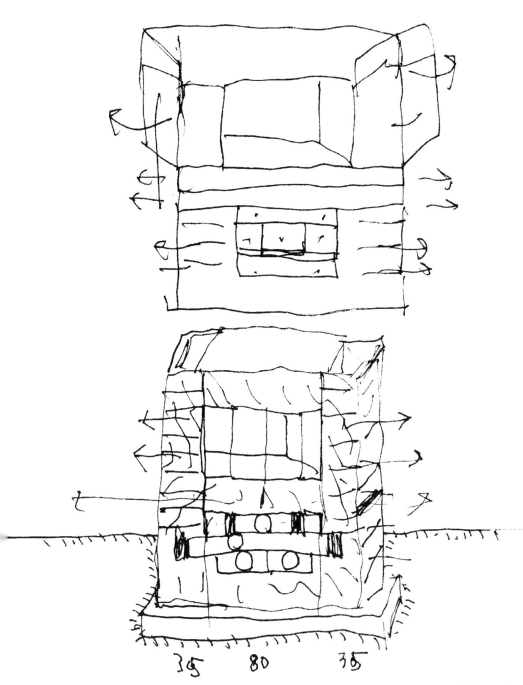

35   80   35

589

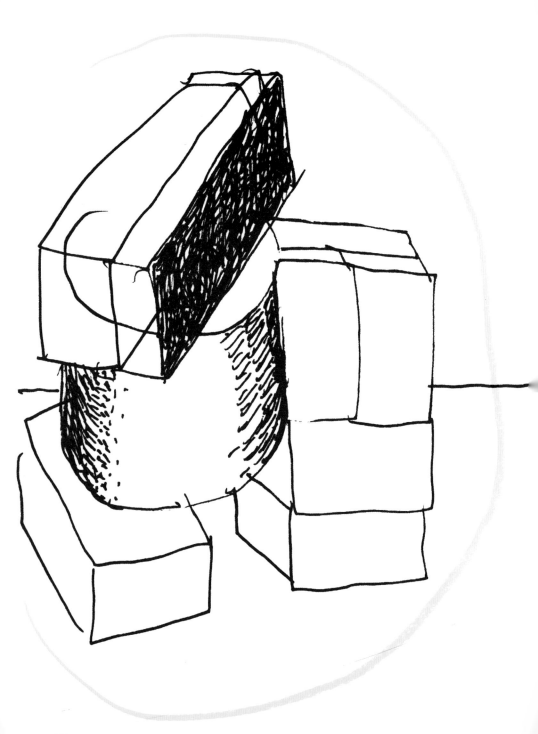

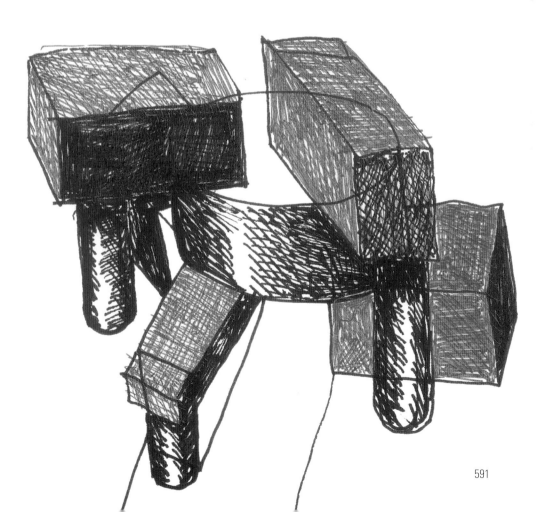

591

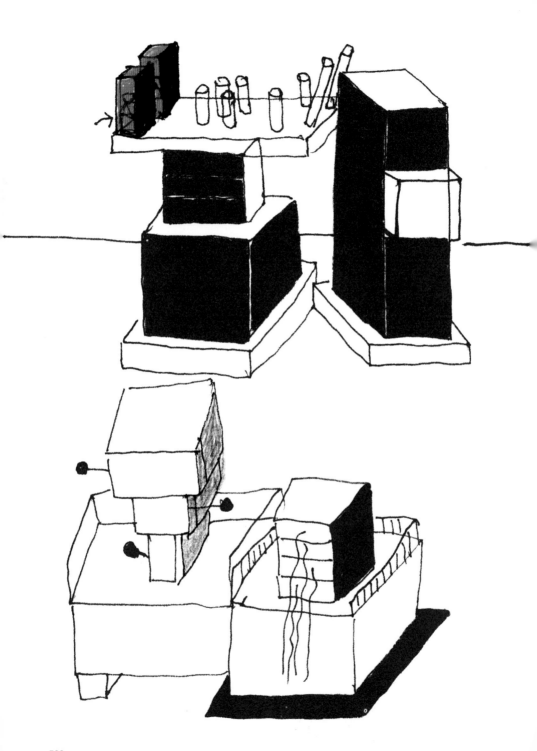

592

PICCOLI MOBILI

593

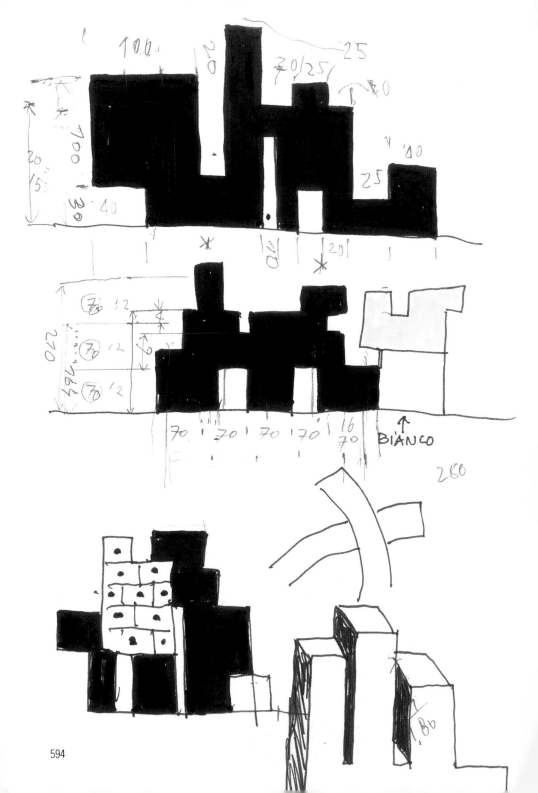

BIANCO

260

594

598

602

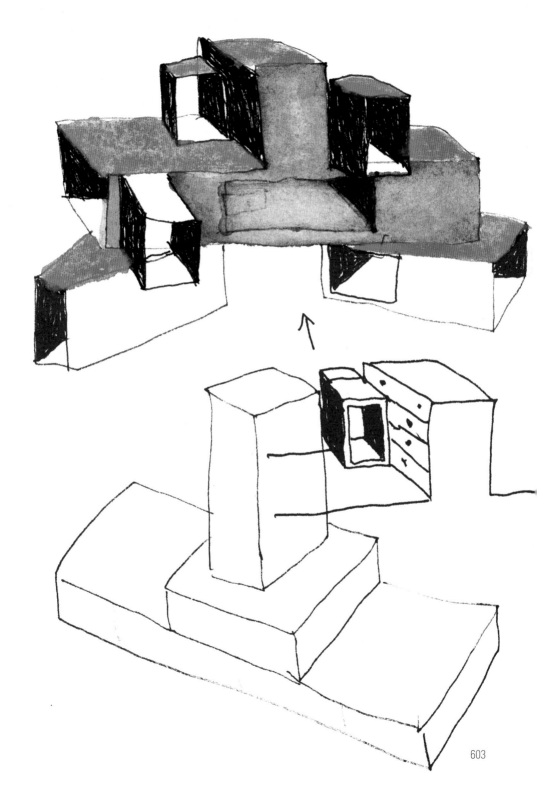

603

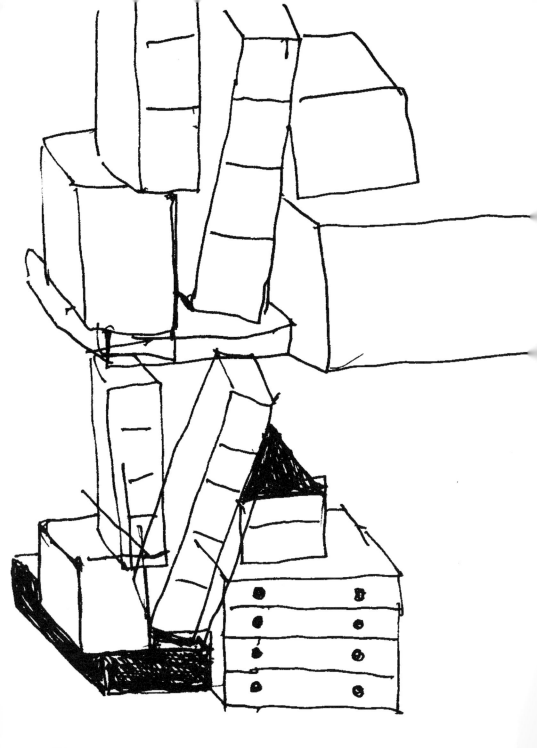

604

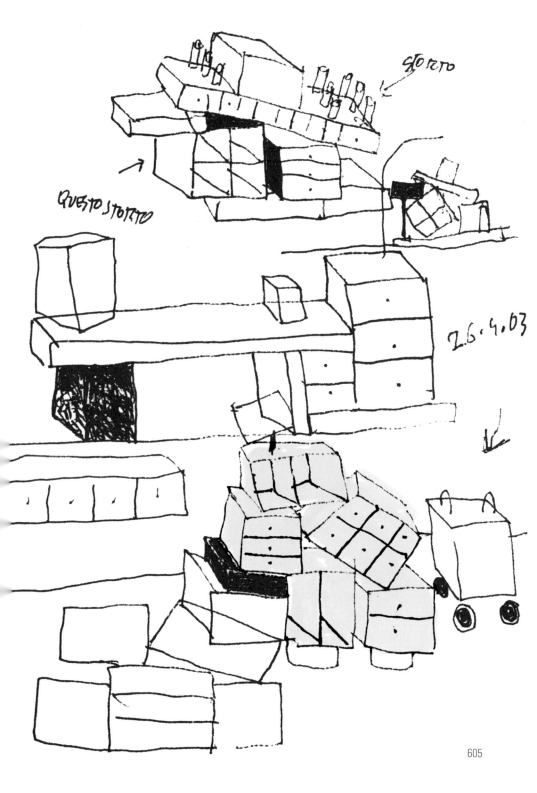

STORTO

QUESTO STORTO

2.6·4·03

608

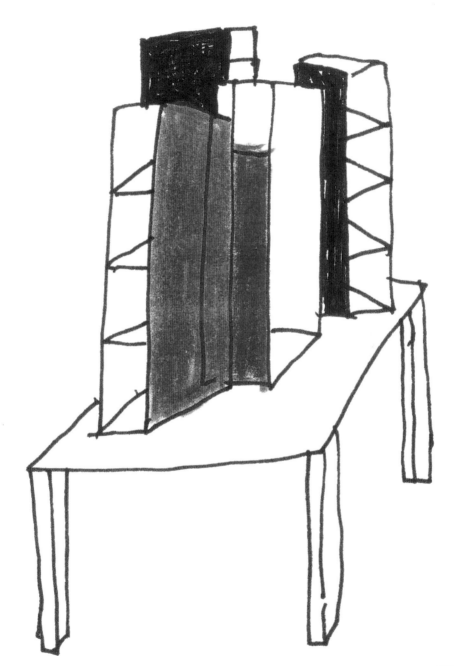

609

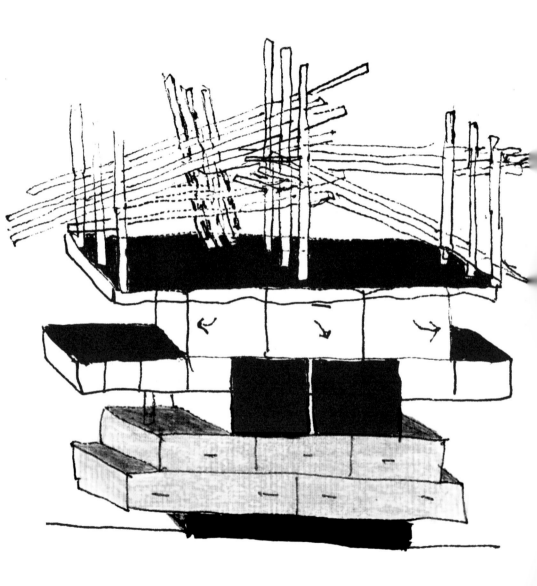

610

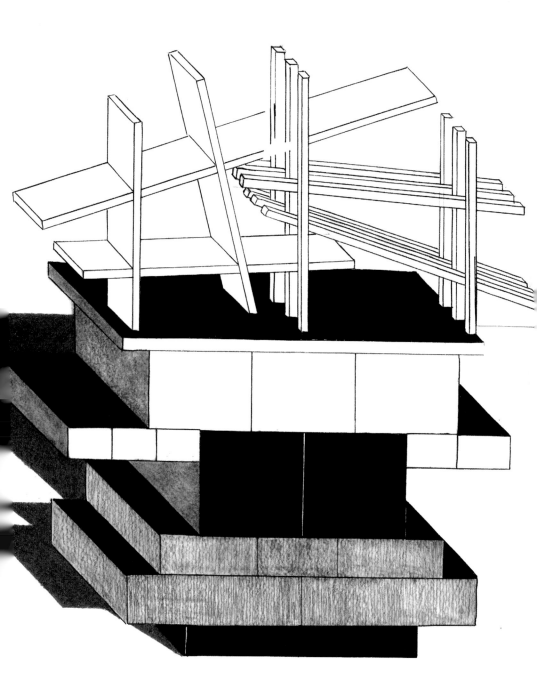

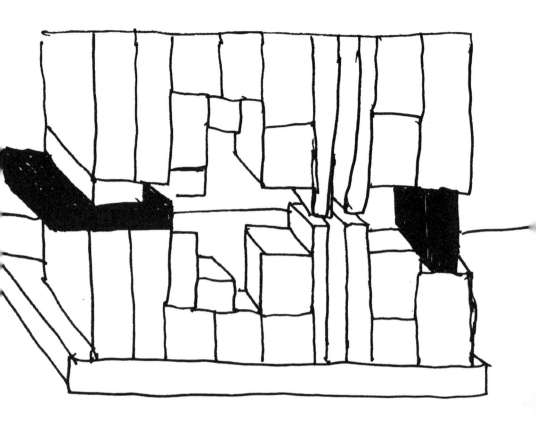

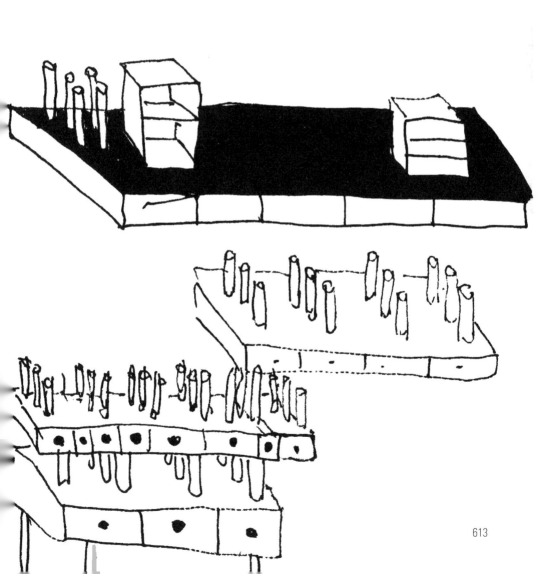

613

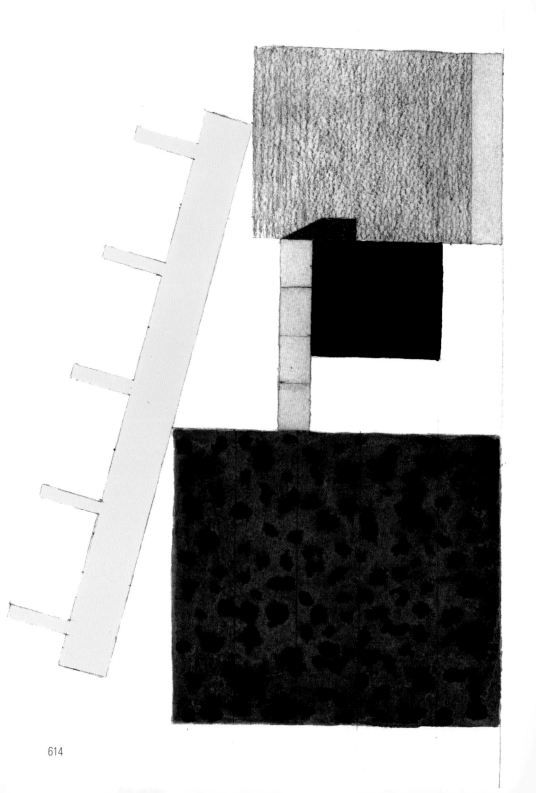

614

615

VETRO
o
FERRO
↓

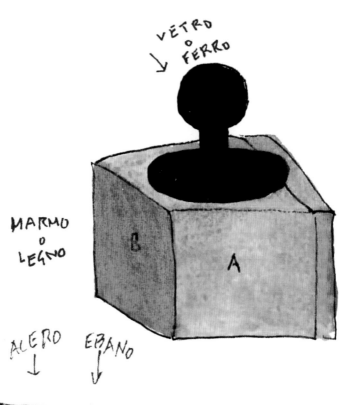

MARMO
o
LEGNO

B

A

ACERO   EBANO
↓   ↓

616

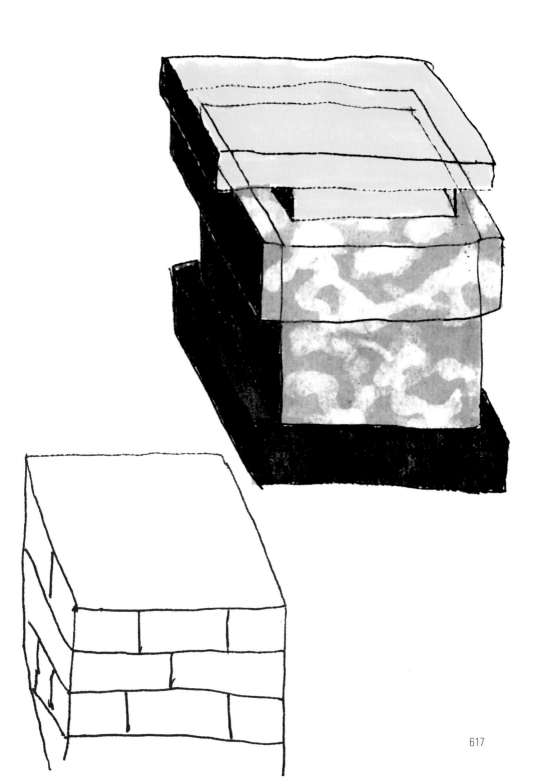

617

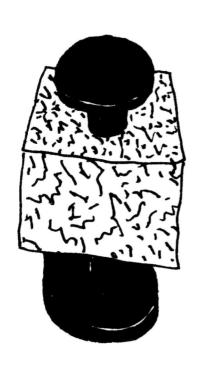

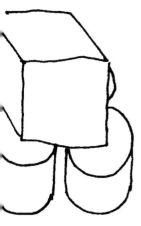

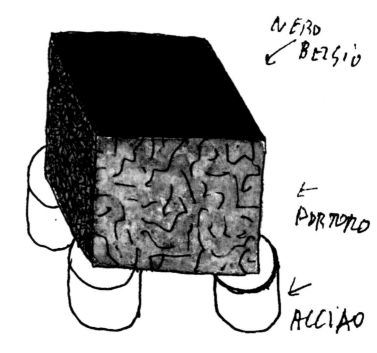

NERO
BERGIO

PORTORO

ACCIAO

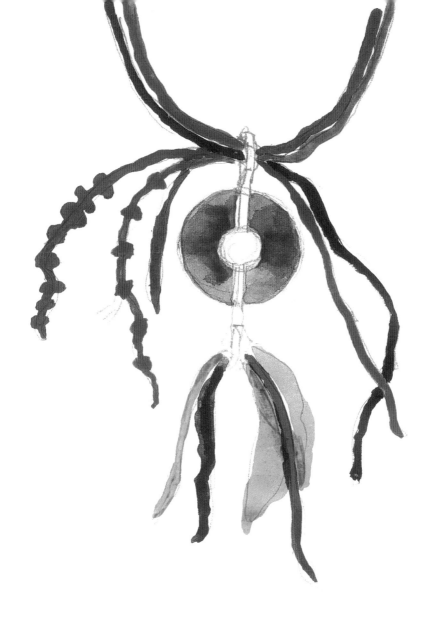

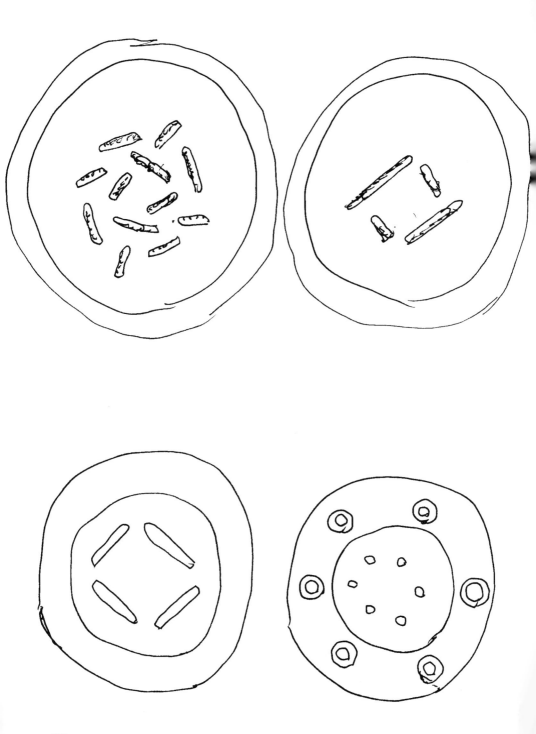

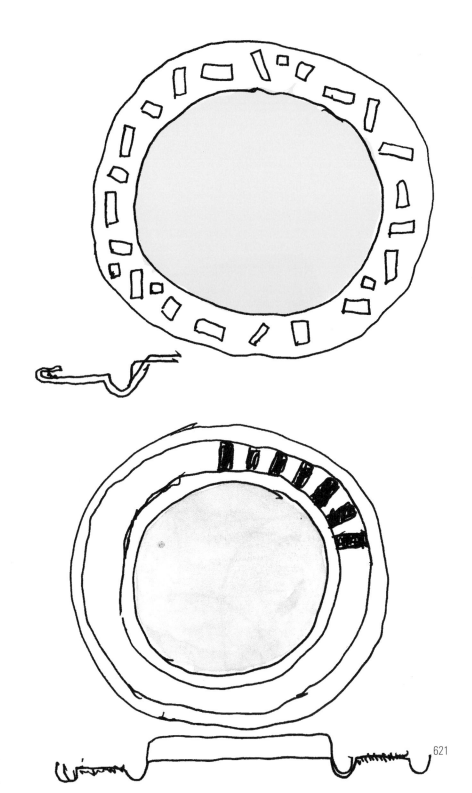

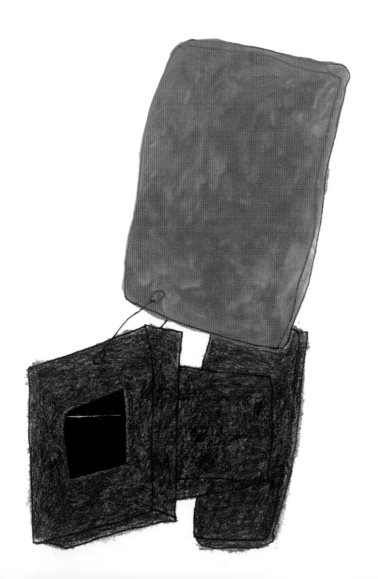

623

624

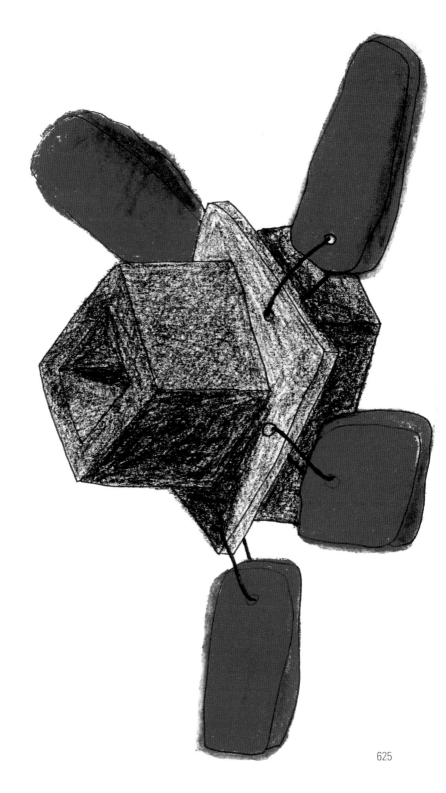

626

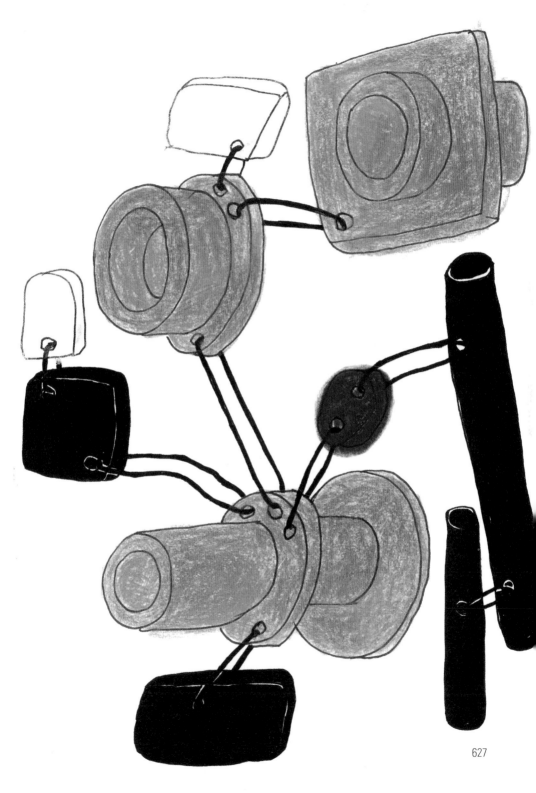

627

③

②

TUTO BIANCO

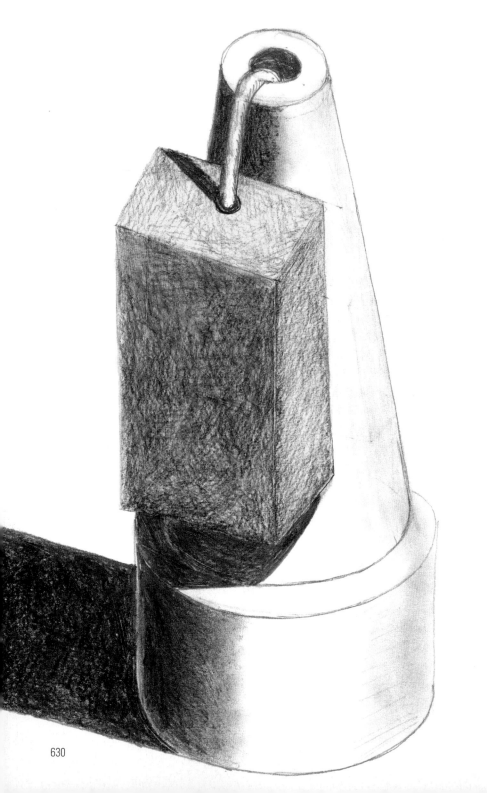

630

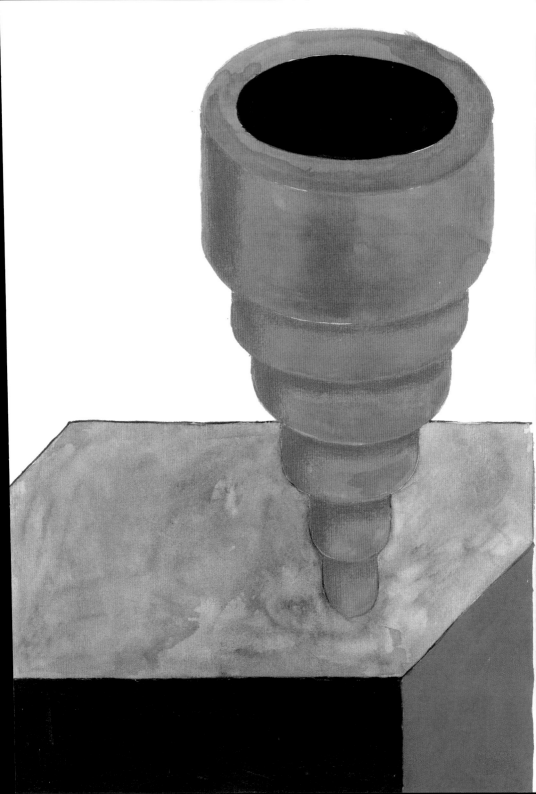

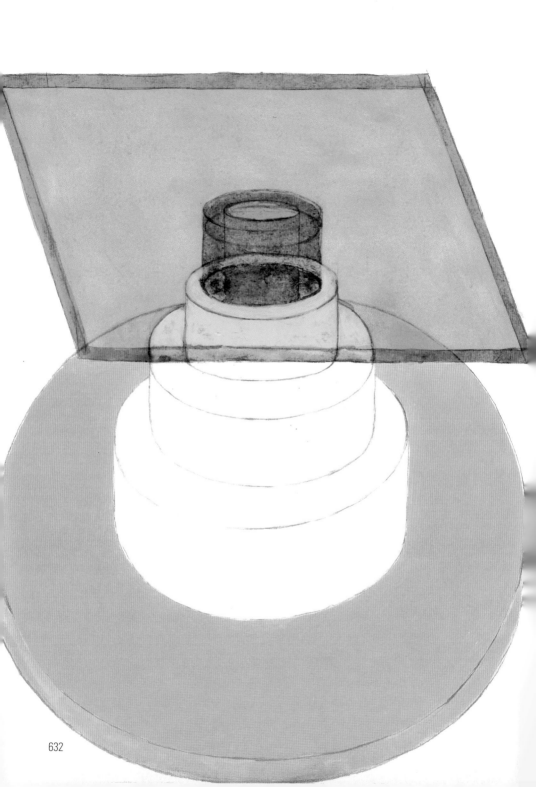

APRILE
2003

633

634

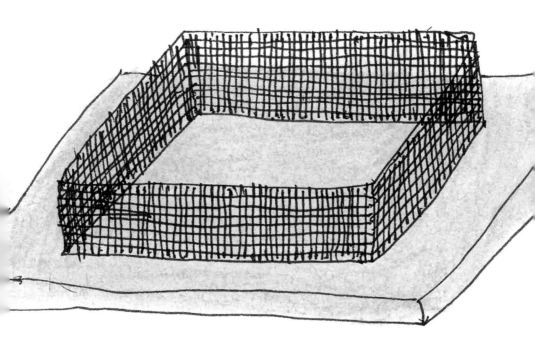

640

642

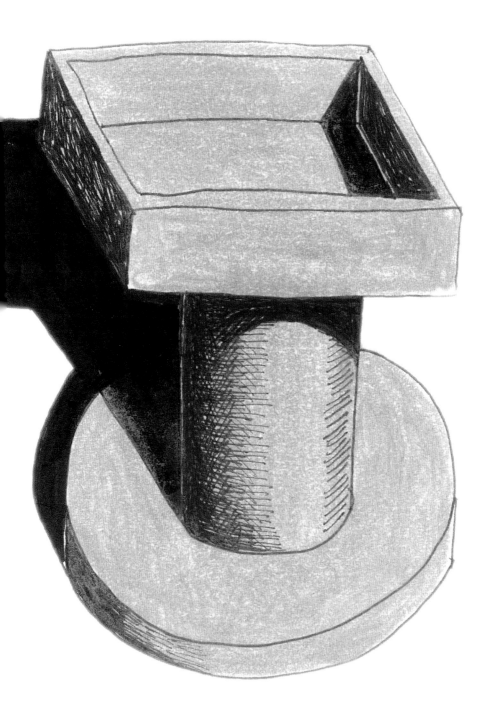

PORTAFRUTTA PER ARANCE E LIMONI – 8/2003 – SOTTSASS

PORTA FRUTTA PER PRUGNE - 8/2003 - SOTTSASS

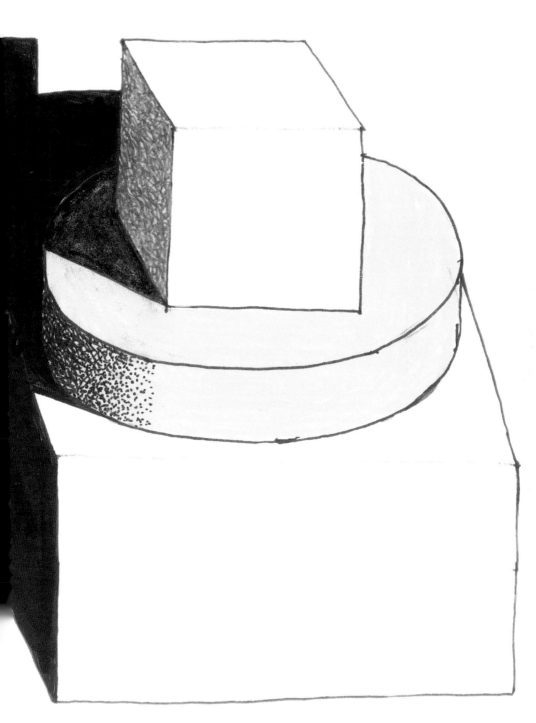

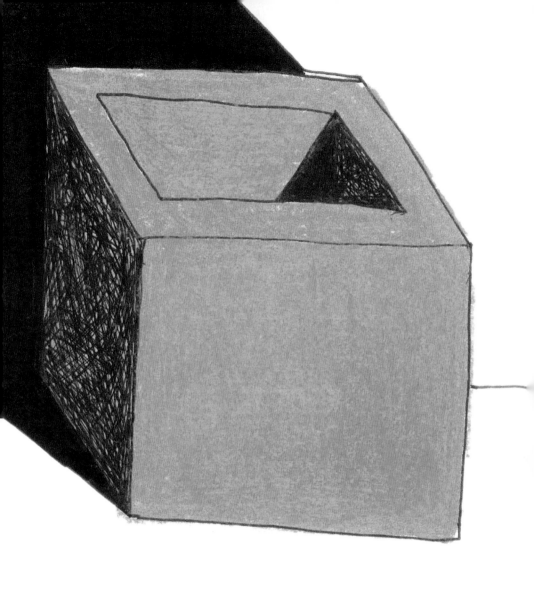

648

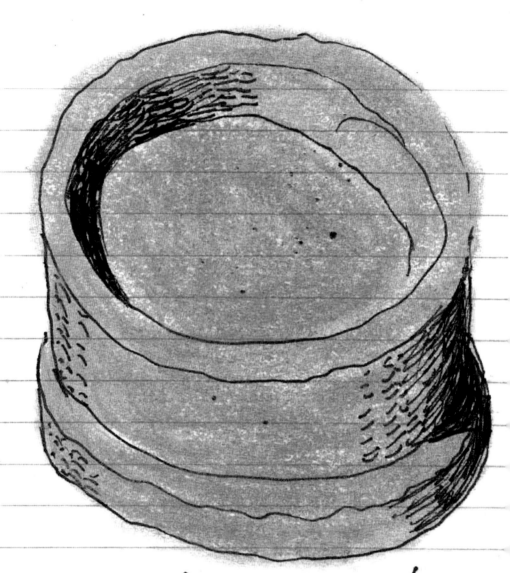

20 PEZZI ANTICHI

651

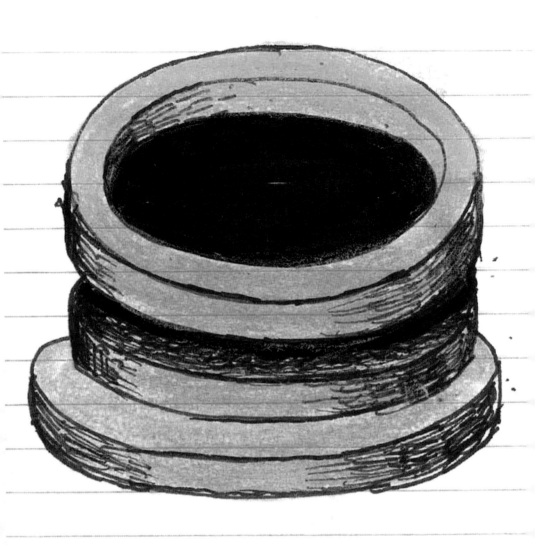

652

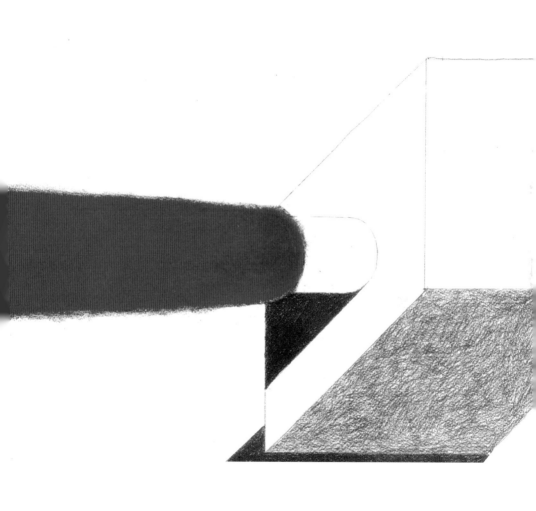

30/6/03 803x

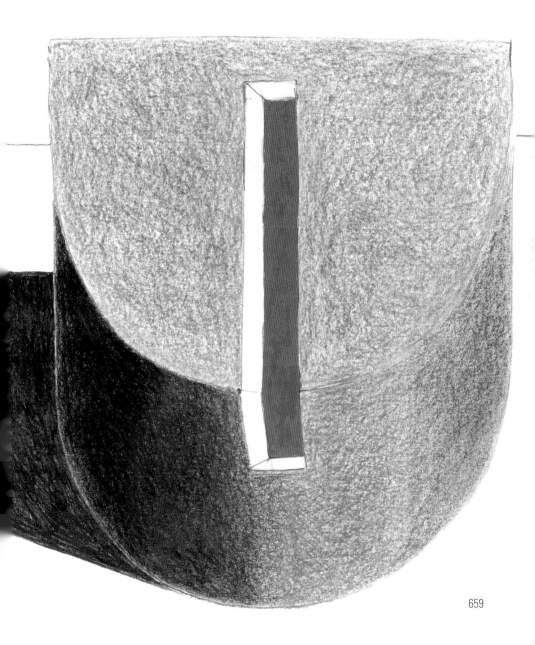

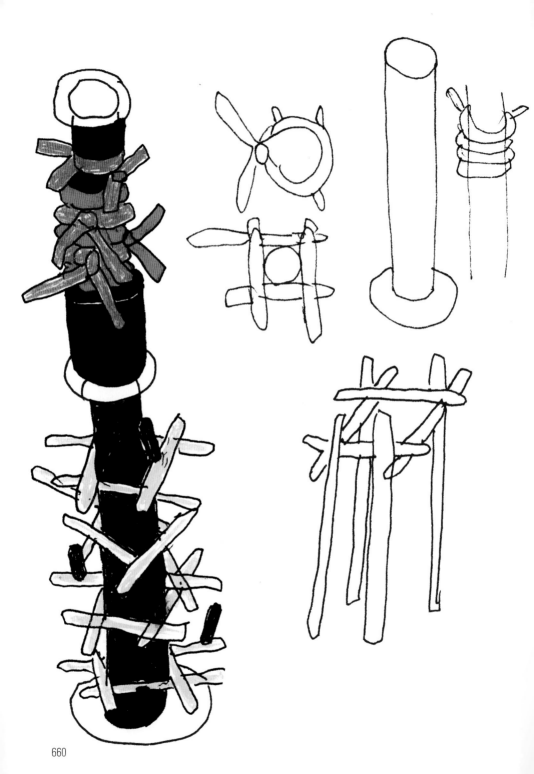

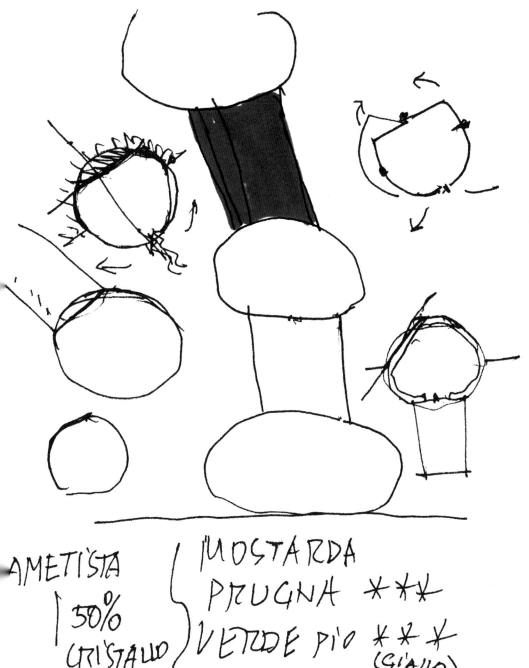

AMETISTA
| 50%
CRISTALLO

* * *

{ MOSTARDA
PRUGNA * * *
VERDE PIO * * *
(GIALLO)
// PETROLIO
ANTRACITE (GRIGIO)

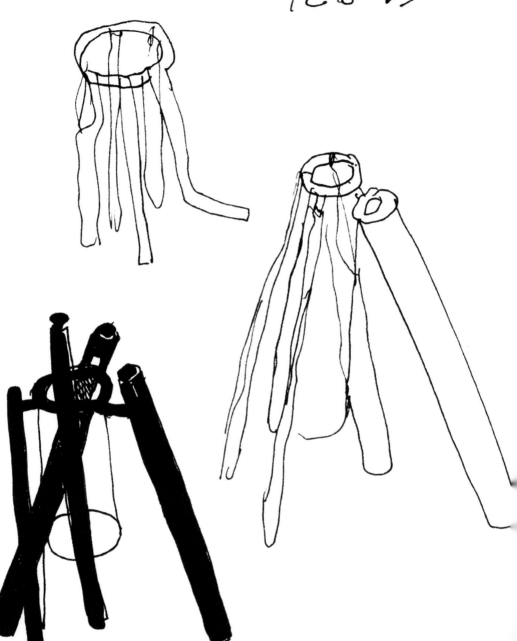

12·6·03

662

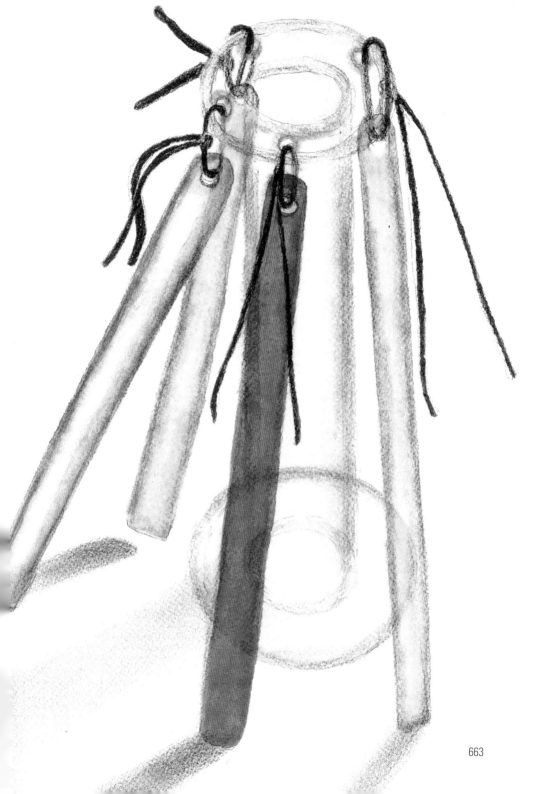

CALABRIA
CATTOLICA DI STILO (RC)

CHIESA RUPESTRE
SANTA MARIA DELLE ARMI (CS)

TRA VIBO
VALENTIA
e TROPEA
LOCALITA'FOSSI

ENOTRI 7sec.A.C.
(SIBARI
CROTONE
↓
MUSEO
ARCHEOLOGICO
STATALE
↓
LOCRI

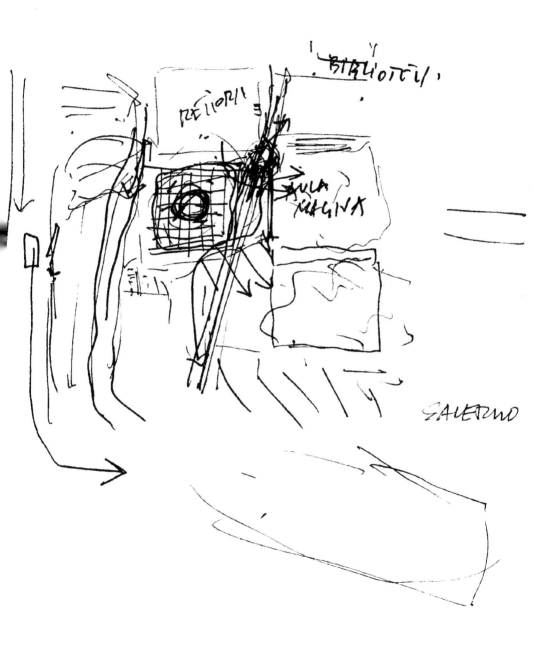

RETTORII

BIBLIOTECA

AULA
MAGNA

SALERNO

665

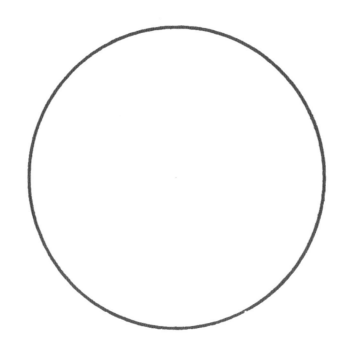

CERCHIO DISEGNATO CON
IL COMPASSO

CERCHIO DISEGNATO A MANO

FORSE PER PIGRIZIA O FORSE
PERCHÈ MI SENTO -IO-
FRAGILE, MI SENTO PIÙ
PROTETTO DAL CERCHIO
FATTO A MANO

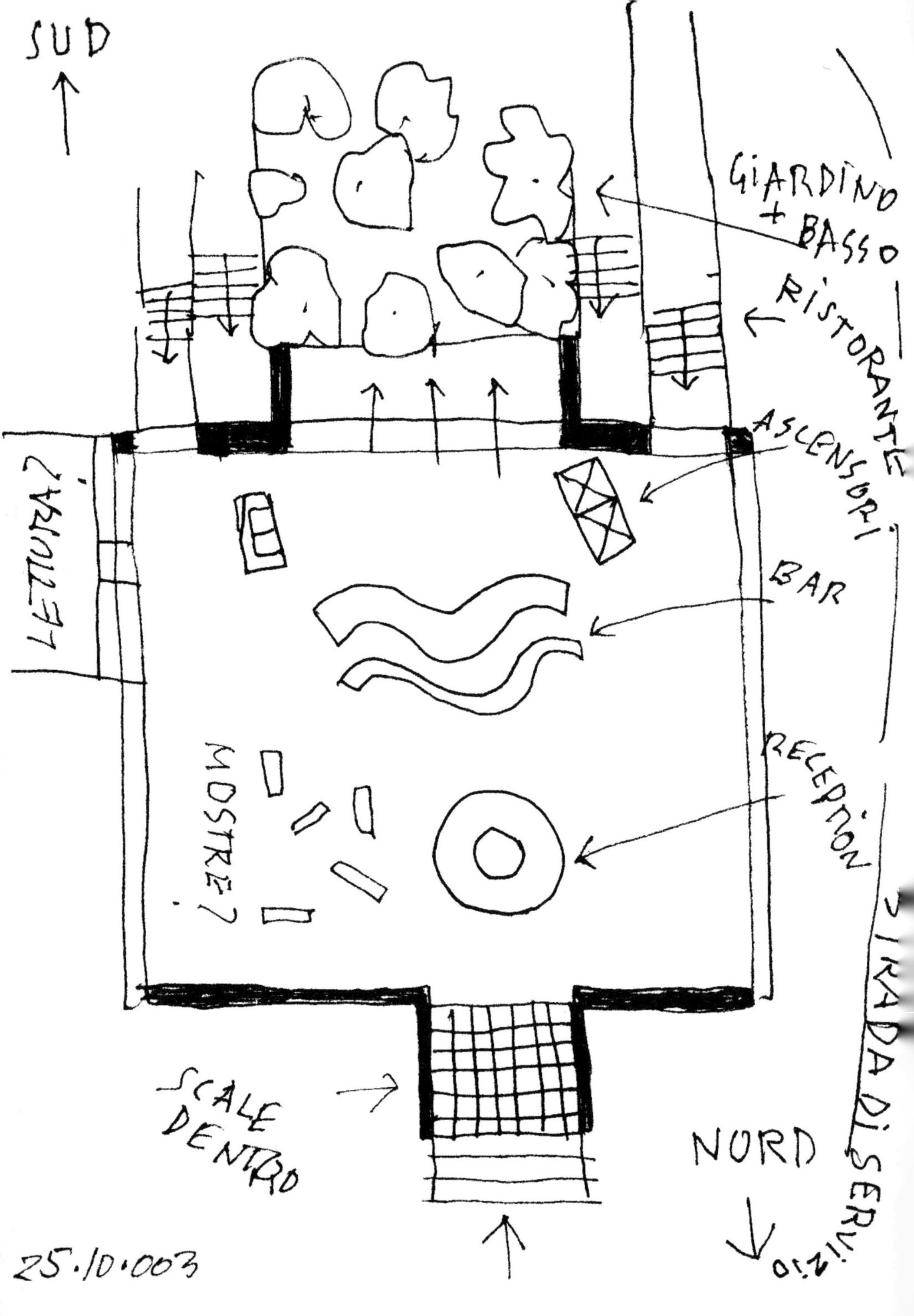

SUD

GIARDINO + BASSO

RISTORANTE

ASCENSORI

BAR

RECEPTION

STRADA DI SERVIZIO

NORD

LETTURA?

MOSTRE?

SCALE DENTRO

25.10.003

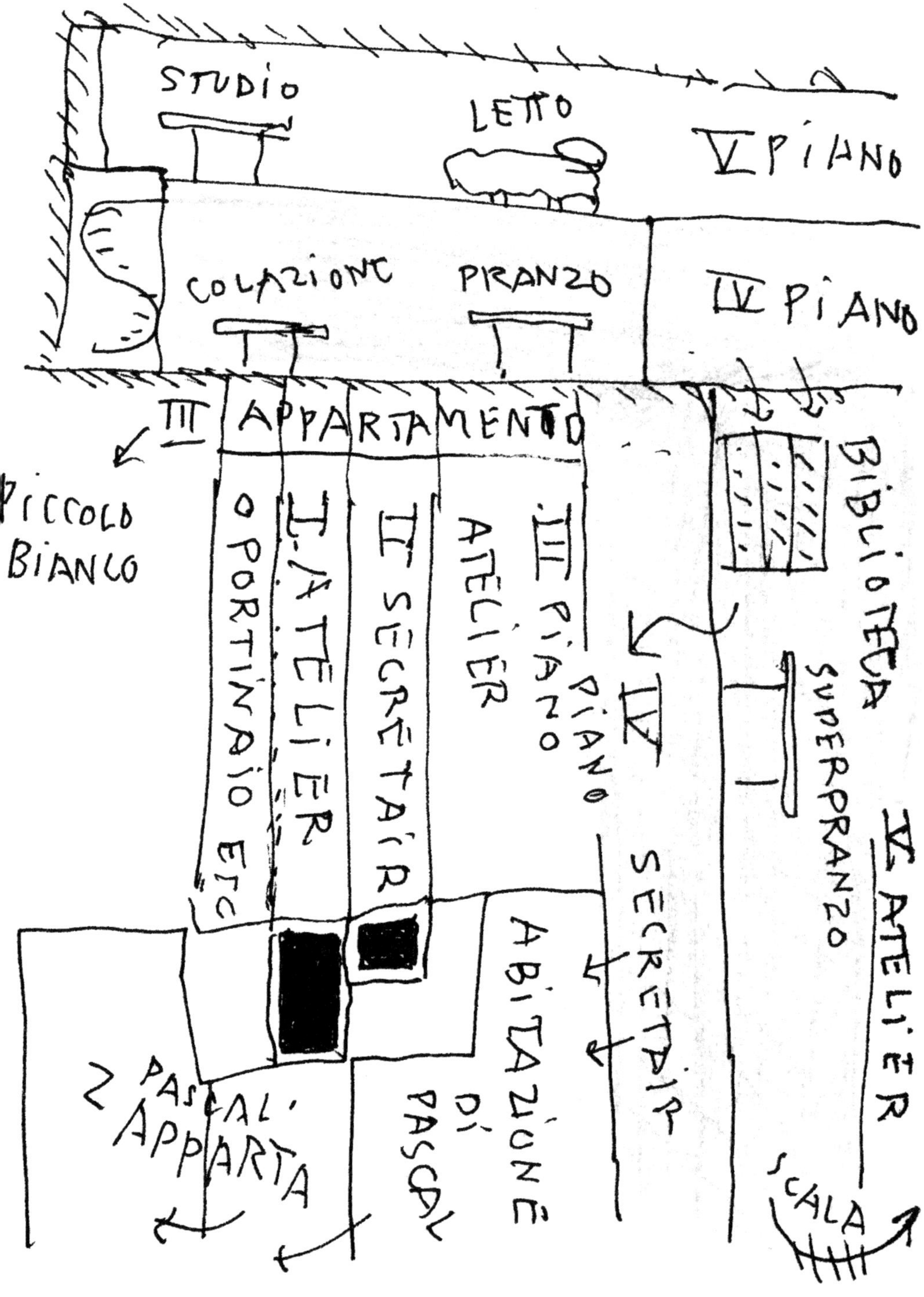
STUDIO
LETTO
V PIANO
COLAZIONE
PRANZO
IV PIANO
III APPARTAMENTO
PICCOLO BIANCO
O PORTINAIO ETC
I. ATELIER
II SECRETAIR
ATELIER
III PIANO
IV PIANO
BIBLIOTECA
SUPERPRANZO
V ATELIER
SECRETAIR
ABITAZIONE DI PASCAL
PASCAL' 2 APPARTA
SCALA

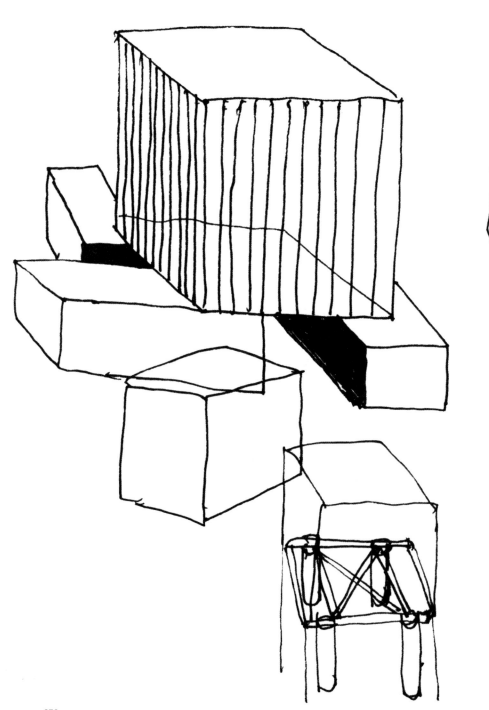

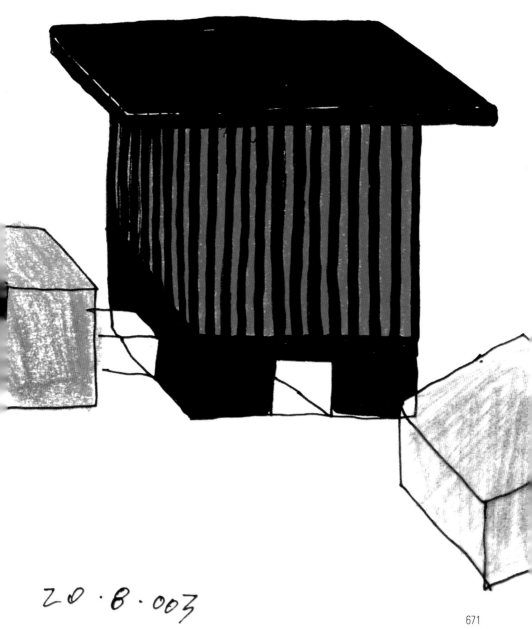

20·8·003

672

CI VUOLE UN INGEGNERE
GIÒVANE E GENIALE
(SUBITO)

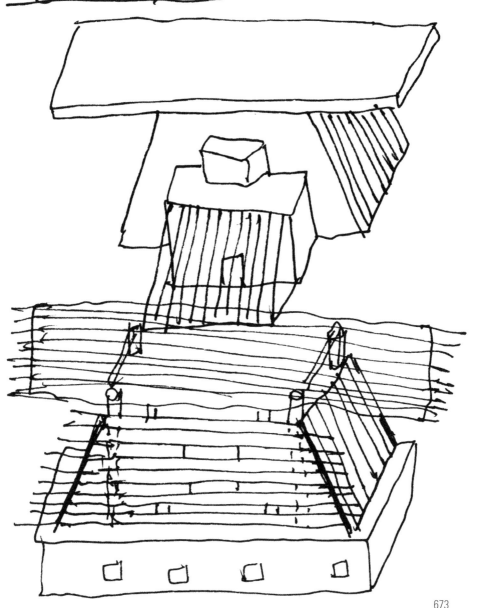

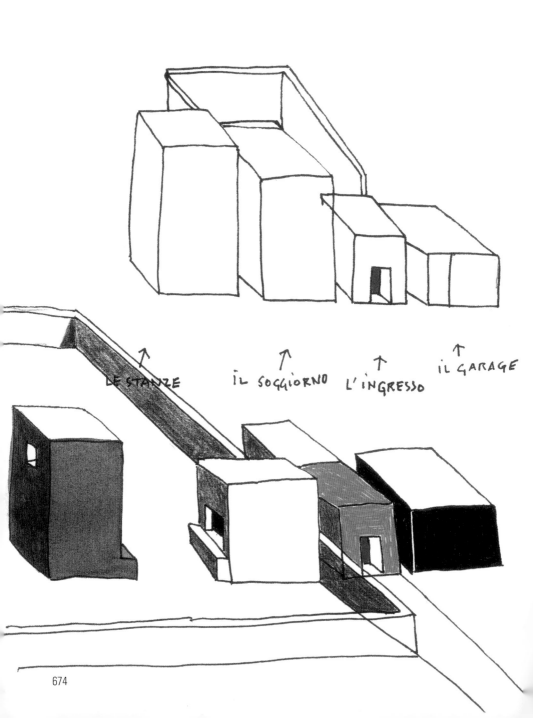

LE STANZE IL SOGGIORNO L'INGRESSO IL GARAGE

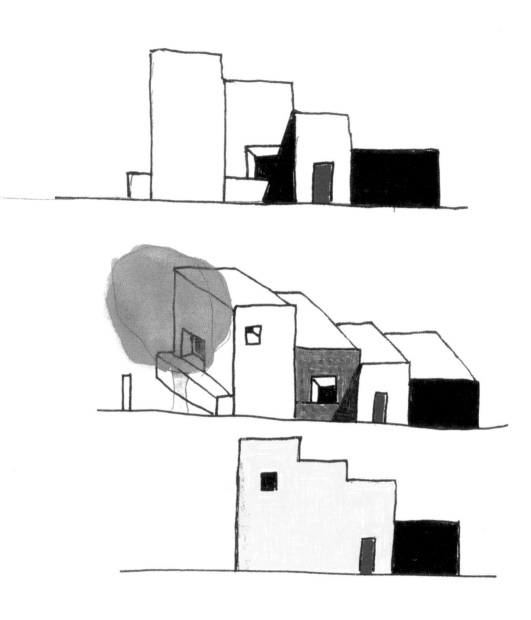

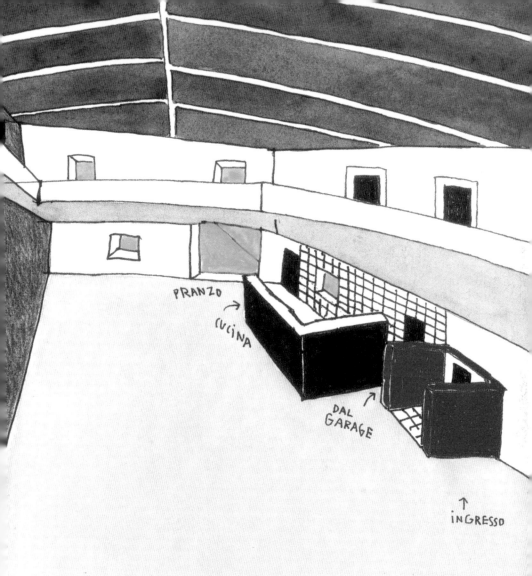

PRANZO

CUCINA

DAL
GARAGE

↑
INGRESSO

CASA TUNISINA (1)

679

USCITA   ENTRATA
AUTORIMESSA   MUSEO
"TEMPIO DELL'ARTE
SULLA RIVE DEL MARE"

687

688

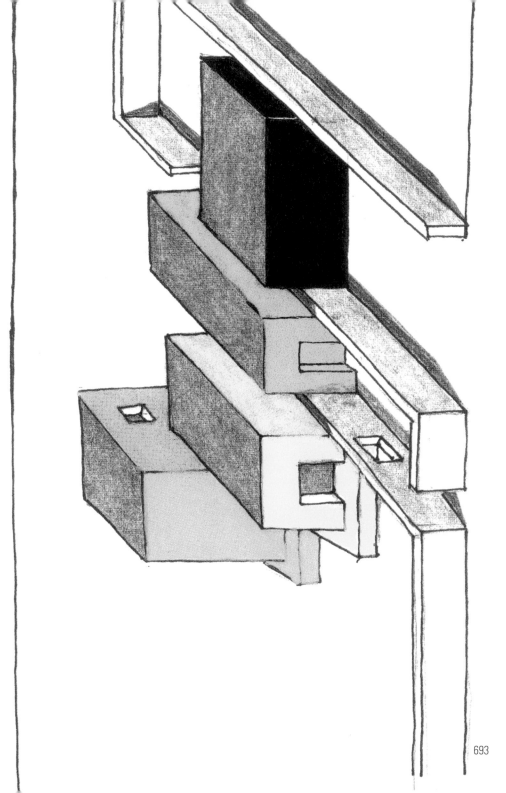

693

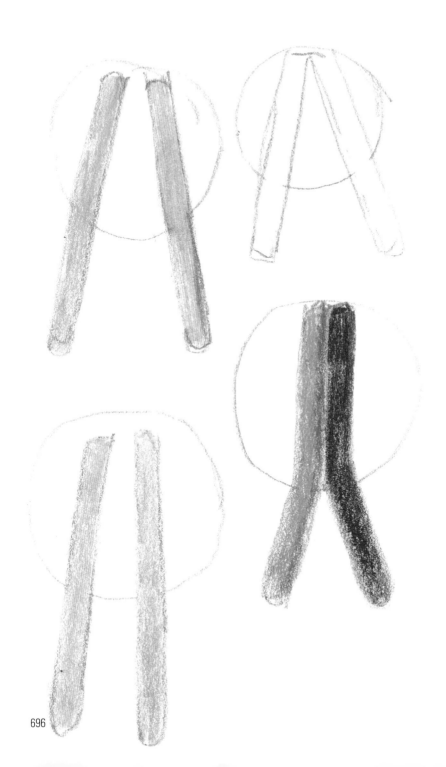

696

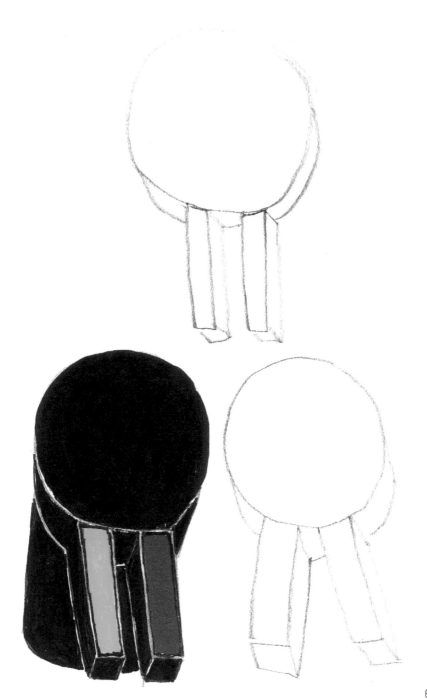

697

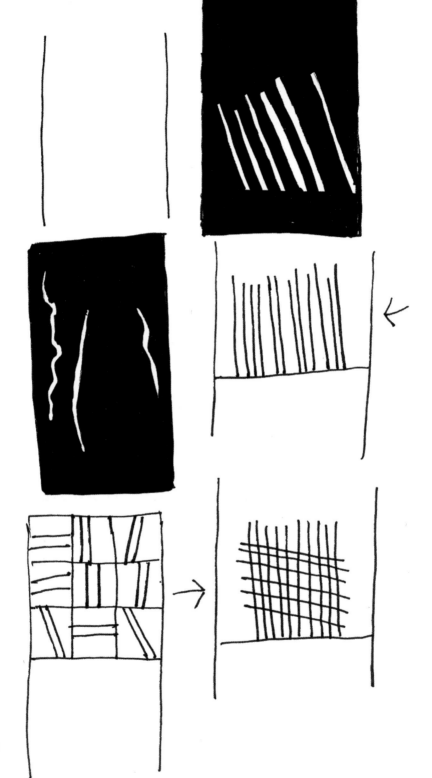

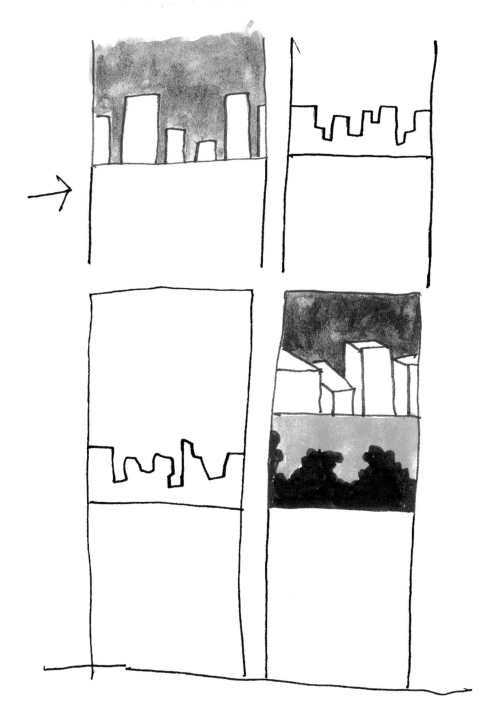

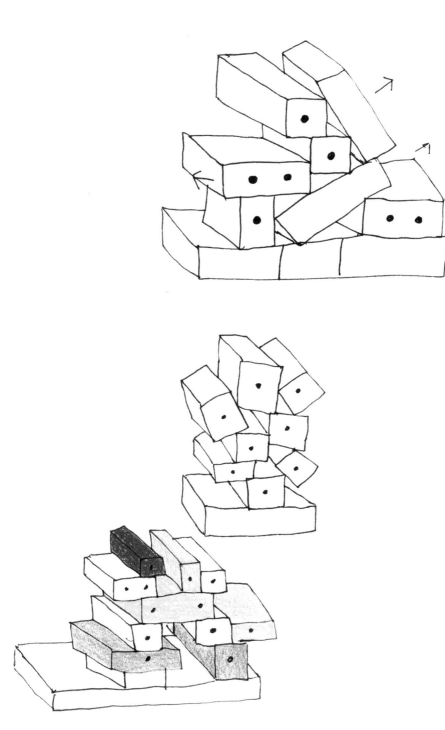

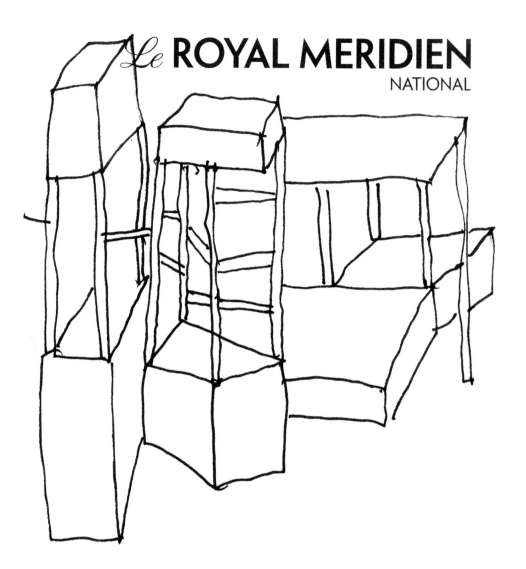

Le ROYAL MERIDIEN
NATIONAL

15/1 Mokhovaya Street Moscow 103009 Russia
Tel.: +7 095 258 7000 **Fax:** +7 095 258 7100
e-mail: hotel@national.ru www.national.ru
IN PARTNERSHIP WITH NIKKO HOTELS

704

13.4.04
MALTA

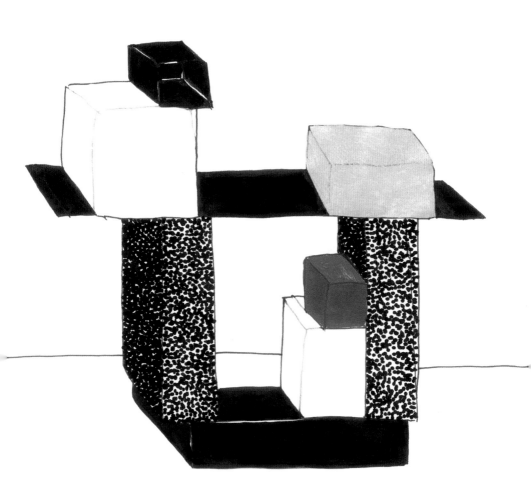

SCRIVANIA PER SIGNORE MANCINO

15·6·04

710

28.6.04

TROVATO
il 6 - 9 . 004

1

23 · 7 · 04

2

DOMENICA

712

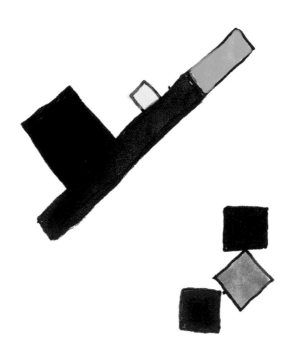

716

Captions of the drawings

XXIV